9-95

MORE
DRESS PATTERN
DESIGNING

NATALIE BRAY

*Former Principal of The Katinka School
of Dress Designing,
London*

FOURTH EDITION

Illustrations by Adrienne Slack

With Fashion Supplement
and illustrations
by Ann Haggar

COLLINS
8 Grafton Street, London W1

Collins Professional and Technical Books
William Collins Sons & Co. Ltd
8 Grafton Street, London W1X 3LA

First published in Great Britain 1964 by
Crosby Lockwood & Son Ltd
Reprinted 1967
Second revised edition 1970
Reprinted 1972
Third edition (metric) published 1974 by
Crosby Lockwood Staples
Reprinted 1976, 1978
Reprinted 1980 by Granada Publishing Ltd (ISBN 0 246 11335 9)
Reissued in paperback by
Granada Publishing Ltd 1982
Fourth edition published by
Collins Professional and Technical Books 1986

Distributed in the United States of America
by Sheridan House, Inc.

Copyright © Natalie Bray 1964, 1970, 1974, 1986
Fashion Supplement © Ann Haggar 1986

British Library Cataloguing in Publication Data
Bray, Natalie
More dress pattern designing.—4th ed.
1. Dressmaking—Pattern design
I. Title II. Haggar, Ann
646.4'3204   TT520

ISBN 0-00-383305-4

Printed and bound in Great Britain by
R. J. Acford, Chichester

Also by Natalie Bray

Dress Pattern Designing 5th Edition
With Fashion Supplement by Ann Haggar
0 00 383304 6

Dress Fitting 2nd Edition
0 00 383220 1

CONTENTS

BIOGRAPHICAL NOTE

Natalie Bray was born in Russia, the daughter of a naval officer, but left the country at the time of the Russian Revolution. She trained as a musician, married an Englishman and became a qualified engineer. She first became interested in technical dressmaking in 1926 when she was asked to help in the management of a business called Katinka – Court Dressmakers, started several years earlier by a member of her family. She went to Paris for a year to learn cutting and in 1927 she obtained the Diploma of the Academie de Coupe de Paris. She then worked for three leading Parisian model houses including Lucien Lelong. Having returned to London, she worked at Katinka but in 1928 decided to start teaching classes as well. At first these were run on the same lines as those she attended in Paris – dealing only with modelling patterns on the dress stand and practical dressmaking. She soon became interested in working out a *simple, quicker and more exact* method of cutting patterns on the flat, which would be based on and could therefore be tested by results obtained by modelling. By 1935 she had evolved her own system of flat pattern cutting, and this method has been taught with various improvements and fashion modifications ever since. The techniques she pioneered and perfected revolutionised dress pattern designing, assisting the rise of the modern fashion industry. Her teaching has had a profound influence on design, production and education. Her works are classics: fashions change but the principles of cutting the flat pattern do not. They remain essential reference books for all students, teachers and practising cutters.

INTRODUCTORY

This book expands and completes the course of pattern designing, the basic part of which was given in an earlier volume. A number of examples and illustrations show how the basic principles are applied to styles of more elaborate design, as well as to the more specialized cutting of patterns for underwear, tailored garments and children's clothes, patterns which have their own particular requirements, difficulties and problems of fit.

At this advanced stage in pattern designing it is just as important as in the earlier work to be thoroughly familiar with the basic principles and proportions for everything goes back to them. The fact that every type of pattern, simple or elaborate, can be developed quite logically from a few foundations representing the figure is of the very essence of these methods, and nothing must be allowed to conceal the obvious inter-connection of all patterns produced from the same few blocks. In order, however, to retain complete control over the many problems and possible difficulties of a complicated style, it is essential to be very sure of the structure of the blocks. It is only when knowledge and understanding of foundation patterns is such that no departure from their basic lines and proportions, whether to follow some intricate detail of a design or a change in fashion, can cause any difficulty or uncertainty, that advanced and *original* work in pattern designing can be attempted successfully.

As already stated in the earlier volume, no practical methods of cutting on the flat can be accepted as reliable unless the result can pass the test of a check on the stand. To no other patterns does this apply so much as to patterns of *draped styles*, which often have to be tested several times before the result can be considered satisfactory. It is therefore useful to repeat an earlier warning about not allowing these methods to degenerate into a system of hard and fast rules, and to preserve throughout the work a flexible, experimental attitude, which is never so important as when dealing with advanced design.

All patterns must be planned against a background of many practical considerations: figure (size, shape and posture), fabric (weight, texture and width), suitability (becomingness and suitability for purpose) and finally the demands of constantly changing fashion. Experienced pattern designers do not usually lose sight of these practical details, and so are generally less in danger of becoming set and limited in their approach and methods of work.

With regard to using these methods for *patterns of tailored garments*, it must be stressed that far from underestimating the value of direct drafting – the basis of all tailor-cutting – they aim at bringing out, i.e. explaining and emphasizing, the special qualities achieved by the classical method. Since pattern development from basic blocks is now generally accepted and often found more convenient, it is most important that in the case of jackets and coats it should be applied in a way which does not lose the special points of cut and fit ensured by direct drafting. Above all, adaptation methods in tailoring demonstrate once again how, through the use of a common foundation, every type of pattern is basically connected with other patterns: the figure is always the same, even if the line and fit of the garment are different. The appreciation of this fact helps considerably in acquiring a more thorough understanding of pattern cutting and fitting, and as a result practical experience is gained much more rapidly.

In conclusion one can only state again that the attributes of a competent and successful pattern designer are both knowledge of fundamental principles, thoroughly analysed and clearly understood, and the ability to apply them in practice in a flexible and imaginative way, guided by good judgement, taste and fashion sense.

ABBREVIATIONS AND REFERENCE LETTERS

CB—Centre Back
CF—Centre Front
B—Bust measurement
NP—Neck Point
SP—Shoulder Point
UP—Underarm Point
U—Underarm Point in Kimono patterns
W—Waist Point, waist level or measurement
WR—Waist Reduction
NW—Natural Waist
H—Hip Point, hip level or Hip measurement
HW—Hip Width, i.e. Hip measurement + allowance
Ch—Chest Point, chest line or measurement
xB—Back measurement
LW—Length to waist
SG—Straight Grain
RS—Right Side
WS—Wrong side

IN SLEEVE PATTERNS
TA—Top Arm measurement
DC—Depth of Crown
B—Back Inset point (or top of Back line)
F—Front Inset point (or top of Forearm line)
T—highest point of sleeve crown (Top line)
U—lowest point of crown (top of Underarm line)
E—Elbow point or elbow level

IN KNICKER PATTERNS, SLACKS, etc.
B—Back Fork point
F—Front Fork point
S—top of back seam
HW—Hip Width (see above)
OX—Depth of Crutch

Point X—highest point of bust
         Crease line point in tailoring patterns
         (e.g. in jackets)
         Crutch point in knickers and slacks
Point D—the point of the Shoulder dart
Point G—Gusset Line point in Kimono patterns

THE PRINCESS DRESS AND
THE PANEL BODICE

The Panel bodice is the classical Bodice block and in the past was used as the principal foundation from which all other styles were developed.

Though replaced by a simpler modern block, more suitable and convenient for present fashion, it still retains considerable importance as a basic pattern, an importance which goes well beyond its purely 'historical' interest. Not only are some versions of it much used in theatrical designing for period, ballet costumes, etc., but some *styles based on it* are nearly always in fashion – in dresses, underwear, jackets and coats.

The importance of the Panel bodice is due mainly to the fact that it embodies a cut which is most suitable for reproducing the shape of the figure, i.e. it can be used better than any other type of pattern to make an *exact replica of the figure*, with all its individual features. In former years considerable use was made of it as a **foundation pattern for individual figures,** and some cutter-fitters may still prefer this method of work. A *tight* Panel bodice is fitted *to the shape of the figure* and then put on the stand and padded, thus providing an 'individual stand' (or form) for each customer on which all patterns and dresses for this person can then be modelled or fitted.

The reason why this particular cut is so suitable for outlining or moulding the figure is that the two Panel seams, back and front, in their *classical position* (if not always in their modern interpretation) pass over all the main curves and hollows of the figure in such a way that they provide quite naturally **the best seams for close shaping.** The bodice can be fitted very tightly, like a skin, following exactly the curves of bust and shoulder blade, and of the hollows below. Even when not required to be close fitting, as is often the case in modern designing and generally in tailoring, it can still *outline* or even just *indicate the shape* of the figure better than any other type of pattern.

The Princess line is merely an extension of the Panel bodice to full dress length, *without a break or join at the waist.*

There are many versions of this classical cut, and it provides endless *style variations*. Whether appearing as a waist-length bodice, much used in theatrical designing and evening dresses, or in its hip-length version (e.g. as a jacket) or as a full-length Princess dress, it is always *basically connected with the classical foundation.*

Since the Panel bodice is no longer so much used as a *foundation*, there is no need to consider it primarily in its very close fitting shape, i.e. as a mould of the figure or a 'fitting lining'. The bodice described here has the usual fit of a well shaped modern *dress bodice*. It can be made tighter or looser, according to the style and type of garment for which it is used (e.g. evening dress bodice or easy fitting jacket). A closer fit is easily achieved by tightening all the seams. Having a minimum of six or seven, but often more, vertical seams, the Panel bodice lends itself better than does a simple bodice to a balanced reduction, *well distributed all round the figure.*

It is important to note, even at this early stage, that in modern pattern designing the Panel line is very largely a 'style line' which, once shaped correctly *according to the design*, should not be changed in fitting, e.g. when tightening the bodice. Classical arrangement apart, panels can be of different shapes, wide or narrow, more or less curved, straighter or more sloping: these are all *style* line variations which must be reproduced so as to be in keeping with the design and which do not necessarily follow the classical position which is mainly a position of 'best fit'. Within the limits of a particular style, however, it is necessary always to bear in mind the best panel position for the *shape* of the figure, and to *be guided by the classical seam* in achieving *the best fit*. For instance, whatever the shape of the seam and wherever it starts from – shoulder or armhole – it should always be made to pass as near as possible to the highest point of the bust, in fact as near to the classical position as the design interpretation permits.

THE CLASSICAL PANEL BODICE
modern version – Plate 1

As already stated, the classical Panel bodice in its present day shape is *not tight fitting* but is adapted from the Standard bodice block, retaining the usual width and fit of a shaped, darted dress bodice.

Some overall tightening must occur however because of the extra vertical seams which extend the waist darts (lengthen them up and down) and so cause some loss of width *between* bust and waist and *above* the hips. This must be borne in mind in style adaptations. Unwanted tightness can be reduced by using smaller 'waist darts' in the Panel seams, i.e. by curving less their *outer* edges – the Side front and the Side back edges. These edges are the 'fitting lines' which can be shaped, i.e. curved more or kept straighter, to make the bodice cling more or less to the figure.

The basic Panel bodice consists of 6 or 7 sections when it is without a CB seam (FIG. 1, Plate 1), or of 8 sections, when there is a CB seam as well as one in the CF (FIG. 3, Plate 1).

The shoulder point of the Panel (S) is usually in the middle of the shoulder. For the back it can be established correctly by measuring half shoulder length from NP and then from SP. On the front it will come a little inside the open Shoulder dart to match the back point S.

The position of the Waist point (W) is marked on both sides of the Waist dart, as the two edges of the seam must *enclose the dart*.

The position of the Hip point (H) is governed by the shape of the Panel seam—straighter or more sloping— and in the basic style is usually placed a little farther out (1–2 cm) from CB/CF than the Waist dart points.

BACK – Plate 1 – FIGS. 1 and 3

For the Back Panel the three basic points are placed as follows:

Point S is marked at half shoulder length from NP.

Point W is placed on the inner side of the Waist dart which will have to be increased by half of the Sl. CB waist suppression (1 cm) *if there is to be no CB seam* (FIG. 1), i.e. in a 6-section Panel bodice. With a CB seam the Sl. CB takes the usual 2 cm suppression and the Waist dart thus remains as on the block (FIG. 3). In either case a note should be made of the distance of W from CB.

For point H, on the Hip level, measure from CB the distance CB—W plus 2 or 1·5 cm: this usually places point H in line with the centre of the Waist dart or just outside it. It is therefore convenient to extend the centre guide lines of the darts above and below the usual length to help in the drawing of the Panel seam.

Connect the three guide points S – W – H by a smooth, slightly curved line, as shown in the diagram.

The Side back is outlined by the *outer* line of the Panel seam which also passes through 3 points: point S on the shoulder, placed at half shoulder length from SP; point W on the *outer* side of the Waist dart which is either increased (FIG. 1) or as on the block (FIG. 3); and point H which coincides with the Panel point on the Hip level. The two lines of the seam meet and run together for 5–6 cm above the *low* hip level and, as will be seen from the diagram, for a few inches above the Waist dart to avoid undue tightening over the hips and over the prominence of the shoulder blades (the bodice often has to be adjusted here—taken in or let out—to conform to the *exact shape* of the figure).

This outer Panel seam line is drawn to enclose the shoulderblade and Waist darts which will, of course, be cut away when the two parts of the pattern are separated.

The underarm seam follows the bodice block. The inner shaped seam is used mainly for waist-length bodices, the outer for jackets and other looser-fitting panel styles.

FRONT – Plate 1 – FIG. 2

For the Front Panel mark point S again at half shoulder length from NP, to match the back. This will bring it slightly (1 cm) inside the open Shoulder dart, so that the other side of the dart will have to be moved the same distance *out*, towards the armhole.

Point W is placed on the inner side of the Waist dart.
Point H is 1–1·5 cm farther out from CF than CF—W.

To help with the drawing of the panel curve, an additional guide point may be marked on the bust level, just inside the point of the Shoulder dart (0·5 cm).

The Side front is outlined by the outer line of the Panel seam which encloses both Shoulder dart and Waist dart and joins the other line for a short distance on the bust level (see balance marks) and on the hips.

WAIST SHAPING

The basic front Waist dart is seldom increased except in *short*, close-fitting dress bodices having no CF seam. In the hip-length version, unless a very close fit is wanted, it is preferable to use an additional dart halfway between the basic Waist dart and the side seam, to avoid over-shaping below the bustline.

It must be noted that the waist dart arrangement described here gives the easy fit of an ordinary dress bodice (waist measurement+4–5 cm). For a looser fit, e.g. for a jacket, the waist would naturally be reduced less, so that the question of Waist dart increase would not arise. On the other hand, in closer fitting styles, such as hip-length evening dress bodices or tight Princess styles, some *tightening of side seams* would probably be required *in addition to dart increase* (FIGS. 3, 5, 6, Plate I and Plate II).

Waist tightness is therefore very important and must be considered at an early stage as it affects the very *shape of the seam lines*. It is also necessary to bear in mind that any tightening of the waist is bound to influence considerably (tighten or loosen) the fit *above* and *below* the waist, and there is a tendency for this pattern to work out *too tight between waist and hips*.

Once the method of planning Panel seams and the allied problem of waist shaping are understood, the fitting of these styles does not present any particular difficulty. Provided one has taken sufficient care with the initial planning of the seams, letting out or taking in at the fitting will be done mainly on the Side front and the Side back. Only exceptionally will the Panel line itself be altered.

Some possible fitting corrections are shown in FIGS. 5 and 6 at the bottom of Plate 1.

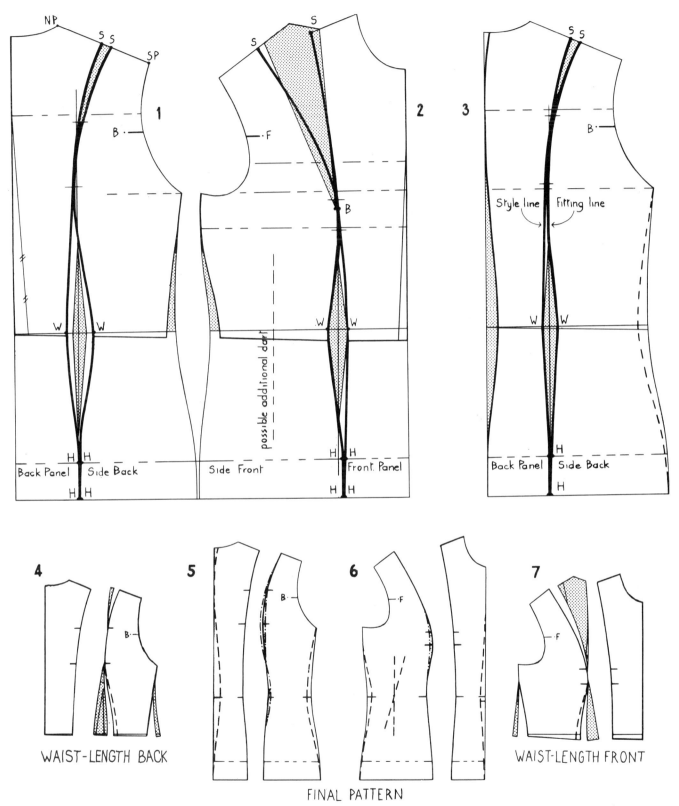

WAIST-LENGTH BACK

FINAL PATTERN

WAIST-LENGTH FRONT

PLATE 1

THE PRINCESS DRESS

The Princess dress is the Panel bodice continued to full dress length, with more or less width at the hem, according to the style.

The classical method was to place the metre stick along each side of the *lower part of the Waist darts* and side seams, touching in each case points W and H (the latter marked on a higher 18 cm Hip line) and then, along the rule so placed, to draw the skirt seams down to their full length. This gave *differently sloped skirt seams* according to the slope obtained in each case between W and H. Thus where the Waist dart was deep, as was often the case, for instance, in the hollow of the back, the *outer* line of the Waist dart was more sloping, so that the skirt seam shot out more and gave more width to the hem.

The total hem width, therefore, was dependent on the size of the Waist darts, i.e. on the Waist measurement, and a smaller, more 'pinched-in' waist went with a fuller hem. The back usually worked out fuller than the front, and this was in keeping with the line of the *classical* Princess dress and in general with the line of all skirts worn at the turn of the century which, with or without a train, always had a 'sweep' towards the back.

This method is obviously too limiting for modern style designing where total hem width and its distribution are entirely a *matter of 'line'* and not of shape of figure. A present day Princess dress may have a moderate hem width of 2¼ m, or even less (when the line is almost straight the style is usually described as a *Panel dress*); or it can be quite full, sometimes very full in the hem (4–5 m or more), particularly in long dresses. The fullness can be evenly distributed, slightly or much reduced in the front, or concentrated mainly in the back, often in an even more exaggerated way than *happened* in the classical style.

Because of all these possible variations the most usual method now is to *decide on the total hem width*, according to style, then *plan it on the hem level*, and finally draw the sloping skirt seams *from the hem points upwards*, to join the bodice, instead of ruling them downwards from the waist, as before.

METHOD OF WORK—Plate 2

Using a 6-, 7- or 8-piece Panel bodice, continue the CF and CB lines straight down, exactly as for a one-piece dress, ignoring any waist shaping on CF/CB. From Hip line level draw four more vertical lines, parallel to CF/CB, and complete the hem. The skirt part is now a rectangle with a hem width equal to the width of the hips, in this case 52 cm on the half pattern (just over ½ m).

After making a note of the **total basic hem** (1+ m), decide on the **extra width** required for the style to obtain, say, a total hem width of 2½ or 3 m (approximately). Adding about 150 cm to the *basic one metre* to obtain 2½ m, or 200 cm to obtain 3 m round the hem of a Princess dress, would mean an addition of 9 or 12 cm

on every one of the 16 seam edges of an 8-gore pattern, or 12–16 cm on the 12 edges of a 6-gore style. The additions are measured at hem level, right and left from the vertical lines of each rectangle, and the seams are ruled *up* from here to run into the bodice *at least 5–6 cm above* the low Hip line (FIG. 1), but often much higher. As already stated, this pattern tends to work out too tight between waist and hips on many figures and needs 'easing' by means of a *higher crossing of seams*, generally 8–10 cm above low Hip line or more.

This is a general outline of the method, and Plate 2 gives a diagrammatic representation of it, showing the hem additions as overlapping wedge-shaped sections. It is possible to make the pattern in this way, by cutting it and by pasting extra paper for the extensions on every edge. But in practice it is usually more convenient to *work on each section separately*, to avoid pasting or joining of paper. Using therefore another large sheet of paper, first *trace through* the complete Side back and Side front, *with all their hem additions*. The traced-through sections thus contain all the hem width required and represent the final pattern, though if necessary, more width can be added before cutting out (FIG. 4). The original 'working pattern' is then used for the front and the back Panels, which can now be cut out with their full hem addition (FIG. 3). Any CF/CB hem additions can be made at the same time, on paper previously left beyond the CB/CF of the block.

It must be understood that in many Princess styles the planning of the bodice lines will be very different from the basic Panel bodice given in Plate 1 and so, instead of using this bodice as a block, it is usual nowadays to plan each Princess style direct on the standard Bodice block. However, in spite of all the variations, the *principle* of the cut remains the same, and in all Princess styles one is always *guided* by the basic pattern as giving the best possible fit.

VARIATIONS OF THE PRINCESS DRESS PATTERN

The Panel—back and front—may begin **from almost any point on the shoulder,** further from NP or nearer to it (see 10- and 12-gore styles). It may also start **from the armhole,** from a higher or lower point on it, but generally near the inset points B and F.

The line of the Panel may be more or less curved and may *slope in* more or less towards the waist.

The Side front and Side back follow, of course, the shape of the Panels and will vary with them. They control the fit, i.e. the tightness of the bodice, by increasing or decreasing the Waist dart curve. To prevent their overshaping, **additional waist darts** are often used, mainly in the front.

Skirt width addition can be varied considerably by sloping out from different levels, higher or lower, or differently on front and back.

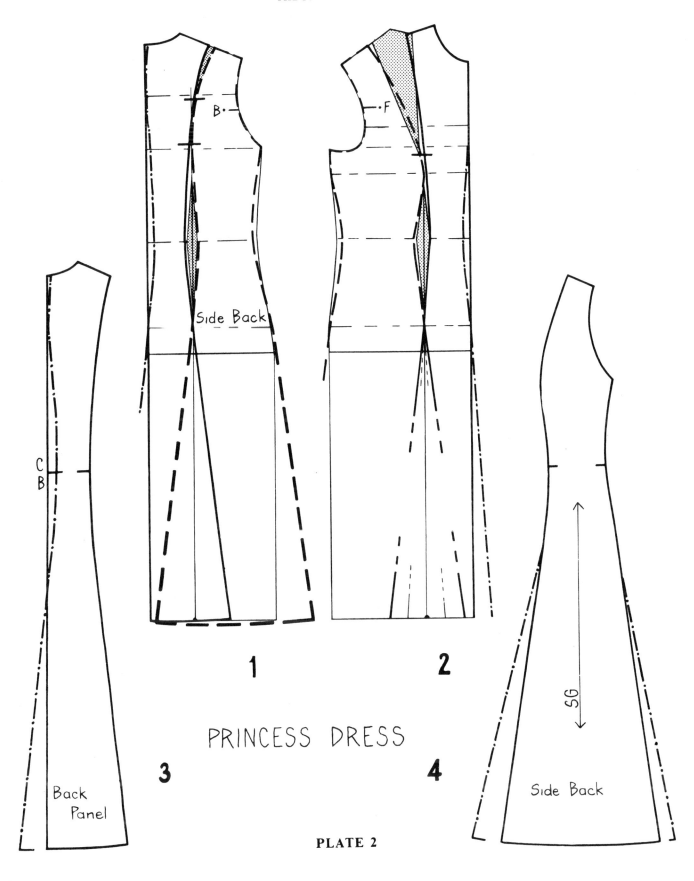

Side Back

B·

·F

C
B

Side Back

SG

1   2

PRINCESS DRESS

3   4

Back
Panel

Side Back

PLATE 2

Further style variations can be produced by cutting away the top and replacing it by a different type of bodice, usually with a high-waisted effect (See Plate 3, styles C and D); or the lower part of the pattern is cut away and replaced by a flounce (Plate 4, style C); or the side gores are replaced by gathered or pleated sections from below the hip level, and so on. Pleats, pressed or unpressed may also be added to the edges of the gores of a moderately full Princess dress. In fact the possibilities of varying the basic style are endless.

Finally, **the number of gores** can be increased to 10 or 12 and a slightly different method has to be used in planning the pattern whenever the bodice is to be divided into more than the basic 8 sections.

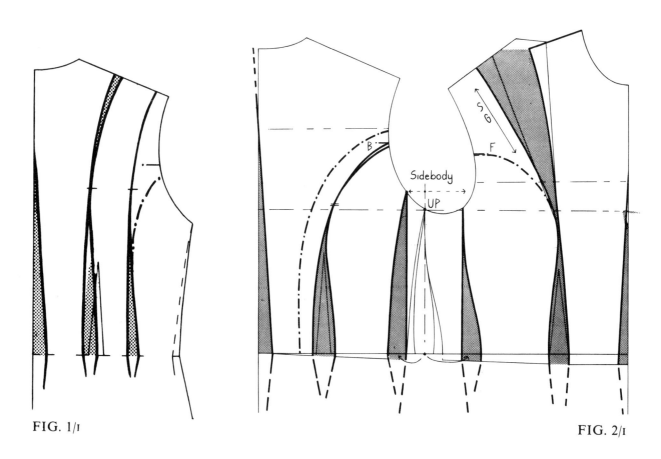

FIG. 1/I   FIG. 2/I

12-PIECE PANEL BODICE
and 12-gore Princess Dress — FIG. 1

FIG. 1 shows the planning of three instead of the two basic sections on the back of a bodice. With the front planned in a similar way this gives a 12-piece bodice which can be extended into a 12-gore Princess dress.

Referring to the *finished waist width* required, divide waist into three approximately equal parts, but with underarm part slightly wider and the middle one often narrower (to balance its small shoulder width). In this case, therefore, measure 5 cm from the Sl. CB and then allow 2 cm space for the Waist dart of the block. Mark the width of the second section 5 cm or slightly less, followed by a 1+ cm dart space. The rest goes into the last section as far as the *outer* shaped seam, since the *extra* dart *replaces* the *inner seam* shaping. All this can, of course, be tightened a little, i.e. all the darts slightly increased, if the fit of the style requires it (e.g. in a period or ballet dress).

On the shoulder, from NP, measure 5·5 cm (slightly

more than at the waist), then allow for the 1·5 cm shoulder blade dart. Make the second section 5 cm wide and leave the rest of the shoulder to the third part. Draw the first and *second* Panel lines, curving them slightly as shown in the diagram, then complete the panel seams, i.e. draw their outer lines, enclosing the darts, as usual.

The front is planned in a similar way, with *shoulder points matching those in the back*. At the waist, however, the underarm part is definitely wider than the other two: it may be almost twice as wide as the narrower middle section (e.g. front section 5, middle 4·5, side 9 cm).

For **a 12-gore Dress** plan the bodice down to the Hip line, then mark a level 6–8 cm above it on which all the lines will meet and overlap, thus making the hips wider. Extend to full length, as described above (i.e. as a rectangle), and complete the seams from the hem up, as usual.

10-PIECE PANEL BODICE
and 10-gore Princess Dress—FIG. 2

Dividing into 10 sections presents a slightly bigger problem because the usual side seam cannot be used: it must be replaced by **an underarm section—a sidebody.** The width of this underarm piece is taken as approximately $\frac{1}{10}$ of the *finished* waist (to round off the figure it is usually slightly more). Thus 7·5 cm width can be used for a 68–72 cm *finished waist*, remembering that even in a *tight* waist an extra 2–3 cm is allowed for fit.

Place back and front of the bodice block with UP touching and with Waist and Bust lines *on the same level:* this will give a gap at the waist—*the underarm WR,*

which must be reduced elsewhere since it cannot be taken out in a side seam.

From UP drop a perpendicular on to the waistline level and plan the underarm section, $\frac{1}{3}$, i.e. 2·5 cm, to the back and $\frac{2}{3}$ (5 cm or just under) to the front of it. Draw two lines parallel to perpendicular, to outline the sidebody. Outside these lines take out the 5 cm WR, 2·5 on each side.

Plan the two sections of the back and of the front, following the style, but generally guided by the usual waist darts and panel arrangement. In FIG. 2 an ordinary panel is shown in the front, and curved armhole panels in the back and front. The dot-dash lines show another, more extreme panel version, used in some period costumes. If the waist tightness is to be increased, it is usually the back Waist dart—the Panel seam dart—which takes the excess. It will also be increased if Sl. CB is not used (i.e. if there is no CB seam).

For a **full length dress** again plan the bodice down to the hips but, as already mentioned above, the overlapping is usually done on a higher level, and may even be just 5–7 cm below the waist, so that much extra fullness is added round the hips. The higher overlapping goes with a wider hem.

FIG. 3 gives a slightly different method for the planning of a similar 10-piece bodice. Instead of taking out the underarm WR (the waist 'gap') each side of the underarm section, it can be eliminated at once by overlapping the side seams (5 cm). This eliminates the actual gap, including the 1 cm *inner shaping* at side seams. There is nothing to take out beyond the sidebody. The rest of the pattern is planned in the same way.

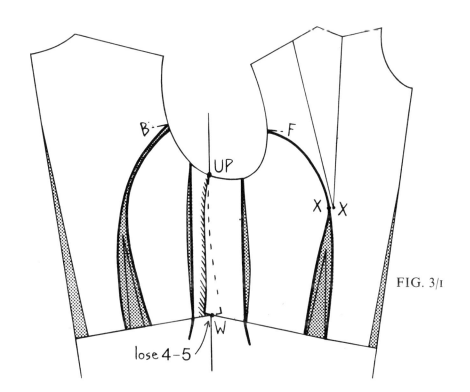

FIG. 3/I

lose 4–5

PLATE 3—PRINCESS DRESS VARIATIONS

This Plate shows an important variation of the Princess cut in which the panels start at the armhole instead of shoulder. Many modern styles are based on this pattern.

The highest point of the panel—Point A—is usually placed on or near the sleeve Inset points B and F. In some styles it may come a little above, in others—and this happens more frequently—it is just below these points. Each position affects the shape of the Panel seam, either flattening it or curving it more.

At the waist point W is in its usual position, just on or sometimes inside the Waist dart, which can be made smaller or increased for a tighter fit when a 'pinched-in' waist effect is important for style interpretation.

N.B. It must be noted that it is often better to have an additional dart on the Side front (occasionally back) than to exaggerate the Panel seam dart (see styles B and D, Plate 3). Another important point to remember is that it is desirable for the front Panel seam, whatever its shape, to pass through point X (highest point of bust), or as close to it as possible.

The crossing point of the seams—point H—is seldom, if, ever, on the low Hip line but, as already shown in Plate 2, at least 5 cm above it. It is often very much higher and may be just under the waist. In some styles these points may be on different levels: higher in the back and lower in the front. Additional fullness therefore may be released from different levels, and generally the fuller the dress, the higher are the points at which the seams run into the bodice.

The armhole Panel seam is much used in classical short bodices, period costumes and ballet dresses—when the actual fit is usually tight (see FIGS. 2 and 3). It is also very popular in modern designing, both for close fitting styles with much hem fullness and for the less fitted styles with a moderate hem width.

FIVE PRINCESS DRESS STYLES

Style A is a simple summer dress which more or less follows the basic pattern given in Plate 2. It has a moderate hem width of 2–2¼ m, as the skirt, supported by a petticoat, shows no fluting at the hem and so cannot be very full. As there are 8 seams (there may, of course, be only 7 without a CB seam), an addition of 6–8 cm on the 16 seam edges should be correct for this effect. Allow less in the front because of large pockets on the side gores.

Style B is a short evening or cocktail dress which is based on the armhole Panel version given in this Plate. It is much fuller round the hem and so requires a bigger addition on all the 16 seam edges. 13–15 cm will have to be added, from a higher level (11–12 cm below the waist), on every seam edge, including CB and CF (the latter may be slightly less full), to obtain a suitable hem width of 3–3½ m. For closer waist fit additional waist darts may be used.

At the top, a wide V-neckline, cut out more than half-way down the shoulder, and deeper in the back than in the front, is 'matched' by the Panel seam running *across* the armhole to form a shoulder extension which covers the top of the arm (see the adaptation shown by dot-dash lines in the main diagram). The front Panel line crosses armhole at F, the back—above point B (at point Z), to obtain a shoulder width suitable to go with the front extension. The shoulder seam is centred and is curved slightly to fit over the top of the arm.

Style C is a pinafore dress, i.e. a skirt with a corselet top and shoulder straps. This is a simple variation of the basic pattern, with the top cut away, 13–15 cm above the waist. Extra hem width is pressed into godet pleats.

Style D is a bigger departure from the basic pattern. The top is cut away and replaced by an ordinary bodice with sleeves and a draped neckline. The pattern for it can be obtained by 'joining' the Panel seams, i.e. omitting them above the raised waistline. The Shoulder dart is transferred into the 'waist', showing as a little fullness above it, but some may be left in the neckline to ease it before adding the 10–12 cm extra height for the draped fold. The neckline is well cut away on the shoulder which has a *centre* seam. The skirt is fairly full and as there appear to be only 6 gores (if the back is as the front) or 7 (if the back has a CB seam), the addition must be fairly big, 12–14 cm, to obtain a 2¾–3 m hem width. For the same reason (i.e. fewer gores) the waist is more difficult to shape without an additional dart.

Style E is a dressing gown or housecoat, with much fullness starting from a high level. The style may also be interpreted as having unpressed pleats or folds in each seam, caught at the waist. As the skirt is long, a hem width of at least 4 m would be only moderately full. The extra width is divided between the 6 or 7 seams, but no fullness can be added down CF as this has a wrap and buttons. For method of adding width to long hems see Plate 4, style D.

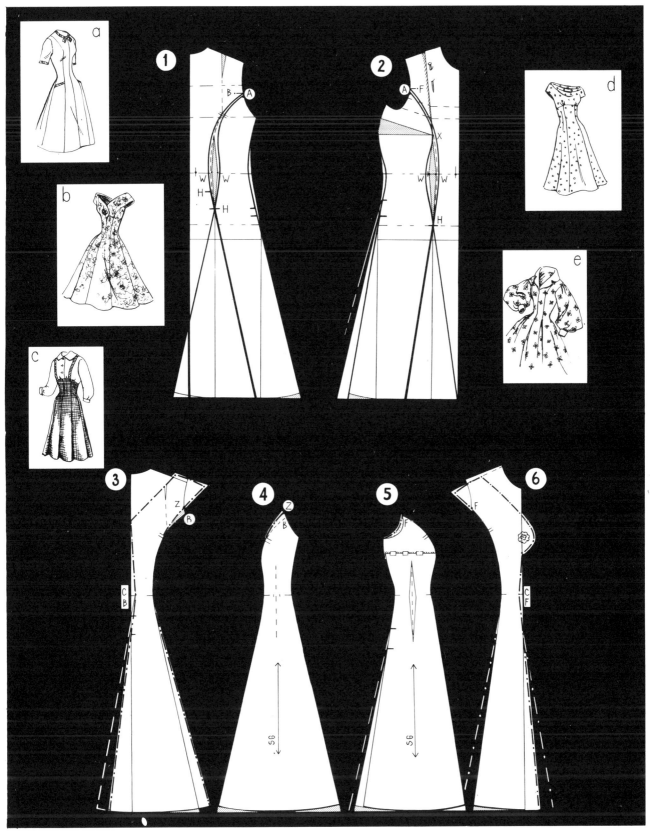

PLATE 3

PLATE 4—PRINCESS DRESS STYLES

A further selection of styles based on the Princess cut is given here. These dresses—two long, two very short—illustrate the addition of hem width from different levels.

Style A—a sports or play dress, suitable for beach wear. It has a strapless top and a very full, short skirt. The seams run into the bodice part on a very high level, just below the waist, increasing the fullness of the skirt all the way up.

Add the rectangular extensions below the Hip level, as usual, but only to the required length. Then plan the hem additions, to increase the basic width (e.g. of 1+ m) to the required total hem width of 2½–3 m suitable for the style. This means adding about 1½–1¾ m to the basic width, which gives 10 or 12 cm on each of the 16 seam edges.

From the points marked on the required hem level draw the seams to run into the bodice part 3–5 cm (average 4 cm) below the waist, which obviously gives a considerable addition round the hips as well, i.e. it produces a flared skirt.

For strapless top see style C and FIGS. 3 and 4.

Style B, another **sports dress** for tennis or—with long sleeves—for skating, has again a very short skirt (40–42 cm) and considerable hem fullness, springing out from a high level to produce flares all round the figure. The top follows the basic pattern but with some increase in panel width on the shoulder where the Panel seam is placed ⅔ out or 9 cm from NP. Width is therefore added here to the basic pattern, and reduced on the side pieces, as shown in FIGS. 1 and 2.

The skirt part is completed as for style A.

Style C—Evening dress: This is a full-length dress (106–110 cm) with a strapless top and a skirt with a deep flounce which may be of different material (e.g. lace, net, chiffon etc.).

The bodice is simply cut away at the top, is often higher in the front than in the back, and is tightened on the side seams, FIGS. 3 and 4. The Shoulder dart depth is doubled for a closer fit *above* the bust, which is essential for all strapless styles. The front panel may be widened at the top, as shown in FIG. 4, adding to the Panel and reducing the Side front (see detail).

The Princess dress may be cut to its full length so that the lower part serves as a foundation over which to mount the full gathered flounce. The lower part (under the flounce) can also be replaced by a flat but more shaped flounce, with more hem width to hold out the gathered flounce covering it. Or, the lower part can be cut away completely and the gathered flounce simply attached to the lower edge and supported by a full petticoat or stiffened slip.

In this case, when planning the Princess dress, one must consider the width of the skirt *on the level where the flounce joins it,* i.e. a little more than half-way down the full skirt length. The width should not be excessive otherwise this part of the skirt will not *stand out* round the figure but will tend to fall into deep folds. Plan the dress therefore 60–65 cm long to go with a 45–50 cm

flounce and make it only about 1¾ m at the lower edge, which means a 5–6 cm addition on each seam edge. If this works out too full for the effect desired, it can easily be reduced by taking 1–2 cm off every seam edge.

The flounce is a straight piece which, according to the fabric used, is two, two-and-a-half or three times as wide as the lower edge to which it is attached. But, if preferred, to increase the hem width without adding any more to the gathers at the top, the flounce may be slightly shaped by slashing and opening out the pattern from the hem.

Style D—a Wedding dress: This is a 7-gore Princess dress which has a CB but no CF seam. The Panel seams curve from the armholes. Considerable width is added to the hem and there is a short train which develops from just beyond the side seams to a 40–45 cm length on the CB (or more).

The pattern is planned in the usual way, first down to hip level. The rectangle extensions are then added to full length, 106–112 cm below the waist. After cutting out the pattern, each section is placed separately on a large sheet of paper to make the necessary additions for the extra hem width and, in the back, for the extra length of the train.

The total hem width in this style is about 6 m or just over, and more than half of this goes to the back. Distribute the total hem width between 6 gores (counting the two narrow back gores as *one*), allowing less than 1 m for the front panel (e.g. 70–80 cm), approximately 1 m for each of the four side gores, and more, i.e. 1½ m, for the *double* back gore.

As the basic hem width of the rectangle is only 104 cm, or 52 cm (½+ m) on the half-pattern, something like 2⅜–2½ m must be added to the half-pattern to make up the required total width of 3 m or just over. Of this addition 1 m approximately will go to the front gores, and about 1½ m to the back gores. Since these have a train which increases the hem width, what is measured on the *full length level* will have to be a little less, say 120 instead of 150 cm, to allow for the increase caused by later lengthening. Divide the 120 cm more or less equally between the 4 seam edges (see FIGS. 5 and 6): the slightly smaller addition on the CB is made because of the very narrow width of the half-gore.

From all these points obtained on the *full length hem* draw the seams upwards, taking them to 3–4 cm below the waist on the CB to a slightly lower point in the next seam and still lower (8–9 cm down) on the side seam. In the front the fullness can be added from a still lower level, i.e. the seams can run into the bodice part 12–13 cm below the waist.

Add the length for the train to the back gores, as shown in the diagram: this will increase the hem width, as planned.

The CB seam can be made into a soft, unpressed, inverted pleat, ending on hip level, just below the fastening (zip). A little extra width should then be added at the top to form the pleat (dot-dash lines), while above it all extra width beyond the bodice CB is cut away.

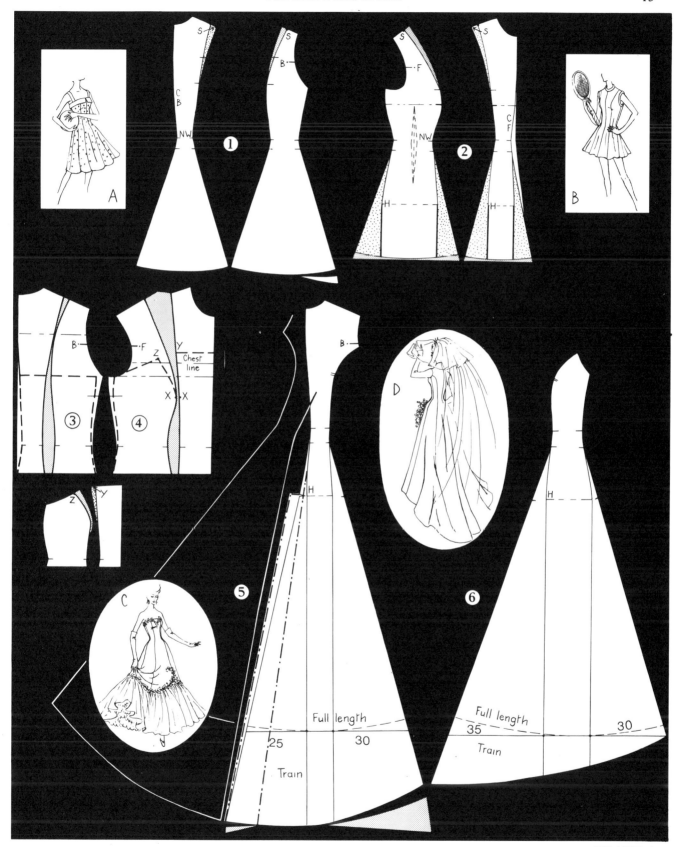

PLATE 4

THE KIMONO
BLOCK PATTERN

Historically the Kimono or Magyar is the oldest 'pattern' and represents a very simple way of shaping fabric to the body—a primitive cut. Though now a highly developed pattern, it still appears in its primitive shape in stage costume designing, in baby wear, knit wear and at times in fashion wear.

The simplest shape of a kimono pattern, corresponding to the first arm position in the sketch opposite, has absolutely *no shoulder slope* or any other *shaping* to the figure: it cannot *fit*, it can only drape on the figure. Now and again fashion brings back this rather crude draped effect (e.g. to achieve a 'chunky' line), and so revives the original simple cut which *suits the style*, even if it does not, strictly speaking, *fit* the figure.

But on the whole, under the influence of modern ideas of design and fit, the kimono has undergone many changes and transformations and so has gradually become a complicated pattern. In its more elaborate, sophisticated shape it belongs, therefore, to advanced pattern designing and, when the kimono is in fashion, designers often aim at effects which can be achieved only with great skill and a thorough understanding of the various cutting and fitting problems involved.

The kimono appears nowadays in a great variety of styles, whereas before the range was small and change of style was limited almost entirely to decorative work. Now a whole technique of special adjustments and manipulations has developed around it to 'improve' its cut and *fit* and to increase its possibilities in fashion and style variation. It is as a result of all this that it can no longer be considered a simple pattern, though some versions of it are still simple enough.

Most of the improvements introduced into the kimono are directed towards making it fit more like an ordinary bodice with set-in sleeves, yet without losing the attractive effect and smooth, graceful line of the continuous shoulder and sleeve. This creates various problems to the solving of which are due the many difficulties of kimono pattern cutting. It is more important to under-

stand these difficulties and the reasons why they occur than to try and produce the perfect kimono pattern which will fit all figures and suit all styles: this is hardly possible. As with collar cutting, kimono cutting is largely a question of *arriving at good results* through understanding the problems involved and knowing how to deal with them.

If one considers the sketches on the opposite page, it becomes clear that the arm position has an effect on the *length* of the line A–B–C which is the Top line (NP to wrist) and the line D–E–F which is the underarm (waist to wrist). In the top sketch A–B–C is shortest and D–E–F is longest. In the bottom sketch A–B–C is longest and D–E–F shortest. The two middle figures show intermediate lengths. All this can be established and checked on the figure by direct measurement.

Only a sleeve cut separately and set into an armhole can adjust itself to this change of length and allow for complete freedom of movement. As will be seen from FIG. 1 below, a set-in sleeve actually has some excess length in each position: this appears as a 'fluting' fold above the shoulder when arm is raised or under the arm when arm is held down (it shows better on a bodice laid flat on the table than on the figure). This adjustable reserve of length is the result of the way the crown and armhole are shaped and joined.

It is impossible to have this *automatic adjustment* in a sleeve which is cut in one with the bodice, where there

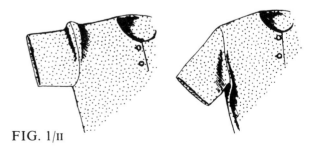

FIG. 1/II

is neither crown nor armhole, and so this becomes the *central problem in kimono fitting*. A correct choice of sleeve position, i.e. sleeve 'slant' has to be made in every case. If a position similar to the top sketch is chosen, then there is enough *underarm length* to allow the arm to move upwards comfortably, but the *sleeve fits badly on the top* as soon as the arm is lowered, developing creases and drags from SP and tightness over the Top arm muscle. If, on the other hand, the sleeve is cut with a good 'slant' and a 'break' at SP (as the lower sketches), it will have a smooth fit along the top due to the extra length achieved by slanting, but will lose length under the arm and feel uncomfortable as soon as the arm is raised.

The problem is solved by first choosing a suitable slant for the sleeve to ensure its good fit on the top, and then introducing extra length into the shortened underarm by means of a 'gusset' which releases the sleeve to allow freedom of movement.

It must be noted that there are several suitable slants to choose from for the top of the sleeve (basically represented by the two middle sketches on the right), and there exists quite a variety of 'gussets' to ease the underarm fit: both are varied according to fashion, style, the fit aimed at, length of sleeve and texture of fabric.

The more slanted kimono sleeve, particularly in the closer-fitting styles, usually needs a 'break' at SP to accommodate the shoulder bone, the angle of which becomes more pronounced as the arm moves down (lowest sketch on the right). With some exceptions (mainly loose sleeves with large 'armholes'), kimono sleeves fit better when there is a break at SP. Not only does this add length to the Top line of a kimono, but it does so at the right point, at SP, where it is needed, not at the wrist where it would be useless.

The Kimono block is produced from the standard Bodice block and the Straight sleeve block. Before using the bodice it is necessary to adjust it to suit the special requirements of a kimono fit:

(*a*) **The shoulder seam must be centred** since shoulder and sleeve are cut in one: this ensures a better line for the kimono Top seam which must run down the middle of the arm.

(*b*) **The bust width must be re-distributed** to reduce difference between back and front and to place side seam well under the arm so that it runs smoothly into the sleeve seam.

(*c*) **The Bust (Shoulder) dart must lose width** to provide some *ease* for the front 'armhole part' which in a kimono *drapes* over the hollow and shoulder bone instead of moulding it.

(*d*) **The rest of the Shoulder dart must be moved** to another position to facilitate kimono construction.

(*e*) **The Back shoulderblade dart must be used to its full depth** to tighten back 'armhole part' which tends to sag (unless shoulder padding is used, when dart is less important).

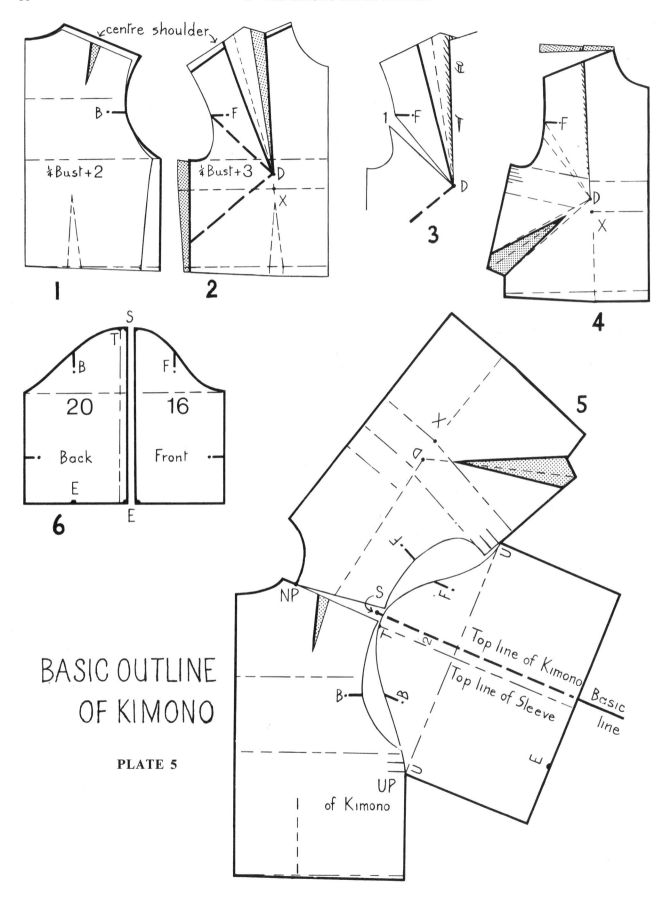

centre shoulder

¼Bust+2

1

¼Bust+3

2

3

4

20
Back

16
Front

6

BASIC OUTLINE
OF KIMONO

PLATE 5

5

Top line of Kimono

Top line of Sleeve

Basic line

UP
of Kimono

PREPARING BODICE BLOCK FOR THE ADAPTATION – Plate 5

The Back – FIG. 1: Outline to the waist and before cutting out draw a *Centre shoulder seam*, as usual (0·5+ cm above NP, 1 cm above SP). The shoulder must be long enough to allow for a full shoulderblade dart (1·5–2 cm extra length).

Along the Bust line measure from CB ¼ Bust + 2 cm and mark the new UP. Repeat measurement (25 cm for B 92) along the Waist line and drop a perpendicular for provisional side seam, thus forming a rectangle below the Bust line. Cut out the pattern.

The Front – FIG. 2: Outline to the waist and measure ¼ Bust + 3 cm for new UP (26 cm for size B 92). Repeat on the waist level and draw the perpendicular side seam.

From the point of the Shoulder dart – point D – draw a line to point F on the armhole and cut on it (FIG. 3). Close enough of the Shoulder dart to open a gap of 1 cm in the armhole slash; then secure (paste) the gap which can now be ignored (it should not be more than 1 cm).

Transfer the remainder of the Shoulder dart to a new *diagonal underarm position*, the line running from 4–4·5 cm above the waist to point D (FIG. 2). Shorten dart to just below the True Bust line (FIG. 4). With Shoulder dart closed complete the Centre shoulder seam.

On the side seams of both back and front mark several 1 cm divisions, measuring down from UP (Bust line) 1–2–3 cm, etc.: they will be used at the next stage.

Sleeve: Outline and cut out a Straight sleeve to the elbow, straight at the bottom, and the same width right through, i.e. 36 cm in size IV (B 92).

THE KIMONO BLOCK – basic position – Plate 5

Using a large sheet of paper (75 × 50) place the back in the lower left hand corner, 2 cm away from the edge, and secure in this position. Place the front as shown in FIG. 5 with SP's on the same level but *with a 1 cm gap between* them and with the front NP touching the back shoulder 1·5–2 cm below the back NP: excess shoulder length will be taken out by the shoulderblade dart. Secure the front in this position. Then place the sleeve to the armhole in such a way that the two U points of the sleeve are *the same distance down each underarm* of the bodice. The 1 cm divisions help to adjust and check this equidistant position.

This is **the basic Kimono position** which can already be used as a pattern, though in modern cutting its use is limited. It is used mainly to produce a *more advanced Kimono block*.

Note that the Top of the sleeve (point T) may either touch the armhole or overlap it or not reach it: this will vary with individual shape and size, but is of no importance at this stage. Any overlapping, however, should be noted as it usually indicates a square, long shoulder, for which provision can be made later.

With the sleeve in this position (absolutely equidistant

down the side seams), note which point of the crown comes to the *middle of the gap* between the two SP's: this is the **Kimono Shoulder point** (S) from which runs the **Kimono Top line** (or seam), *parallel* to the Top line or middle of the sleeve block and usually 2 cm (or 1·5) to the front of it. Mark this line through on to the paper underneath and remove the sleeve pattern. This is *the basic line for the planning of the different slants* of the Kimono sleeve.

The sleeve pattern is cut in half along the new Kimono Top line, the back part being usually wider than the front (FIG. 6). Each part is used separately for the next stage of construction.

Having established **the basic Kimono line** (i.e. Kimono Top line), it is now possible to work *from it* to find the more sloping positions of the sleeve, and to provide extra length at SP by breaking the continuous line at that point (over the shoulder bone).

It is convenient to mark the various 'slants' for the different sleeve positions on the basic block without necessarily completing the whole sleeve: any type of sleeve can then be planned from it, as required (FIG. 2). In practice it is also usual to have a separate block for a short-sleeved kimono and one for a long-sleeved kimono with a more slanted sleeve.

Along the basic line (FIG. 2 – broken line) measure from point S the sleeve length to elbow (32 cm) and mark point E. Then at E measure, at right angles to the line, 2·5 cm down and draw a line from S through this new Elbow point. Since the line slopes more, when the kimono is outlined there will be more break in the line at SP. This slant, known as the 2·5 cm slant, is used mainly for short, loose sleeves.

From the new E point measure 2·5 cm down to obtain the 5 cm slant, and from the latter, again measuring 2·5 cm, the 7·5 cm slant line. All the lines go up to point S. With increase in slant, the 'break' also increases and becomes more obvious (FIGS. 2 and 3). **N.B.** If preferred, a 3–5 and 8 cm slant can be used instead.

For the front the various slanted lines are measured in the same way. Accurate measuring is important.

FIG. 2/II

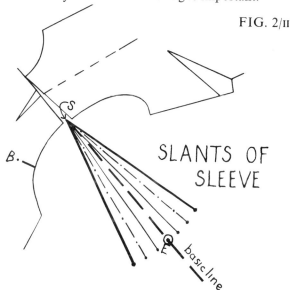

SLANTS OF SLEEVE

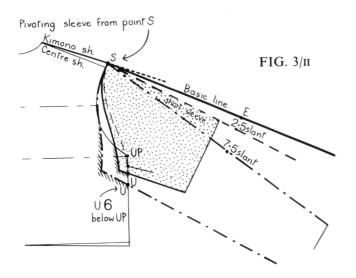

FIG. 3/II

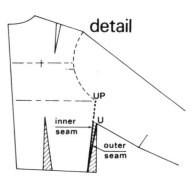

detail

SHORT SLEEVE KIMONO BLOCK
FIGS. 4 and 5

To complete the Kimono pattern for a short sleeve, which may be less slanted than a long kimono sleeve, proceed as follows: take the back of the sleeve (the wider part) and place it with its highest point to S (i.e. middle of shoulder gap), and with its Top edge following the slanted line *selected for the style*, i.e. in this case the 2·5 (3) cm slant (FIGS. 3 and 4). The underarm of the sleeve overlaps into the underarm of the bodice (UP moving down to U) and it is quite obvious that some underarm length is lost.

Proceed in the same way with the front part of the sleeve: the overlapping and loss of underarm length should be the same, so that the remaining sleeve and bodice underarm lines match. But there is often a slight difference and this can be adjusted, either by altering the slant a little or simply by *making* the two edges match.

Outline the final kimono as shown in FIGS. 4 and 5, *passing through the middle of the shoulder gap*, and separate back from front. Note the lowering of UP (now point U): this loss of underarm length, can be measured and most of it is usually replaced by a 'gusset'. In some cases, however, patterns with a small slant, such as a 2·5 cm slant, omit the gusset if the fit of the garment is loose and if it is not worn for work or sport involving much movement, particularly raising of arms.

This is a matter which the cutter must decide by judging each case on its merits.

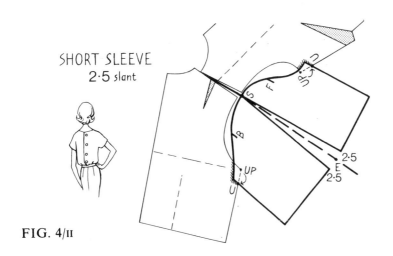

SHORT SLEEVE
2·5 slant

FIG. 4/II

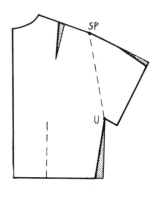

FIG. 5/II

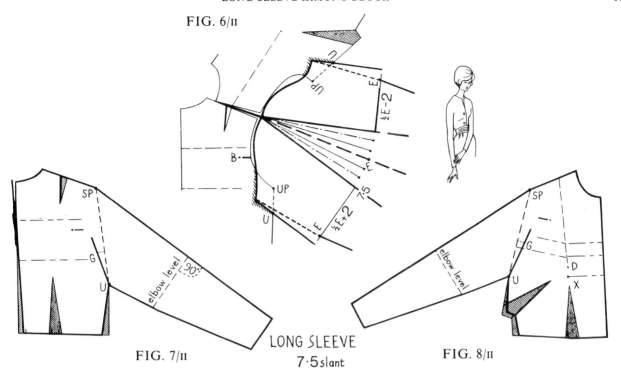

FIG. 6/II

FIG. 7/II

LONG SLEEVE
7·5 slant

FIG. 8/II

LONG SLEEVE KIMONO BLOCK
FIGS. 6, 7, 8, 9

The Kimono block with long sleeves is obtained in the same way, but by following a *more sloping sleeve line* — the 7·5 cm slant (FIG. 6). In the block it is usually presented as a Tight fitting sleeve.

It will be noted that the overlapping of the underarm lines of bodice and sleeve is considerable and so is the loss of underarm length which may be more than 12–13 cm. A *gusset is essential* for this cut which has a *smoother fit along the top*, with more length over the shoulder bone.

The Top line is continued to a full sleeve length (60 cm) and from it are measured, at right angles, the correct elbow and wrist widths for a tight fitting sleeve. Measure $\frac{1}{2}$ Elbow + 2 cm (17) and $\frac{1}{2}$ Wrist + 2 cm (10·5) on the *back* sleeve, and deduct the 2 cm from the *front* part. Then draw the underarm seam of the sleeve through these points (FIGS. 7, 8, 10, 11).

N.B. If point S – top of Basic line – comes only 1·5 cm to the front of the sleeve middle, then only 1·5 cm (not 2 cm) must be added or deducted at Elbow and Wrist.

In adaptations, but not in the block, an elbow dart, similar to the one in the French Tight fitting sleeve, can be introduced into the back part of the *tight* kimono sleeve by slashing it *at elbow level* from underarm up to Top line, and opening 2–3 cm (FIG. 9).

Although it is usual to make this Kimono block with a long and tight sleeve, just as the 2·5 cm slant block is usually made with a short loose sleeve, it must be clearly understood that in adaptations *either block can be used* for a variety of styles, with long or short sleeves. The **distinctive feature of each block is** really **the slant of the sleeve,** and just as there are *long* kimono sleeves which are quite loose and draped, and so can best be cut from the 2·5 cm slant block, so there are *short* sleeves which are very close fitting, moulding the shoulder and Top arm, and for these the long-sleeved block with the 7·5 cm slant is more suitable. The blocks are therefore distinguished mainly by *the fit* of their sleeves.

The underarm seam of the kimono can be taken either from point U (on the intersection of sleeve and bodice) wherever it happens to come according to the sloping of the sleeve, or from point UP *of the original bodice*. The first is **the Outer seam** which gives a looser fit; the second — **the Inner seam** which gives a closer fit under the arms (see Detail on page 18).

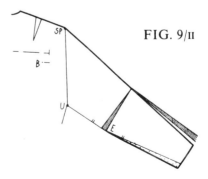

FIG. 9/II

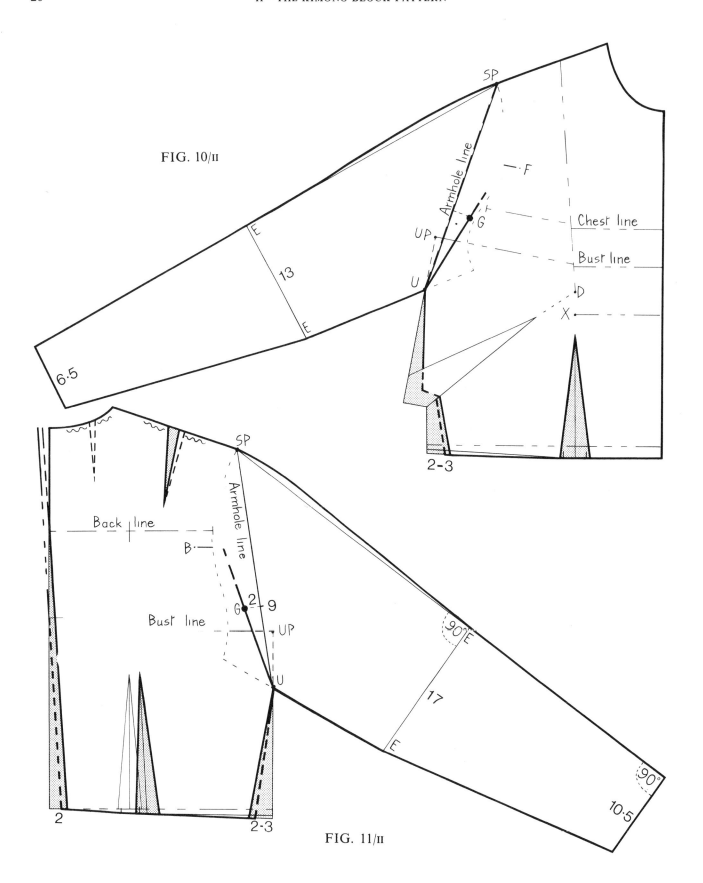

FIG. 10/II

FIG. 11/II

WAIST SHAPING – FIGS. 10, 11

Waist shaping follows the usual method of taking in on the side seams, using the Sl. CB, but seldom the Sl. CF, and taking out the remainder in waist darts.

The final result should equal quarter *finished* waist plus 1 cm for the front and minus 1 cm for the back. Thus with a 70 cm Waist measurement this would give 70 + 5 or 6 = 76 cm (the finished waist), divided by four (19 cm) and therefore 20 cm for the front and 18 cm for the back half pattern. **N.B.** For a tighter fit only 4 cm should be added to the Waist measurement.

Draw the inner side seams from U down to a point 3 (or 2) cm *inside the perpendicular*. For the Sl. CB use either the 2 cm slant, taking it, as usual, through the *Back line level*, or a 1·5 cm slant (from 1·5 cm inside the CB), taking it through a *lower point*, i.e. half-way up the CB line. The latter gives more 'dart fullness' to the neckline and more Back width (which is suitable for some figures and some styles) and loses less width round the bust than the 2 cm slant, which, however, is more generally used.

The waist darts, which are often deeper than usual, can be stitched higher (13–15 cm). An excessive front waist dart can be reduced by moving some of its width into the diagonal underarm (Bust) dart, or simply by 'easing' into skirt waist.

The kimono is essentially an easy fitting, draping pattern and the frequent overfitting of the waist to suit some present day styles often creates fitting problems, such as tightness round the bust and a tendency for the bodice to 'ride up' and puff out at the top *because of the close fit below*. Care must be taken not to lose too much bust width and to retain at least a 5–6 cm fitting allowance. This applies particularly to patterns for larger figures: they should be checked carefully just below the True Bust line. If necessary, width can be increased by small additions beyond CB and CF (adjusting neckline accordingly), without disturbing the underarm part and the sleeve (see also 'width addition' in Chapter Three).

REFERENCE LINES ON THE KIMONO BLOCK – FIGS. 10, 11

It is useful to indicate on the Kimono block the position of some **construction lines and points of the Bodice block,** such as Bust, Back and Chest lines, points B and F, etc. There are also a few special kimono reference lines such as the kimono 'Armhole', the 'Gusset line', points G, SP and the movable point U. They are necessary for reference both when adjusting the fit of a kimono pattern and when developing the pattern of a fancy style, particularly one with an elaborate gusset problem.

The Bust Line level is sometimes referred to in more advanced kimono pattern designing and, as well as this line, one can mark the *original* UP of the Bodice block which is referred to, for example, when planning the so-called 'High armhole' gusset, much used nowadays.

The Back Line and Chest line levels should also be drawn in or at least indicated, mainly on the 7·5 slant block. Their usefulness in planning fancy styles is obvious. They must, of course, be on the same level as in the ordinary bodice, and their correct position is established by measuring from the neckline down CB and CF, e.g., for B 92, 11 and 13 cm down respectively.

Points B and F of the bodice armhole are two other useful points of reference which one has to bear in mind when planning, for instance, some of the gussets.

The two special kimono reference lines are the **'Armhole line'** and the **'Gusset line'**. Point SP (the kimono SP), point G and point U – the *movable* kimono Underarm point, replacing the *fixed* bodice UP – are also important.

In a pattern which has no armhole, it is useful to be aware of the position of the 'arm scye' or 'arm's eye' (in French 'entournure du bras', which is a *line on the body* as distinct from the 'emmanchure', i.e. armhole, which is a *line on the garment*). It can only be indicated approximately by a straight line between SP and U, and is known as the kimono 'Armhole'. It is useful mainly for controlling the *armhole size* of a kimono which in some cases may get too tight. The *combined* SP–U of front and back must never be less than a standard bodice armhole and is usually more. It *increases* as point U *moves down* with the *slanting of the sleeve*. The Armhole line is referred to in many cases, e.g. when planning the Gusset line.

The Gusset line indicates the correct position for a gusset and corresponds approximately to the *lower part of a bodice armhole*.

From U measure along the Armhole line 9 cm up and from here take 2 cm inwards for point G – the point through which the Gusset line runs. This is the **construction line for every type of gusset,** whatever its shape, and the line on which the slashing from point U is done (FIGS. 10, 11). **N.B.** This position and the highest point (G) of the gusset are usually *checked on the figure before cutting* into the garment. It sometimes needs adjusting, i.e. moving farther in (towards CB and CF). It must come as near to the arm scye as possible, though making full allowance for a good Chest and Back width necessary in a kimono pattern.

It will be noted that the Gusset line, both on back and front, slopes in the direction of the end of the Back and Chest lines respectively, and towards points B and F (if these are marked on the kimono). On the figure these points indicate the position of the line where the arm begins. Hence the importance of being aware of all these points and lines in a kimono.

N.B. If the Kimono underarm seam is changed from the Outer to the Inner (see Detail on page 18), the Armhole and Gusset lines must also be changed to follow the new intersection of lines.

VARYING THE SLANT OF THE KIMONO SLEEVE

This is a question of both design and fit, and it must be clearly understood that besides using the three slants shown in FIGS. 2 and 3 it is possible to follow any slant one may consider suitable for a style, sloping the sleeve even beyond 7·5 cm, if necessary, e.g. 10 cm and more. Examples of this are given later. It all depends on the details of the design, on the length of the sleeve, its fullness, fit round the shoulders and also on the fabric, shape of figure and on fashion generally.

As an example, a sleeve in a soft, stretchy fabric can do with less slanting because it stretches and shapes itself to the shoulder bone and so forms a 'break'. With a stiff material, and particularly with a long sleeve (all troubles are worse in long kimono sleeves), more slanting is essential. Broadly speaking, **loose sleeves** of any length, and most, but not all, short sleeves need less slanting. **Sleeves moulding the arm,** long or short styles, and most sleeves below the elbow need more sloping and a 7·5 slant would generally be used for them.

Actually, the slant of most long and tight sleeves is often increased by a very popular adjustment known as **'squaring of the shoulder',** explained in detail in Chapter Three, which has the effect of sloping the line further (i.e. more than 7·5 cm) and at the same time of providing more room for the shoulder bone. For many figures it is advisable to have it as *a permanent adjustment* made on the block (see FIG. 3/III in the next chapter).

THE SIMPLIFIED KIMONO BLOCK
—Plate 6

This is a more simply constructed Kimono pattern useful mainly for simpler styles of kimono blouses, dresses, etc., with cap sleeves, short sleeves and sometimes long but loose sleeves. It is given in two stages.

STAGE I

The size of the paper must be equal to

$$\tfrac{1}{2}\textbf{ Bust} + 5\text{ cm} \times \textbf{LW} + 1\text{ cm}$$

Fold the paper lengthwise in half to mark the *centre crease.*

Back (left half): from top edge, down CB, measure 1 cm for point O (the nape). From O square Neck line and measure 7 (6·5) cm out and 1 cm up for NP.

The lower edge of the paper is the waist. Halve O to waist and take this point 4·5 cm down for the Bust line, ruled right across the paper (4 cm down for small sizes).

Along the top edge measure from NP the length of the shoulder, 12·5 cm, and take this point 4·5 cm down for SP. Rule the basic sleeve line from NP, through SP, as far as X on the centre crease.

Reduce the waist by 3 cm and rule the slanted side seam up to the Bust line (to point U).

Front (right half): Everything here is measured as in the back and could be traced through. The exception is the neckline depth measured 7·5 (7) cm down CF and curved up as usual. **Cut out the draft** along the 'shoulder-sleeve' lines and along the side seams.

STAGE II

Use a second sheet of paper 7 cm longer (higher) and 22 cm wider, and rule **a line** 1·5 cm **below the top edge.** Place the cut out back and front on it, with NP's touching the ruled line, i.e. 1·5 cm below the top edge, and with CF along the right and the CB along the left edge. Outline and remove the cut-out patterns or simply secure the back and front in this position by pasting. The kimono is completed by working round these outlines.

To improve the fit of this very simple kimono and to give it **a better balance on the figure** add height to the back by adding 1·5 cm above NP, SP, X (and Z), and ruling a new, *higher* line through these points. Back NP now touches the top edge of the paper. The Front can lose 0·5+ cm below SP, and so have a lower, more sloping shoulder–sleeve line, to balance the gain in the back (see Plate 6—Stage II).

The sleeve, which is now only a *short cap sleeve,* is *extended* to a basic short sleeve length by placing one side of a set square along the 'shoulder–sleeve' line and the other to touch the underarm at point U. Rule line Z–U which must measure Top Arm + 2·5 cm, i.e. half of sleeve width (**N.B.** if it is much less point U must come down). This gives now a *long* cap sleeve, but still *without an underarm.* For a complete sleeve, with an underarm, rule a line 3 cm farther out and parallel to Z–U. This sleeve measures about 15 cm from SP. Further length can be added in the same way. Repeat everything on the front or trace it all through.

Draw a 2–3 cm underarm Dart 4 cm below the Bust line.

Complete the pattern by sloping the waistline from CB towards the side seam as usual. Then, in the front, add the 2–3 cm dart allowance *below the waist* and drop the CF 2–3 cm, before completing the waistline.

Plan the waist shaping, as required, following the usual method (see Final Pattern). The CB line can be slanted from 1+ cm inside CB through a point half-way up: this adds to width of neckline and provides a 'dart' which can eventually be moved into the shoulder. If the 2 cm Sl. CB is used (tighter back), it will go through the Back line level, found 11–12 cm down CB from O.

The top line of this kimono has no break at SP. To introduce it, and also to give the sleeve **a bigger slant,** slash from point U up to SP and *overlap at U* 1–2 cm (see the last two FIGS. of Plate 6). Re-trace the whole pattern: it can now be used for closer-fitting sleeves and

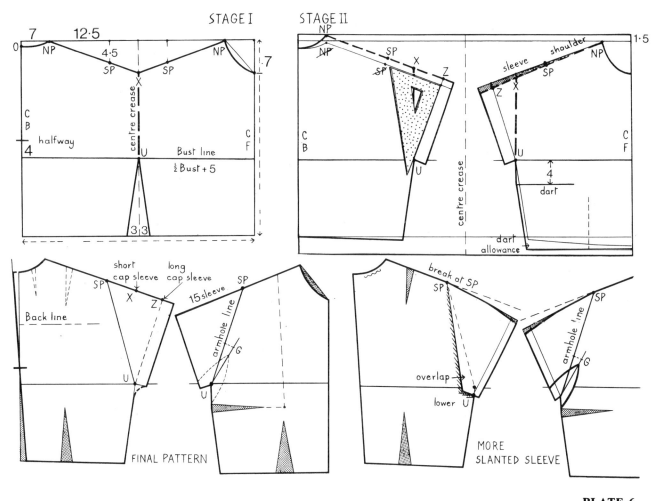

STAGE I STAGE II

FINAL PATTERN

MORE SLANTED SLEEVE

PLATE 6

would in many cases require a gusset which, of course, is optional for the basic pattern.

Because of the slightly different slope of back and front sleeve, the underarms may not match perfectly and would have to be adjusted a little at the final stage.

N.B. If one wants to avoid doing this pattern twice, on two different sheets of paper, one allows, of course, straight away an extra 1·5 cm at the top (ruling a line, as in Stage II) and combines the two stages by simply drafting the back 1·5 cm higher than the front.

Kimono style adaptations involve methods and adjustments of the basic pattern, such as adding width, length, transferring darts, planning WR, etc. which, but for details, are very much like the methods used for ordinary Bodice block adaptations.

But there are also some special adjustments and ways of using the pattern which are more specifically connected with the basic structure of a kimono and with the special difficulties of its cut and fit. Reducing or increasing the slant of the sleeve, improving the fit of the shoulder and, above all, solving the central problem of kimono fit — that of obtaining a well fitting sleeve at the top with sufficient length under the arm — these are the *special* problems in designing, cutting and fitting kimono styles. Of these the biggest is that of skilfully combining an attractive appearance with a comfortable fit, and this naturally leads to the question of gussets — visible and invisible — which have now become so important to the pattern designer.

Various methods exist for dealing with all these problems: the most important are presented in this chapter. It must be stressed from the beginning, however, that their application is never controlled by any definite rules and that their choice will always be influenced by many factors — shape of figure, fabric, details of style and, of course, fashion. In fact, the use of the kimono in advanced pattern designing makes considerable demands on the skill, experience and good judgement of the cutter.

ADDING LENGTH TO KIMONO BLOCK: THE ONE-PIECE DRESS — FIG. 1

The waist-length Kimono block can be **extended to Hip level** by continuing the *straight* CB line (not Sl. CB) 22 cm down and then drawing the Hip line across (FIG. 1). After measuring on it, from CB, $\frac{1}{4}$ Hips + 1·5 cm for point H, complete the side seam up to the waist, curving it as usual (FIG. 1). This is a **Hip-length Kimono block**. The front is obtained in the same way ($\frac{1}{4}$ Hips + 1·5 cm) because the kimono has a *centred* under-arm seam.

The full-length Kimono block is just a continuation of the hip-length pattern. Continue CB line down to full skirt length, preferably the basic length, to be shortened (or lengthened) later, as required by fashion. Draw the hemline on the level and measure on it $\frac{1}{4}$ HW + 4·5 cm. Again the front is completed in exactly the same way as

the back, because of the centring of the kimono underarm.

In adaptations the basic hem width can of course be increased (or reduced), more often with the help of additional seams.

ADDING WIDTH TO KIMONO BLOCK — FIG. 2

A distinction must be made between adding width for style and adding width for a bigger size.

Addition of width for style, i.e. for a design which has a looser fit and a fuller line, is generally made under the arm, as shown in FIG. 2. It actually *shows* as increased width or fullness under the arm (e.g. in a coat).

The addition to bodice and sleeve underarm is not necessarily the same: it is often less on the sleeve than on the side seam. The addition may be only on the bust or Top arm level, *running off to nothing* at the waist or elbow, or it may go right through (as shown in FIG. 2). In the latter case, measure the addition, e.g. 2–3 cm, in two places, at the waist and somewhere higher (or lower) and draw the line parallel to the original seam, either shaped or straight. After measuring in the same way for the sleeve, let **the two lines meet and intersect.** Where the lines cross is **the new- point U.** Note that in all cases the bigger the addition, the lower point U comes down and the shorter the side seam becomes. For example of increase *at Bust level only* see Plate 14 at the end of the chapter.

N.B. It must be noted that because of a slight difference in the angle of back and front kimono, after an addition of width the two side seams may *no longer match*, and may have to be adjusted at the end by moving point U slightly up or down to make the length from waist to point U the same. This can be done either on the front or back (or both, half and half). The sleeve is altered accordingly, i.e. made narrower or, more often, wider at point U.

Addition of width for size, to increase the fitting *for a larger figure*, is usually made down the CB/CF and above the sleeve.

As well as increasing the width round the bust and arm, this addition increases also what in an ordinary bodice pattern would be the Back width and Chest width, neckline and shoulder length: it makes the whole pattern larger without making it looser *as a style*.

SQUARING THE KIMONO SHOULDER
—FIG. 3

The fit of a kimono sleeve, particularly of a long one, is much improved by what can be described as 'squaring of the shoulder'. This is an important adjustment which for some people is *added permanently to the block*.

The small sketch at the top of FIG. 3 shows the defect which this adjustment corrects. It eases the tight fit at SP and provides more room for the shoulder bone: it is therefore particularly important **for figures with square shoulders** on whom the kimono is more likely to produce folds or drags of this type. It is, however, also an adjustment that is usually done **for most Tight fitting sleeves,** since the closer fit is apt to develop this defect. It is also much used in the case of firm materials which do not stretch and 'give' over the shoulder bone and thus do not *improve* in wear.

These are the main cases when squaring is advisable. But, **when squared and padded shoulders are in fashion,** then the adjustment is used in all cases, to provide the room necessary for the shoulder pad.

As well as easing the fit of the shoulder, squaring results in an increased slant of the sleeve, and it does so

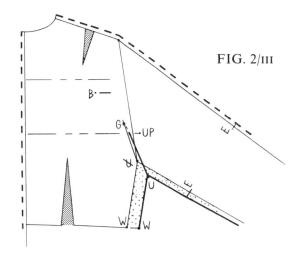

FIG. 2/III

without lowering point U any further. It is therefore also **a method for sloping the kimono more,** whenever this is necessary for style or fashion (see below).

The pattern is slashed from SP down the Armhole line, as far as point U, and opened at SP 2–3 cm or more. In a few exceptional cases this may be as much as 5–6 cm, but the average is 3–4 cm.

Note the **final shape of the Top line**—back and front. The 'squaring' at SP should not be exaggerated, except when the figure has a very pronounced shoulder bone or the shoulder is to be well padded. In the back the line usually passes on or just above the inner side and below the outer side of the slash; in the front it should be slightly lower.

If this adjustment is exaggerated, it may—as well as overshaping the shoulder—increase too much the width across the Back and the Chest.

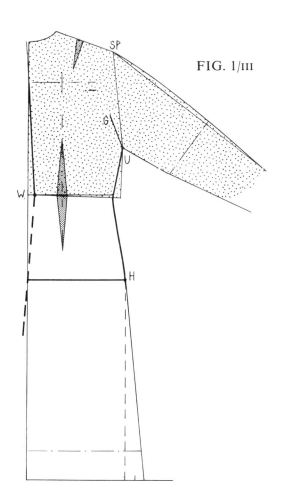

FIG. 1/III

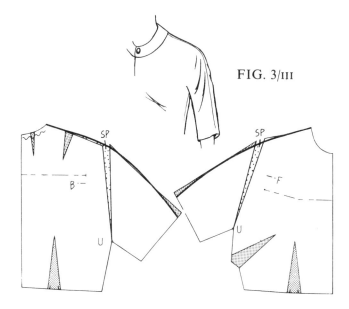

FIG. 3/III

INCREASING THE SLANT OF THE KIMONO SLEEVE – FIGS. 4, 5, 6

It has already been stated in Chapter Two that when style and fashion demand it, the slant of the sleeve is often increased *beyond* that of the 'Long sleeve block' (i.e. the 7·5 (8) cm slant). Basically this is done in the same way as obtaining the other slants of the sleeve, i.e. by pivoting the sleeve from point S and moving it down at Elbow point (E).

Not only does the sleeve Top line slope more, but its underarm overlaps more into the underarm of the bodice, moving point U down and losing length on both sleeve and bodice underarm (more than 1 cm on each). The Armhole line slightly changes its position and so does the Gusset line which must be replanned from the new line.

A quick way of achieving this effect is shown in FIG. 5 where a 7·5 cm slant sleeve is sloped more after slashing from point U as far as SP and then overlapping the two edges at U, 1·5 cm or more. The same result is obtained, and again underarm length is unavoidably lost and the fit of the underarm made less comfortable. Adjust the Armhole and Gusset lines *from the new point* U.

A combined method of sleeve sloping, as shown in FIG. 6, is often very useful. Here the **slant of the sleeve is increased considerably,** first by using a 10 instead of 7·5 cm slant, and then by 'squaring' it as well, 2–4 cm at SP. To compare the new slant with the basic slant, measure from a horizontal line (i.e. one at right angles to CB) which passes through NP, down to point E (elbow). The distance from this line or from the top edge of the paper to point E in FIG. 4 is 23 cm and in FIG. 6 it is 28 cm. Note, that by this test the use of the Sl. CB gives a more sloping sleeve in the back.

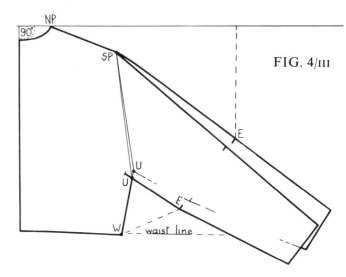

FIG. 4/III

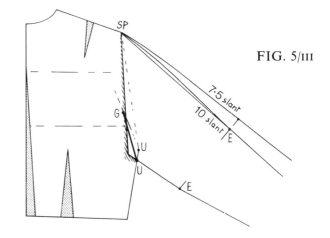

FIG. 5/III

REDUCING THE SLANT OF THE KIMONO SLEEVE: THE DOLMAN

The Dolman is a very popular classical kimono style. The name is often used to describe kimono sleeves in general, but this is not quite correct since the 'Batwing sleeve' kimono has a distinctive cut and line of its own, different from other kimono styles.

Its most characteristic feature is a low, **draped underarm.** There is no *visible* gusset, but the method of lengthening the underarm is achieved by **reducing the slant of the kimono sleeve.**

After outlining a 7·5 cm slant kimono, measure the *combined* length of bodice and sleeve underarm, from waist to elbow, i.e. W–U plus U–E. It will measure about 27–28 cm in an average size. Then measure distance W to E in a *straight* line across (18–19 cm) and compare with the underarm length W–U–E to establish the probable loss of length if a seam is drawn on that low level. Though the final seam, when *curved*, will be slightly longer, it is still much too short for comfortable wear and the distance W–E must be lengthened *by raising the sleeve.*

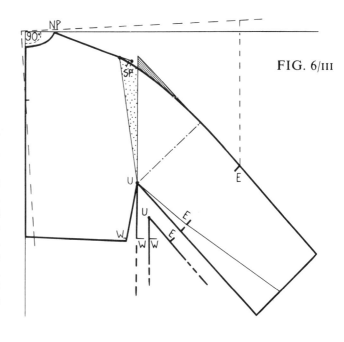

FIG. 6/III

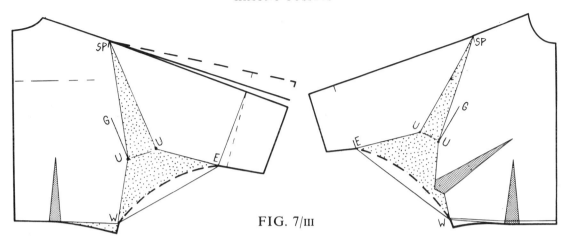

FIG. 7/III

Slash from U as far as SP and open at U a sufficiently big gap (6–7 cm) to increase the length of line W–E to 25 cm, i.e. 2–3 less than the necessary 28 cm: the extra will be gained by curving the seam above the straight line, and also by dropping the waist point as in FIG. 7.

In the front the same distance of 25 cm between W and E is obtained with a smaller gap at U (only 4 cm approx.) because in these draped styles the underarm Dart can be included in the seam: it simply *drapes* under the arm.

Length beyond point E does not affect the result and the sleeve can be simply continued to any length required by the style.

The slant of the sleeve is so much **reduced,** that the 'shoulder-sleeve' line becomes almost, and sometimes quite straight, without a break at SP. It is, in fact, very much **like the original basic kimono** (see FIG. 5/II). In some cases it may even swing in the opposite direction (upwards): this will happen when a still longer and *more draped* underarm is wanted.

Should it be necessary to transfer the Bust dart to another position, instead of 'losing' it in the draped underarm, e.g. to use it in the neckline for a draped fold (very popular in kimono styles), then the front gap at U must be opened more to obtain the full 25 cm length between W and E. The two lines W–E — back and front — must always match, since they are sewn together.

Finally, it must be noted that, although the underarm length of the Dolman was increased to 28 cm, this is still a *reduced length,* corresponding only to the 7·5 cm slant kimono underarm which, in most other styles, is generally extended by gussets. As already said above, the underarm can be further lengthened by opening the gap at U more or sometimes by curving the seam higher. But generally speaking the average Dolman style does not have a full underarm length and so is not particularly suitable for wear when freedom of arm movement is important: it has a graceful line, an easy fit round the bust, but is essentially a *draped* style in which arm movement is restricted.

KIMONO GUSSETS – general remarks

Coming to the fundamental problem of kimono fit, it is useful to repeat that the lengthening of the Top line, though improving the fit of the sleeve itself, invariably reduces the length of the underarm to such an extent that the arm can no longer be moved or raised freely. The basic cause of this defect has already been explained in Chapter Two and illustrated by the sketches on page 15. Here will be given the methods for overcoming this difficulty, i.e. the planning and adding of various gussets which, in one shape or another, have now become a necessary feature of more advanced kimono pattern designing.

First, however, mention must be made of some cases of kimono styles in which gussets can be omitted and of the circumstances in which this can be done. Basically, all simple kimono styles cut with a 2·5 (3) cm slant or on the Dolman principle can omit gussets provided ease of arm movement is of no particular importance and allowance is made for the strain at point U where the garment often tears.

N.B. Curving at point U minimises this danger but on the other hand reduces the underarm length even more.

In many *easy fitting* summer dresses, for instance, with short kimono sleeves (cap sleeves) one can ignore the slight discomfort and so omit gussets, reinforcing the underarm at U with double stitching or in some other way.

There is also the case of the soft, *stretchy* fabric, particularly 'knitted' fabric which often helps to solve the problem by providing some 'stretch' under the arm, and also over the shoulder bone, thus helping to *improve in wear* the fit of a kimono sleeve originally cut with a smaller slant. In such cases it is possible to use the 2·5 or 5 cm slant block which has a longer, more comfortable underarm, and to expect the sleeve *to adjust itself* to the figure in wear, i.e. to 'grow' over the shoulder because of the stretchy material. With a non-yielding texture, such as a brocade, this would be impossible. All this is taken into consideration by an experienced designer and pattern cutter.

Finally, in very voluminous kimono garments, particularly coats, one can sometimes ignore the gusset problem because, with the extra *deep 'armhole'*, the fit is almost that of a cape, and with the way a cape is worn (i.e. wrapped round the figure and with arms moving freely *inside* the garment), the necessity to move or raise the arms is usually not taken into consideration. In such cases either no gusset is used at all or only a very small one (to a certain extent this consideration applies also to Dolmans).

Apart from these and possibly a few other similar cases, all smooth-fitting kimono sleeves, particularly when cut to elbow length or lower, must adopt some method of relieving the underarm strain.

To understand the construction and effect of a gusset more clearly it is useful to examine the two cases illustrated in FIGS. 8 and 9. In the first diagram is shown **the addition at point U** of a square, folded diagonally, which can do little to release the strain because being added **outside the underarm** it does not really lengthen it: in fact, it may replace the original length by a shorter one. What it really does is to provide some 'bias' *stretch* and so prevent tearing at point U. It was obviously for this purpose that it was so much used in primitive kimono garments which, with sleeves at right angles to CB/CF, already had quite enough underarm length.

To obtain real benefit from a gusset, i.e. actual lengthening of the underarm and release of strain in the lower part of a kimono 'armhole', it is essential that the **gusset should be set into the garment,** after cutting precisely where the pull is felt when the elbows are moved out, i.e. **in the lower part of what would normally be the armhole,** just above point U (FIG. 9). It is not, therefore, only the extra length provided by the gusset, but also the easing of strain above point U which is its aim and object. In fact it aims at reproducing in a kimono the fit of an ordinary set-in sleeve.

Having established the importance of *setting in* a

gusset, one must now consider its **exact position on the Kimono pattern** and, finally, the **various types of gusset** used in modern pattern designing.

The gusset has quite a definite position on the pattern: it is always on or near the Armhole line, (see Chapter Two, FIGS. 10, 11). It must be placed so as to point in the direction of Back width and point B or Chest width and point F, all these being definite points on the standard bodice armhole.

Method—FIGS. 8 and 9 (also 10. 11/II):
From point U measure along the Armhole line 9 cm and from here measure 2 cm *in* for point G—the **Gusset point** through which **the Gusset line** is drawn from point U: the slash for the gusset is made along this line. It does not necessarily indicate the actual *length* of the slash, which is usually shorter, 7–8 cm (though sometimes it may be longer): it gives the correct direction and is therefore a construction line for every gusset, whatever its shape.

N.B. As already stated in Chapter Two, this position and the highest point of the gusset are usually *checked on the figure before cutting* into the garment. It sometimes needs adjusting, by *sloping in a little more* towards CB or CF.

A variety of gussets will now be explained: the Standard set-in gusset—the most frequently used; the Strip gusset; the Built-in or invisible gusset; the various Gusset Extensions and the High-fitting gusset.

THE STANDARD SET-IN GUSSET—Plate 7

This is always a cut-away section of the kimono underarm, varying in shape and size, which is expanded to gain underarm length and then set back into its original position. It is an elaboration of the simple square gusset (FIG. 9 below) which is less used in advanced pattern cutting because, though essentially correct, it can often be clumsy and difficult to set in.

The minimum size which can be conveniently cut away from the underarm usually takes the shape shown

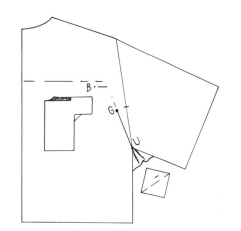

FIG. 8/III

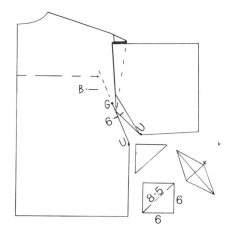

FIG. 9/III

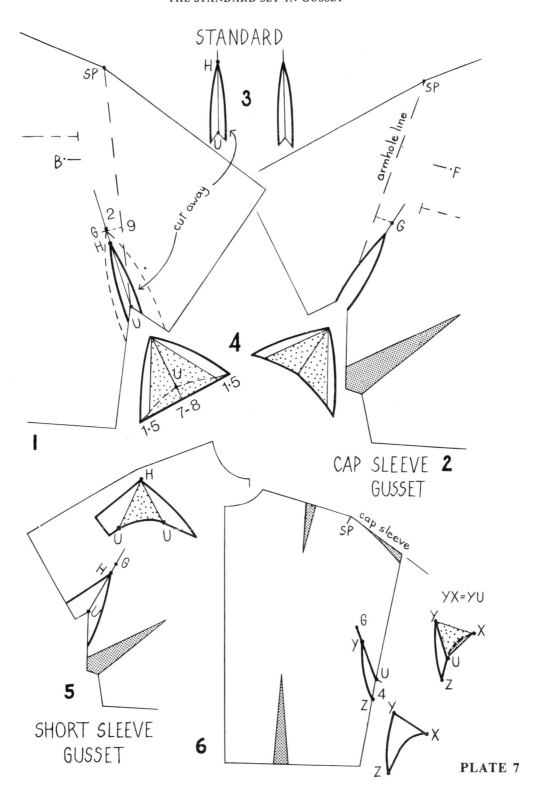

STANDARD

3

B

F

armhole line

SP

cut away

4

1

CAP SLEEVE **2**
GUSSET

5

SHORT SLEEVE
GUSSET

6

YX=YU

cap sleeve

SP

PLATE 7

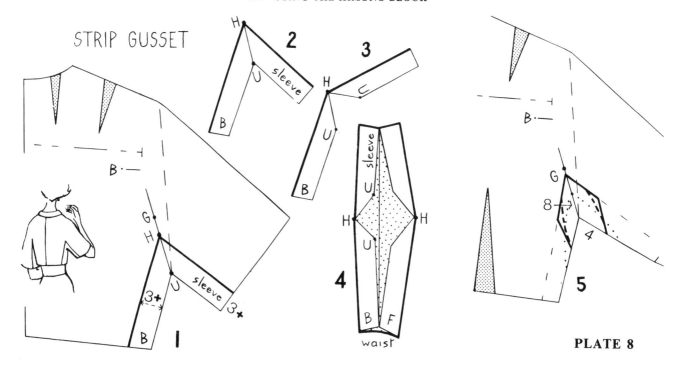

STRIP GUSSET

PLATE 8

in FIGS. 1 and 2 of Plate 7. Along the Gusset line mark 8 cm up from point U; then measure 1·5–2 cm down each underarm – sleeve and bodice – and connect the three points. Cut away this piece (FIG. 3), slash from U along Gusset line (FIG. 4), open over another piece of paper and paste down. Curve the lower edge 1–2 cm up. The amount added in the slash may be as little as 5–6 cm, but is usually 8 and may be 9 cm, bearing in mind, however, that in wear the edge may gain a little in length as it is usually cut on the bias (true bias along Gusset line). It is not essential therefore, in the gusset pattern, to regain the whole underarm length lost: this is seldom done. The two parts – back and front – are cut and set into the kimono separately and joined only when the whole underarm seam is sewn. The lower edges, therefore, *must match* in length.

The broken lines (in FIG. 1) show a different and bigger shape of the same gusset, made longer down the two underarm lines.

Another popular version is the **Short sleeve gusset** shown in FIG. 5: the diagram is self-explanatory. Finally FIG. 6 shows how the same principle is applied in a **style with cap sleeves,** i.e. with the shortest possible kimono sleeve, which has *no underarm.* Although in many such styles gussets are omitted, there are cases when it is advisable to have a gusset even with a cap sleeve (e.g. for sportswear). Such a sleeve usually fits close to the arm at the top and is cut on a 7·5 cm slant Kimono block. The gusset is outlined 4 cm down the *bodice underarm* (to Z). On the other side it simply follows the gusset line 6 cm up (to Y). After cutting away U–Y–Z, with a slight curve on Y–Z, add to one side of it (U–Y) an extension

(5–6 cm) to X, the outer edge of which, X–Y, must be equal to the length U–Y since it goes into the slash U–Y. Cut on the bias as usual.

The principle of the Standard set-in gusset may, of course, be applied to other shapes, but the ones given above are the most usual.

THE STRIP GUSSET – Plate 8

This is a very popular type of gusset much used in modern pattern designing. It is either a simple **continuous underarm strip** going from waist to sleeve edge or, more often, a **'shortened strip'** well concealed and quite inconspicuous under the arm. It can also be a **fancy underarm section** which is *part of the design* and so does not have to be concealed in any way.

Method; The **basic strip gusset** is first outlined as a narrow band (strip) 3–4 cm wide along the whole underarm – bodice and sleeve – separately on back and front. No measurement is taken up the Gusset line but highest point H is *where the two lines meet,* which usually works out about 5–6 cm up from point U.

The outlined strip, forming an angle at U–H, is cut away as a complete section (FIG. 2), then slashed from U up to H and opened out into a long strip (FIG. 3). The two long strips – back and front – are then placed on a sheet of paper to a straight line, waist and sleeve ends matching, as shown in FIG. 4.

Theoretically, it should be possible to open out each section until it is quite straight. In practice, however, it is better to leave them with a slight curve, so that a little width is gained in the middle (under the arm, where there is most strain). This also makes it easier to match the waists and sleeve edges, as one section is usually a little longer (as a result of unequal underarm angle of kimono back and front), and so in any case has to be curved slightly to match the shorter strip. Outline the whole wide 'strip' and insert it into the bodice with two seams — one each side — replacing the original underarm seam.

The advantage of this type of gusset is not only that it is so inconspicuous and on the whole easy to put in, but mainly that it gains considerable underarm length (almost replacing the whole loss) and, as a result of this, fits very high under the arm. More often than not it is cut on the bias and so adjusts itself even better to the shape of the figure.

There are many variants of this type of gusset, the most popular being a 'shortened' strip, only a few inches long and pointed at each end, which runs into the side seam, as shown in FIG. 5, Plate 8 (see also Plate 12). It is particularly suitable for long, tight, kimono sleeves.

The 'strip gusset' method is very useful to the modern designer as it is often possible to incorporate it in the fancy lines of a design. Instead of a simple strip, a whole fancy underarm section — part of the design — can be dealt with in this way (for example see Plate 15).

CONCEALED OR BUILT-IN GUSSETS
— FIG. 10

These gussets form quite an important group, and the lengthening of the underarm here depends entirely on the style of the kimono. It is possible in some kimono styles to work in an extension of underarm length without using a separate and visible gusset: the gusset is, so to say, built into the style and is thus concealed.

The Dolman gusset is really an example of such a concealed gusset which it is possible to have in this case because of the draped underarm of the style.

A more typical example, however, is a **kimono style with an extended yoke** (FIG. 10) in which the yoke part continues into the sleeve, i.e. forms the upper part of it. Whenever the kimono sleeve is thus divided horizontally by a fancy style line, it is possible, after separating the two parts, to make a slash in the lower part from U up to the highest point on the top edge, and to open at U 4–6 cm to increase the underarm length. The slash is always made in the direction of SP or along the Gusset line. The effect of this underarm extension is to reduce the slant of the lower part of the kimono sleeve and so lengthen it on the underarm while retaining the smooth fit of the 7·5 cm slant in the top part.

There are quite a number of kimono styles designed on these lines, i.e. divided horizontally. There may also be other cases where the design is suitable for building-in a concealed gusset and providing underarm length without either interfering with the style or using a separate set-in gusset.

The additional length at point U forms a draped fold under the arm, not very noticeable unless it is rather big: hence the amount added is generally comparatively small. Much depends of course on the texture of the fabric: in a stiff material, such as cotton or linen the fold would of course be more noticeable, and the addition is therefore usually smaller.

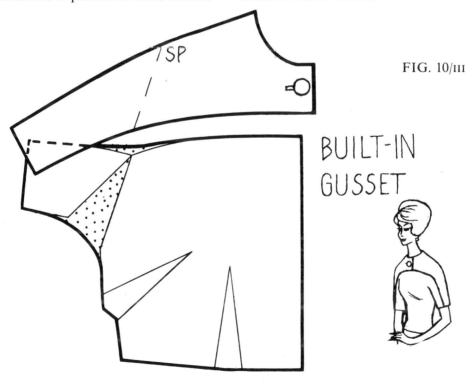

SP

FIG. 10/III

BUILT-IN GUSSET

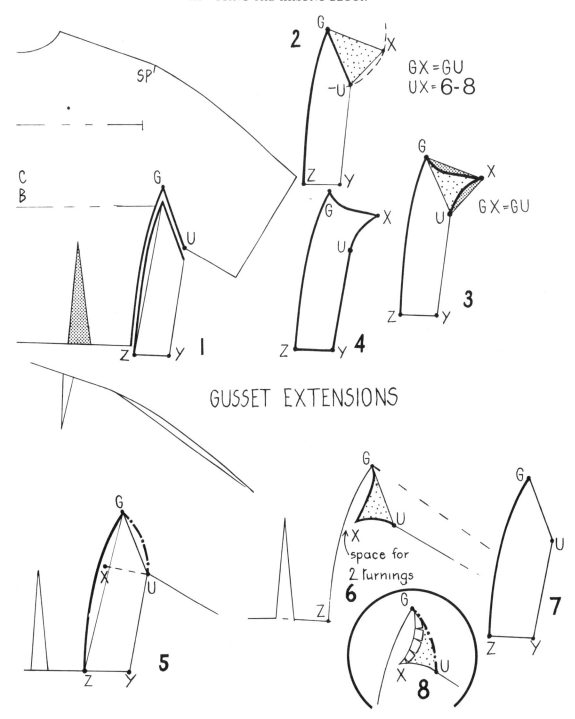

GUSSET EXTENSIONS

GUSSET EXTENSIONS—Plate 9

This is another useful method for dealing with insufficient underarm length in a kimono pattern. It is based on introducing the extra length as **an extension of a part of the kimono bodice,** without the use of a separate gusset piece.

The extension may be added to the sleeve part or to the bodice part, and occasionally to both, but in each case the style must be such that there is *a separate section* in it, e.g. a yoke or a panel, which is cut away from the main part of the pattern before an extension can be added to it. The method cannot be applied to a *simple* kimono style, without any fancy lines.

There are a number of such styles in present day fashion—styles which are particularly suitable for this method. In fact, the popularity of some kimono styles is largely due to the ease with which their gusset problem can be solved, for gusset *extensions* are generally easier to deal with than set-in gussets. Such are the various styles with yokes and panels, particularly with curved panels starting from the 'armhole'. Most of these, more or less curved, Panel lines start from point G, or a point just below or above G, but always on the Gusset line — the line which is nearest to a real armhole position. One of these curved Panel styles is used in Plate 9 to explain and illustrate the general method.

Method — FIGS. 1, 2, 3 and 4 show the extension **added to the bodice,** i.e. to the underarm section. FIGS. 5, 6, 7 and 8 show a similar **addition made on the sleeve part** of the kimono. In each case the same style is used with only a slight variation in the width of the underarm piece.

Plan and draw the Panel line from point G on the Gusset line (9 cm above U) down to a point (Z) 6 cm in from the side seam. This outlines a very narrow underarm section, only 6·5 cm in the widest part, which is then cut away along a very slightly curving line and, at the top, along the Gusset line U–G.

To this underarm section a gusset extension is then added as shown in FIG. 2. The addition of a 7 (8) cm gusset is made along line U–G, either by sweeping a circular line from G through point U, to obtain an equal length X–G at a distance of 7 cm; or, simply by measuring and making X–G equal to U–G, with X 7 cm away from U.

After adding the extension, trim it to the shape shown in FIG. 3, but taking care not to lose any length on the line X–G since this is the line which will have to be sewn to U–G on the main pattern (see FIG. 1) and so must equal it. FIG. 4 shows the shape of the final pattern incorporating the extension. No special 'setting-in' is involved since the seam edges will simply come together when the bodice is assembled.

FIGS. 5, 6, 7 and 8 show the same extension made this time on the sleeve part. It must be noted here, that in order to have sufficient room for the sleeve extension, the underarm part which is cut away must be of such shape and size that *the remaining gap*, between sleeve and Panel seam, is *big enough* for a full-size gusset extension *plus an allowance for two seam turnings*. The underarm section, therefore, is wider and curves out a little more *into* the back and front than was necessary in the first case, where it could be kept quite narrow. On the other hand, all difficulties and limitations disappear if the sleeve part is also cut away (dotted line from G FIG. 6) as is actually done in many of these styles. All these points, of course, have to be considered at the designing stage.

For the rest, the addition is made in the same way, always along the line U–G, this time U–G of the sleeve, and again the lines U–G and X–G must match. FIG. 8 shows an alternative way of producing the extension which is sometimes preferred because it ensures a correct length and shape on the edge X–G.

The question of whether it is better to make the extension on the bodice or on the sleeve *depends very much on the details of the style*. In the style given here either method can be used, mainly because the underarm sections are comparatively small and therefore the gussets are in any case well concealed under the arm. But, as a rule, although the sleeve extension is less visible, the bodice extension is simpler to plan and join and is, on the whole, more often used. There are cases, however, where a gusset extension added to the bodice may spoil an important line of the style, for instance a yoke, a panel, a raglan line, etc. In such cases the extension should always be made on the sleeve (with or without a separate underarm sleeve section). An example of this is given in Plate 11.

It is also possible, and in some cases suitable, to make smaller extensions on both bodice and sleeve parts, so that there is a seam in the middle of the gusset part. For various reasons, this has been found on the whole to be less satisfactory, mainly because the seam is not always in the best position and tends to make the extension more conspicuous and clumsy. On the other hand, this type of gusset extension can be expanded into a Dolman effect, by adding both width and depth under the arm; it can also be shaped to produce the opposite effect — the effect of a high-fitting underarm, similar in fit to the underarm of an ordinary bodice with set-in sleeves (see next section).

HIGH-FITTING GUSSET EXTENSION
or built-up gusset – Plate 10

This is a special case of gusset extension which in its final shape gives the appearance of an underarm with an ordinary armhole and set-in sleeve, while at the top the sleeve remains connected with the shoulder as a kimono sleeve. The special advantage of this 'building-up' of the underarm until it reaches its usual high level, is that the fit under the arm is made as comfortable as in an ordinary bodice with set-in sleeves while at the top the special features and attractive line of the kimono are retained.

It is an ingenious way of dealing with the main problem in kimono fitting, but is restricted to only a few suitable styles. There is actually more than one way of producing patterns of these particular styles and at least one other method is given in Chapter Five (as a Drop-shoulder method – in Plate 23, style C).

The method is explained here in detail through several stages of building up a gusset extension, but once the principle is understood, the final result can be achieved in a more direct way, as shown in FIG. 7. The same style with an underarm section starting from point G is used since it is mainly in these styles with a separate underarm or sidebody that the possibility of building up the underarm exists. The Panel lines divide the 'armhole' into a kimono part (approximately the upper $\frac{2}{3}$) and a lower part which can be changed into an ordinary armhole.

Before planning the style, it is useful to refer to the basic 7·5 cm slant Kimono block given in Chapter Two, to see how far point U drops below the bodice underarm point UP when the sleeve is pivoted from S for a 7·5 cm slant (FIG. 3/II). It will be found that UP which is on the original Bust line of the bodice block is over 5 cm above point U of the kimono, so that at least 5 cm underarm length is lost. The same will be found about the sleeve underarm which loses over 5 cm through overlapping at U. Therefore if 5 cm can be added above point U on the kimono side seam and sleeve underarm, the complete bodice block underarm can be re-established, which is precisely what this method achieves.

After outlining the underarm section (FIG. 1) and cutting it away (FIG. 2), plan a 6·5 cm gusset extension as usual. Then measure from U *straight up* 4–5 cm and cut away the part which projects beyond, but not before ascertaining that the *reduced* line G–X at the top is sufficiently long for the armhole part, approximately 6–6·5 cm or just under $\frac{1}{6}$ of an average easy fitting armhole (of 42–43 cm). The final back and front lines G–X should make up about $\frac{1}{3}$ of the armhole size, more than $\frac{2}{3}$ of which still remains *in the kimono part*, between SP and point G (see FIG. 6).

By measuring between SP and G, i.e. the point where the real armhole begins (back and front), and between G and X (FIG. 7), it is possible to work out the *total size*

of the armhole quite correctly and make sure that the lower part is not made too small.

It will be seen (FIG. 7) that if the line taken up from U towards UP simply follows a *slanted side seam*, the top (i.e. G–X) works out wider; if a straight side seam is followed, it may be too small. The checking of the top edge G–X is therefore important: if necessary to increase it, width can be added on the side seam, at U, as shown in FIG. 4 – the final pattern of the bodice underarm section.

The same applies to **the sleeve part** which in any case **must match the 'armhole'** G–X, to which it will be sewn. FIG. 5 shows the under-sleeve section cut away from the kimono and extended upwards in the same way: G–X equal to G–X of bodice section and the rest trimmed away. FIG. 6 shows a sleeve extension which is *not* separated from the main pattern. Note that the Panel line in this case must be sufficiently curved to provide the necessary turnings as well as the built-up sleeve underarm.

Once the idea of this construction is understood, it is of course unnecessary to go through the stage of first adding a full gusset extension and then trimming away the projecting part: the **upward extension** can simply be made to the required height – 4–5 cm. The more usual 4 or 4·5 cm addition (for a loss of over 5 cm) simply means a slightly *lower final armhole*, which is generally preferred, as is also a looser underarm fit.

When joined together, the 'armhole' and sleeve in the lower part should have the same ease of fit and the same underarm length as in an ordinary bodice pattern. Any possible 'drag' may come only from point G being *too low* a point *on the total armhole*, i.e. having too much kimono armhole in proportion to real armhole. In many of these styles, therefore, the curved Panel seam starts higher, i.e. above point G, though still on the Gusset line.

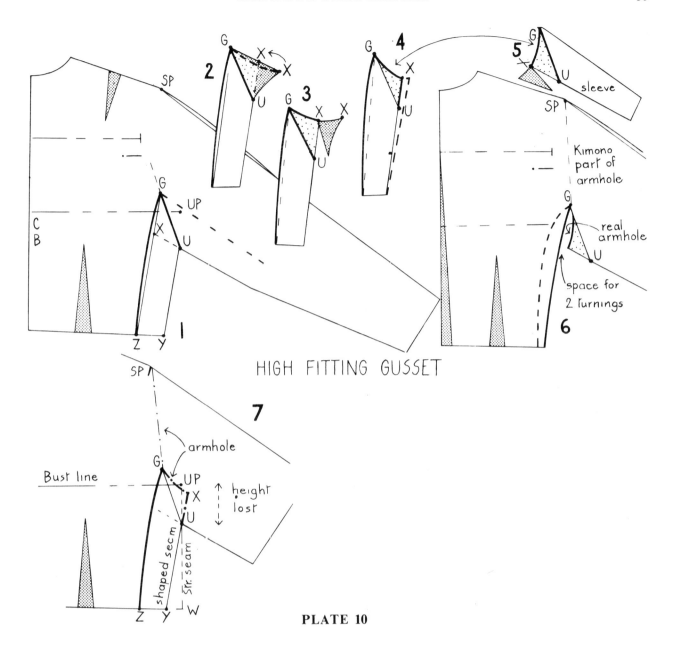

HIGH FITTING GUSSET

PLATE 10

In conclusion it must be stated that in present day designing the Kimono occupies quite a special place. It will be easily appreciated that in its more sophisticated modern shape it can often replace the ordinary Bodice block, imitating the fit of the latter and even reproducing details of its cut, such as sleeve and armhole, while still retaining distinctive features of its own in a softer, more 'draped' silhouette and easy fit. Indeed some designers seem to prefer the kimono to the ordinary block not only for raglan or drop-shoulder styles, but for a variety of other designs, adding set-in sleeves and armholes and treating it very much like an ordinary bodice block.

The two patterns nowadays are almost interchangeable and each can be made to acquire more and more features of the other. This is an interesting development, mainly to be found in haute couture designing: it is a trend which is in keeping with the less formal, more fluid, easy line and fit of many modern clothes.

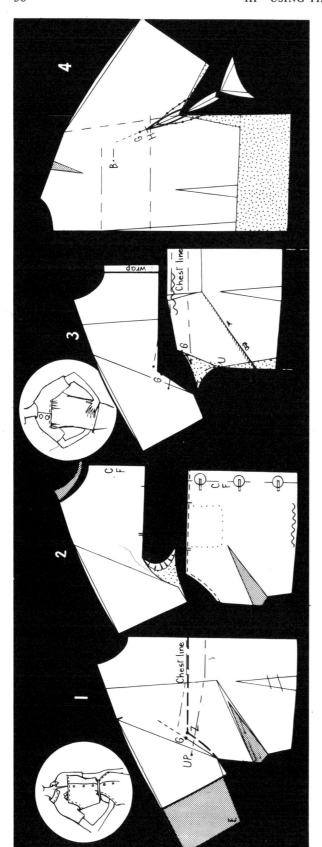

PLATE 11

The Plate shows two **Kimono styles with yokes** which *illustrate how the choice of a gusset is made.* In this case it is the choice of a **Gusset extension**, which can be added either to the bodice part or to the sleeve.

Style A—a dress bodice—could be interpreted in two different ways: with bodice stitched over lower part or, as it is clearly shown here, with lower part stitched over the yoke, *forming a pocket and emphasizing 'armhole'* part (outlined by stitching). The back is either the same or quite plain, with a set-in gusset, as in style B. Use a 7·5 cm slant Kimono block outlined to elbow level.

The yoke is on Chest line level, drawn at right angles to CF, and extends as far as the Gusset line or, preferably, to a point (Z) which is controlled by ½ Chest measurement + 1 cm and so usually comes inside point G. From point Z draw a slightly curved line, like *a flat armhole,* down to point U. Cut the pattern on this line. In order not to spoil this line which is *a feature of the design,* add the gusset extension to the sleeve part, making it 6–7 cm wide, as shown in FIG. 2.

Shorten sleeve to 20–23 cm from SP. Add 2–3 cm wrap to the lower part of the bodice, which can, of course, also be the top of a one-piece dress. Yoke just meets on CF.

Style B is an overblouse with a similar yoke, but in this case clearly stitched *over the lower part* and emphasized in the design, while the underarm (armhole) is quite inconspicuous. The gusset extension is therefore added to the bodice part, giving it a slightly more 'draped' fit under the arm.

The yoke is drawn 1 cm above the Chest line, as far as the Gusset line, along which the pattern is cut, as usual, before adding to it the gusset extension. As the yoke is quite high, its CF opening may be too short and so make it necessary to continue it *sideways* (under the yoke), or else to have an additional opening in the CB (a point of style influencing finishing technique). Add a wrap to the yoke.

Shorten sleeve, straighten side seam and add length required below the waist.

The back is quite plain and so *cannot have a gusset extension* as the front. It must have a **set-in gusset**, matching in width the gusset extension of the front (6–7 cm).

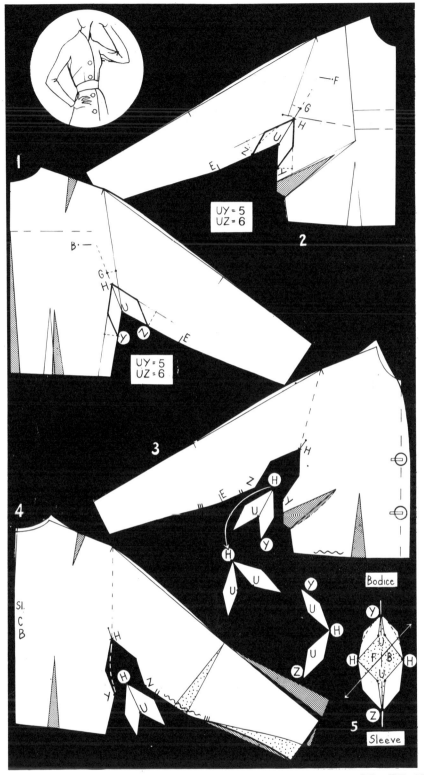

PLATE 12

PLATE 12

This shows a **Kimono bodice with tight long sleeves** for which a **shortened Strip gusset** is particularly suitable, as it is inconspicuous, long enough on the underarm to be comfortable yet not too loose in the lower 'armhole' part, so that it fits quite high under the arm.

Use the Kimono with the Sl. CB and the usual (shaped) side seams and darts of the 7.5 cm slant block. Add some wrap (2 cm) to the lower part of CF, running off to nothing at the top. Raise and widen neckline, back and front, to make it stand away a little.

The Gusset strip, 3 cm wide, is measured separately on back and front, only 5 cm long down the bodice underarm (U–Y) and 6 cm long down the sleeve (U–Z). The points at Y and Z are obtained by raising the opposite sides of the strips 5 cm. (Sometimes the angle is 'rounded off' as shown by dotted line in FIG. 2). Point H—height of gusset—is at the crossing of the two strips, and usually comes well below point G, only 6 cm up from point U.

After cutting away the short strips (FIGS. 3 and 4), slash from U up to H, open gap and place both strips to a straight line, as shown in FIG. 5, with points Y and Z matching and a slight gap at U. Outline the whole gusset.

When finished, the gusset will measure across H–F–B–H a little more than twice the strip width, i.e. about 9–10 cm, *replacing on the pattern* twice U–H, i.e. 12–13 cm, which accounts for the tightening and neatening of the fit under the arm. The underarm length Y–U–U–Z, is now almost equal to that of an ordinary bodice. Cut the gusset on the true bias for a still neater fit.

The sleeve (FIG. 4) is *shaped at the elbow* in the back, as tight fitting sleeves generally are.

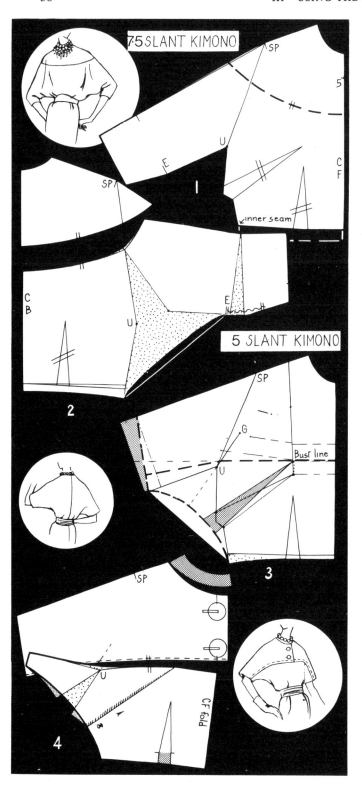

PLATE 13

The Plate shows two **Dolman styles** with **concealed gussets.**
Style A has a deep round yoke, well shaped to the shoulders and
a **very low, full and draped underarm,** the folds of which provide
the necessary length *without any visible gusset.*

Plan the style on a 7·5 cm slant kimono to make the yoke fit closer
to the shoulders and top arm. Outline yoke through points 13 cm
down CF, 9 cm below SP and 15 cm down CB, leaving CF and CB
more or less equal in height below. Add 2–3 cm below the waist
for a small pouch and dip the sides well (FIGS. 1 and 2).

After cutting away yoke, slash from U to the top edge along
Armhole line, and open at U more than usual—8–9 cm—to make
the underarm seam on the lower level, between W and E, at least
30–33 cm long. Curve it only very slightly.

For a sleeve of full or ¾-length it is advisable to shape it as
shown in FIG. 2.

Style B is a **Dolman less full under the arm,** with the underarm
seam shorter (less draped) and curved higher (closer to figure).
The yoke extends into sleeve and runs quite low across the front,
on Bust line level, passing a little *above* point U and down to the
edge of the sleeve 3–4 cm above the underarm seam. The back is
quite plain.

Since the fit over the shoulders appears to be somewhat looser
than in style A, the 2·5 or 5 cm slant Kimono block can be used,
at least *for softer fabrics.* The 7·5 cm slant, however, may be
preferred for a smoother fit at the top and for stiffer fabrics which
have no stretch.

When outlining the block, draw the underarm as shown in
FIG. 3, curving the line well upwards (4 cm). Shorten the sleeve
more on the top. Re-draw the Bust dart so that its point *touches*
the yoke line (FIG. 3) and close it transferring it into the yoke
seam (FIG. 4).

Slash from the underarm towards point U and open a gap
of 4–5 cm, again curving the seam upwards. This underarm is
less long and comfortable than in the previous style, but the style
clearly shows a neater and more *restricted* underarm fit.

PLATE 13

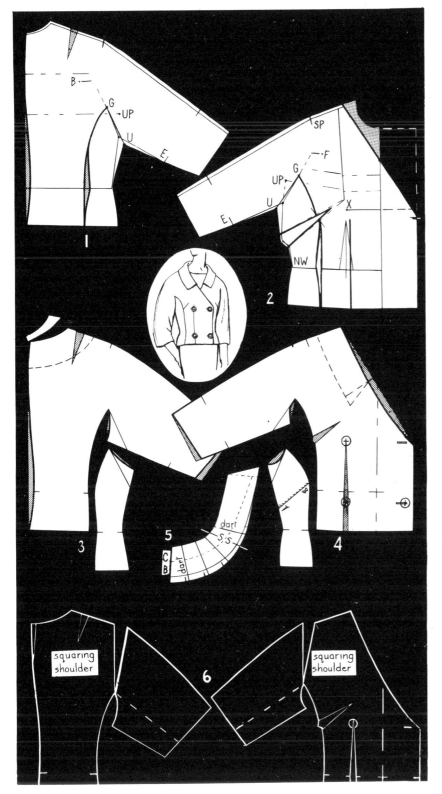

PLATE 14

PLATE 14

This is a kimono jacket which has an under-arm section or 'sidebody' outlined by a curved Panel seam. It can therefore have a **high-fitting, built-up gusset extension** which is, in fact, particularly suitable for such a style.

The jacket is semi-shaped, *outlining* the figure without fitting it closely, and it is cut to Waist measurement + 12–15 cm, with an easy fit on the hips. The style shown here has a wide DB wrap (9–10 cm), a cut-away neckline, a collar rolling high in the back only, and fairly wide sleeves.

Use the 7·5 cm slant kimono with shaped side seam, 2 cm in at the waist. Extend the block below the waist as usual, 10–12 cm down CB, allowing on lower edge ¼ hips + 2 cm. Add 1 cm to the bust width and 0·5 cm to sleeve, running off the lines at waist and elbow (FIGS. 1 and 2). As this is a jacket, add also 0·5 cm above the shoulder and sleeve. Lengthen sleeve to 10 cm below the elbow; later shorten the lower seam (FIGS. 3 and 4). If preferred, the top of the sleeve may be *curved more*, for width and style.

Draw the **Panel seams** from point G (or from 1 cm higher) crossing the waist ⅓ out from seam. To shape the waist use 1–2 cm darts in the Panel seams, suppress 1 cm in CB seam and also in the small front dart, moved slightly forwards so that buttons can come on it. Check waist to make it Waist + 15 cm and adjust darts if necessary.

The gusset extensions are added by simply continuing the slanted side seam and sleeve 4·5 cm higher, taking care not to reduce size of 'armhole' and under-sleeve edge by insufficient sloping out of seams. The curves must match.

Complete pattern by following details of the style.

Finally, it is an advantage in jackets to **square the shoulder,** as described earlier in the chapter (FIG. 3). In this case, this can be done at the end, when it is clear how much the gap at SP can be opened (1–2 cm or more), without losing completely the gap under the arm (which provides the turnings). Had the 'squaring' been done at the beginning, it might have been more difficult to build up the gusset extensions unless, of course, the sleeves were also given *separate underarm sections*, as so often happens in these styles.

FIG. 5 shows the flat collar, before darting it in the back part.

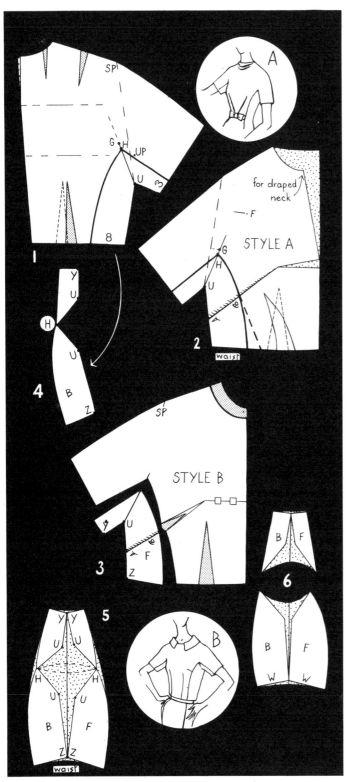

PLATE 15

This is a kimono **style with a fancy Strip gusset** which can be used as a gusset or **transformed into a built-up high-fitting gusset extension.**

The style here is quite simple and it has the same underarm section as the jacket style in Plate 14, except that here it continues into the sleeve as, of course, it must in order to form a strip gusset. The sleeve part is usually narrower (inconspicuous), whatever the shape of the bodice section.

Outline the whole section as shown in FIGS. 1 and 2, taking point H (Height of gusset) to 1 cm below G. To do this conveniently the underarm Bust dart must be closed and moved elsewhere, usually to CF, either permanently (style A) or to be returned later for style B (though in the front *underarm section* the dart is eliminated altogether).

Cut away the front and back underarm sections (FIG. 3), slash from U, open to straighten them out (FIG. 4) and place as usual on to a sheet of paper to a straight line (FIG. 5) with a small gap at U and with waists and sleeve edges matching.

Outline the whole together as one underarm section and use it like this *as a fancy strip gusset.* If it is felt that there is too much length under the arm, a horizontal dart (dotted line) can always be taken out at the fitting. Complete pattern according to style.

Version II: Instead of cutting the whole gusset in one, one can arrange bodice and sleeve pieces separately along a straight line, and then **build up an extension** of 4–4·5 cm above each, so that a high-fitting gusset is obtained, with 'armhole' and under-sleeve matching.

As already stated, the fancy strip gusset may appear in a variety of shapes, its lines always being part of the whole design. It has therefore great possibilities in style development and is very popular with modern designers.

PLATE 15

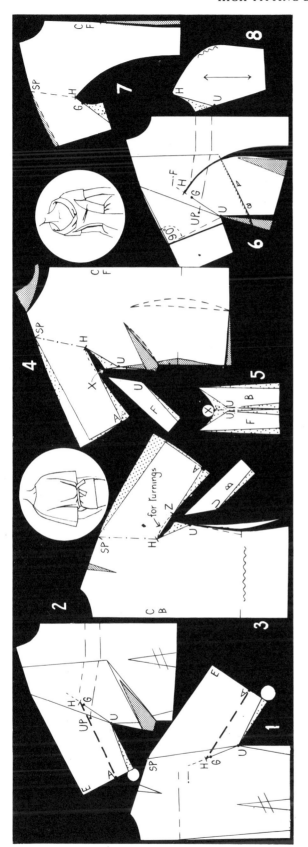

PLATE 16

These are kimono styles **with high-fitting, built-up gussets**. **Style A** is a loose overblouse with bell-shaped sleeves, to which a high-fitting gusset extension is added *after removing a narrow section from the under-part of the sleeve.*

Add 1 cm to lower edge of elbow-length sleeve (since the block is a *tight* sleeve), and then outline a narrow section, 5 cm wide, with the top point H coming just above point G. Cut along U–H–A, back and front. Lengthen the whole pattern 10–12 cm below the waist and, if desired, straighten the side seam (adding 2 cm at W) for a looser fit or make it only slightly shaped (FIGS. 1 and 2).

After removing the narrow under-sleeve section, the upward building-up of the side seam extension must be done *along the original slanted side seam*, as following the straight seam would make the 'armhole' part at the top too small. Add 4 cm above U (FIGS. 3 and 4), as it is difficult to add more here. Measure to check the 'armhole' part. At the lower edge of the sleeve add width for the bell-shaped effect (FIGS. 3 and 4) running the lines into SP

and into H, as shown in diagram (a little of the width may be used for turnings).

Join the two cut-away sections of the under-sleeve into one, leaving a small gap at the top (FIG. 5), and build up the 4 cm height in the middle before drawing the final curve which *must be equal to the combined front and back armhole* curve. Adjust a little if necessary.

If slight shaping of the side seam is desirable, this can very easily be done now by taking 1–2 cm in from the straight seam. Cut out boat-shaped neckline to suit style.

Style B is a close-fitting dress bodice. It has a curved panel seam which makes the building-up of the gusset possible. Use the usual shaped seam of the block, the full depth of the waist dart and, if not tight enough for the bodice, the Sl. CF also (FIGS. 6 and 7).

Since point H is higher above G (than in style A) the armhole part here is bigger and the extension can be built up higher (4–5 cm) —all this being suitable for a closer-fitting style, (but obviously impossible in the first style).

The Bust dart is transferred into the Panel seam. The short sleeve is tightened at the top and at least 3 cm length is allowed under the arm (FIG. 6). The neckline is cut out.

CHAPTER
FOUR

THE RAGLAN

The Raglan is a **sleeve which extends** upwards beyond the crown **into the bodice** and joins the bodice not along the *usual armhole line*, but well above it, along some fancy line unconnected with the shape of the Top arm or the shoulder.

The Raglan *sleeve extension* is, in fact, *part of the bodice* shoulder, and the pattern of a Raglan can therefore be constructed quite logically by detaching a piece from the bodice and adding it to the sleeve. The line along which this is done will vary with style, and there are many different shapes of raglan; but the basic principle which applies to all of them is that what is added to the sleeve must correspond to what is taken from the bodice.

The classical style of raglan extension crosses into the bodice approximately half-way up the front and back armhole, and then gradually reduces itself in width until it reaches the neckline, covering, or more correctly 'replacing', part of the front and part of the back shoulder.

According to where the raglan extension actually crosses into the bodice, and the resulting depth of the armhole, there are **three main types of Raglan:**

The High Raglan
The Low Raglan
The Deep Raglan

The High Raglan always crosses the armhole at points B and F *or higher*—see style *a* above. The lower part of the armhole, below points B and F, is completely untouched and therefore the fit of the sleeve in this part is quite unaffected.

The fit of a High raglan sleeve is, in fact, as comfortable as that of an ordinary set-in sleeve, and allows for all necessary arm movement. It does not, however, provide any extra ease in the armhole (or not enough to be noticeable) as some of the lower-cut raglans do. It is a 'style line' rather than a means of widening the fit of the sleeve.

The Low Raglan either crosses or *touches* the armhole below B and F or, more often, misses it completely, the raglan lines being planned *inside* and well *below* the basic armhole. This affects the fit of the sleeve, and a special adjustment in the pattern is necessary to make it comfortable. Style *b* is representative of this type of raglan, which is at times more fashionable and may completely replace the High raglan.

The Low raglan has a wider armhole and so often gives the impression of greater ease and comfort. It is really a transition to the kimono cut and, like all sleeves with *deep armholes*, it brings in problems of fit similar to those of a kimono (e.g. pull on shortened underarm, etc.). It is in fact often cut from the Kimono block though there does exist a method of producing the pattern from an ordinary Bodice block.

The Deep Raglan—style *c* above—fits like a kimono and is always cut on the Kimono block. It is simply a kimono style (a Raglan Dolman) with a fancy line. Because of this extra line, however, the gusset problem is easier to deal with.

THE HIGH RAGLAN – general remarks

This raglan, as already stated, is as comfortable and neat in fit as an ordinary set-in sleeve, provided the basic condition of sleeve crossing into bodice at B and F or higher has been observed. Whatever its shape – and there exists quite a big variety – the *lower part* of the sleeve head below B and F, and the lower part of the armhole, retain their *usual* shape and fit. The High raglan is therefore built on to the sleeve crown *in its upper part only*.

As with all sleeves cut wholly or partly in one with the bodice, such as Raglan, Drop-shoulder and Kimono, the shoulder seam, or its equivalent – the dart, must not be allowed to slope towards the back but must be placed *well in the middle of the shoulder*. In raglans it is advisable to give it an even more forward position than an ordinary Centre shoulder seam, to ensure a better 'balance' on the figure and to counteract any tendency of the shoulder section to slip backwards. In fact the shoulder seam or dart of a raglan is usually given a slight but quite definite *tilt forward* at NP.

The continuous sleeve-and-shoulder line is seldom without a break at SP, and that is why a dart forms on the shoulder and takes the place of the shoulder seam. The dart angle accommodates the shoulder bone and improves considerably the fit and appearance of the sleeve. Like all darts, it can be moved to other positions.

N.B. A few easy-fitting raglans may have a perfectly plain shoulder, with neither seam nor dart. These correspond in fit and cut to a kimono shoulder cut on the *basic* Kimono block, which has no break at SP and which can be used for some easy-fitting styles (Dolmans, etc.).

The ordinary armhole of the Bodice block is generally used for the High raglan sleeve, but for some styles (and particularly for jackets) the armhole is lowered slightly (1 cm) and the sleeve is adjusted to correspond before the raglan adaptation is made. This gives, of course, an easier-fitting armhole.

METHOD – Plate 17

Outline Bodice block as usual leaving paper for the necessary extensions.

Move the **back side seam** 1+ cm forward, taking the same amount off the front side seam (FIGS. 1 and 2). This *centres the underarm seam*. Re-shape the lower part of the armhole.

Raise the back shoulder 1·5 cm right through, which means a bigger addition at NP than for a Centre shoulder. The same amount is taken off the front shoulder. In some cases, where the basic shoulder is already very forward (as happens sometimes with present fashion), this

addition at NP may prove somewhat excessive; but in general, a slight forward tilt at NP is correct for a raglan shoulder as it gives a better set and a firmer grip on the figure.

After cutting out and before planning the raglan lines, the front Bust dart is closed, as usual (with a temporary underarm slash). The back shoulderblade dart, if less than 1·5 cm, may be disregarded or rather 'transferred' into the neckline. If the dart is over, it is better to close it and to straighten the shoulder seam. If preferred, it can be moved into a *temporary* CB slash (FIG. 3), but usually this can be avoided and the pattern can be manipulated without slashing.

Draw the **raglan lines** on the bodice *following the style*: it is often easier to judge their good shape and balance by placing shoulders together, as in FIG. 4. For a **classical raglan shape** (as sketch) mark 4 cm from NP on back and front and from these points take the lines curving them slightly upwards, through points 5–6 cm down the closed darts, and then down to B and F. For easier assembling use balance marks 4 cm each side of the darts, as well as points B and F. After outlining, cut away the raglan shoulder (FIG. 5).

Outline **the sleeve** (usually the Straight block, but shaped sleeves can also be used). Leave 20 cm of paper above the crown.

Rule a line 1·5 cm to the front of the Top (Middle) Line and parallel to it: this is the 'forward Top line' which matches the forward shoulder seam. Continue it 15–18 cm up as a guide line.

Arrange the cut-away raglan sections above the sleeve, placing them 1 cm *above* the crown and 1 cm apart, i.e. 0·5 cm each side of the guide line (FIG. 6). Bring the back

HIGH RAGLAN

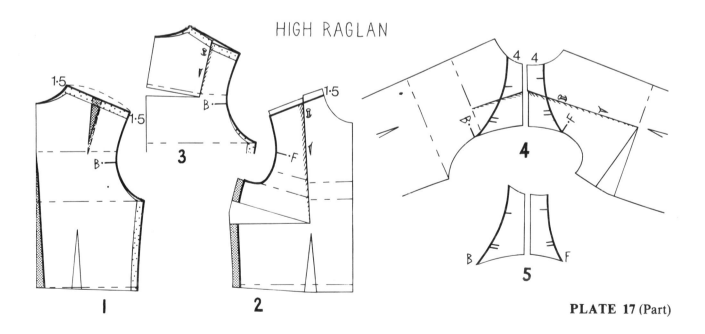

PLATE 17 (Part)

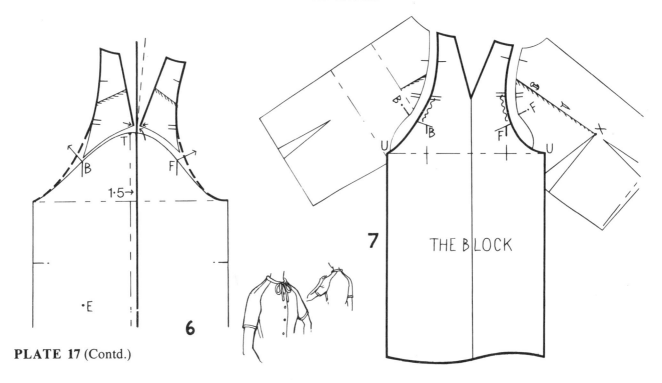

PLATE 17 (Contd.)

section quite close to point B of sleeve and the front section as close to F as possible without exaggerating the gap or *shoulder dart* at the top, for which a width of 8–10 cm is generally used (it may be more for square shoulders or for very long shoulders). Note that the sections are not necessarily equidistant from the guide line at the top, the back being usually closer to it (forward tilt).

Pin or paste the shoulder sections in this position and *outline the whole raglan sleeve*, taking care to draw the final lines slightly outside the shoulder section to provide a little ease across the shoulderpoint and the top of the arm.

On the final pattern (FIG. 7) draw the balance marks, adding to them points B and F, which are transferred from the sleeve crown at right angles to it (FIG. 6). The gap which usually occurs between points F of bodice and F of sleeve (FIG. 7) and to a smaller degree between the B points (which often almost coincide), represents *extra length* in the sleeve edge to be *eased* into the bodice edge near the middle balance mark (just below it), like the ease of an ordinary set-in sleeve. Pushing it down would cause the sleeve to crease: it should be kept well up to improve the hang.

N.B. The small amount remaining from the shoulder-blade dart can also be *eased*, but a little higher, into a flat part of the raglan line, or a dart may be used.

The sleeve seam normally matches the bodice seam, but if any adjustment is required, it is usually quite a simple one.

This classical shape of raglan can be considered as a **basic pattern** which in practice can be used as a founda-

tion for other raglan styles. It gives the *correct dart on the shoulder* so that other shapes of shoulder extension can be planned *over it*, by following the dart (see Plate 20).

DIFFERENT SHAPES OF RAGLAN

There is much variety in the High Raglan styles; less so in the others.

Raglans may be **pointed,** coming to a point at NP (FIG. 1); **square,** i.e. forming a strap or epaulette on the shoulder (FIG. 2); they may form **yokes** of various shapes **attached to sleeve** and often be connected with panels or other fancy sections of the bodice (Plate 20). Just as raglan lines may run far *into the bodice*, front and back, to form yokes, panels, etc., so they may be *shortened*, i.e. stop half-way up the shoulder, to form what is called a *Semi-raglan*, (FIG. 1).

Many of these styles do not cross into the armhole at B and F but higher. Their **position on the armhole** may be measured upwards from B and F, which are approximately on the same level; but in some cases, when the section is narrow, i.e. well above B and F, it is easier to measure it equally both ways from the shoulder (SP).

INTERPRETATION OF RAGLAN STYLES

Sometimes raglan lines are combined with special effects achieved by the use of striped or other patterned materials: thus the back of a raglan yoke may have a CB seam joined in chevron pattern. Care must be taken to

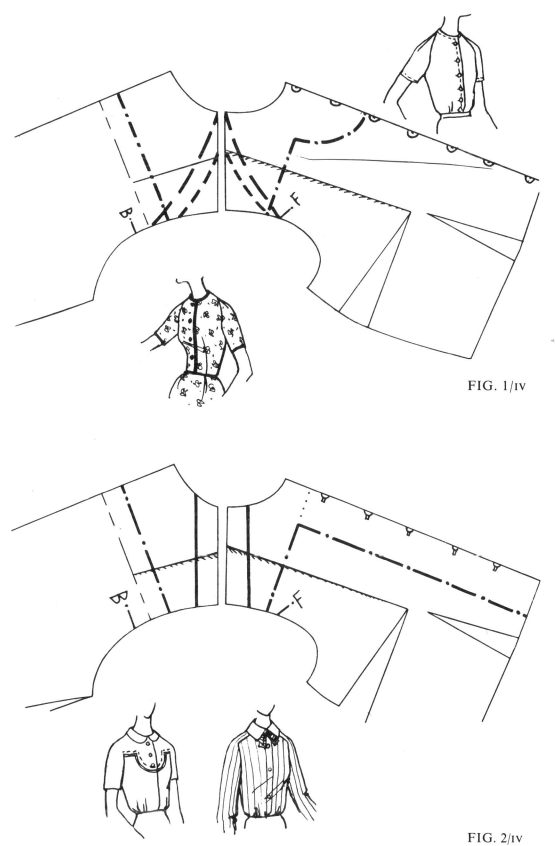

FIG. 1/IV

FIG. 2/IV

plan the pattern so that the desired effect is achieved, and it is usual in such cases to *test the effect* by drawing in the stripes on the pattern, observing, naturally, the correct position of the SG (straight grain) where necessary (e.g. down CF or CB or down the middle of the sleeve). The correct position of stripes, checks, plaids, etc., can thus be ensured at the pattern stage, often by a slight re-arrangement of the pattern. Therefore these styles may sometimes present problems of planning both in the pattern and on the material (the lay).

It is sometimes possible for a cutter to interpret a style as either a High or Low raglan, and to cut it accordingly. With only a slight alteration of the raglan lines, i.e. by straightening them so that they miss B and F and pass entirely *inside* the armhole (not crossing it), one can sometimes change a High raglan into a Low raglan, the cutting technique for which is different (see method lower). In such cases fashion as well as personal preference (e.g. for lower and easier-fitting armholes) is often the deciding factor. There are quite a few raglan styles of this intermediate type which can be interpreted differently according to circumstances. Styles with 'points' at NP are particularly suitable for these variations in cut and fit.

However, just as there are always some raglan styles which are quite obviously High raglans, and which could not be cut otherwise without distorting completely their style lines, so there are many which are unmistakably Low raglans with the lines running well inside the armhole and down to an *underarm point below the usual UP*. Many of these can be cut on the Kimono block — as some cutters prefer to do — and at some fashion periods this seems also the most suitable method to follow, because of the general easy fitting, slightly 'draping' fit of most bodices. It is therefore a point which can only be decided by the cutter. The real Deep raglan, when fashionable, is definitely cut on the Kimono block and its general style and very easy fit, with extra deep armhole, is easily recognizable.

SQUARING OF RAGLAN SLEEVE—FIG. 3

It is sometimes necessary to 'square' a raglan to follow fashion, or for a special style, or simply for an easier fit across the shoulder.

When square padded shoulders are fashionable, all raglan sleeves, particularly the High raglans, are squared to allow for the padded, raised effect. But sometimes this squaring is more a matter of easing the fit across the shoulder bone, as often happens in coats, when even without any particularly square shoulder effect, a little more room is wanted at the top of the sleeve.

The sleeve is slashed along the Top line down to 4–7 cm *below the crown line* (DC line), and then cut across to within 0·3 cm of the seam. The two sections are raised 0·5–1 cm or more, according to the purpose of squaring and the effect aimed at. Even 0·5 cm raising gives

1 cm or more ease at SP. It is clear from the diagram that this gives the sleeve not only height and 'squareness' (i.e. a *deeper dart*), but also more ease across the shoulder bone and round the Top arm (the latter particularly if the slash is made *lower*, i.e. about 7 cm down).

THE LOW RAGLAN—Plate 18

The sketch shows a classical Low raglan, but there exist other shapes. To interpret this style correctly it is quite impossible to draw the raglan lines so that they cross into or even touch the lower part of the armhole: they must miss it completely to end well below the usual UP (5 cm or more). The underarm seam must of course be moved forward the usual 1+ cm.

For this style mark at the top, on front and back, 2 cm from NP (FIGS. 1 and 2) and from these points, curving as shown in the diagrams, take the lines down to a point 5 cm below UP (i.e the UP of the new raglan armhole is moved 5 cm lower). Centre the side seam *before* drawing the lines.

When a raglan line comes very close to the armhole (as here in the front) a little extra width is allowed, *in the pattern only*, for easier manipulation of this part later (FIG. 4). Where the line passes within more than 1 cm of the armhole (as in the back) there is enough width to cut into. This method, used whenever it is necessary to pass very near to the armhole or even just to touch it, will be mentioned again in connection with Deep armholes in Chapter Six.

When the cut-away raglan sections are placed, as usual, above the sleeve (FIG. 3), it will be found that their ends, below B and F, overlap into the sleeve. They must therefore be raised to clear the top of the sleeve. This is done by slashing into them and curving them upwards, as shown in FIG. 4.

On each part to be cut plan 7–8 small sections, starting from B and F (FIGS. 4 and 5). Make the first 4–5 sections slightly wider (approx. 2 cm wide) and the next, except the last, narrower. The cutting is done *from the armhole edge* and of course without cutting right through.

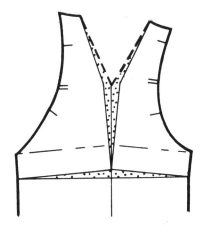

FIG. 3/IV

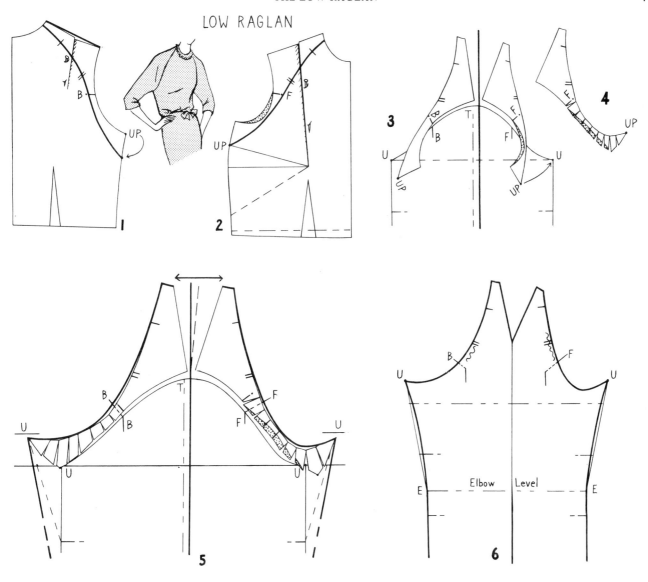

LOW RAGLAN

PLATE 18

After placing the raglan sections in correct position above the sleeve, as for a High raglan (FIG. 5), i.e. 1 cm above sleeve and 1 cm apart (0·5 cm each side of guide line), carefully raise the two ends, curving them in the opposite direction. The basic sleeve line (DC line) extended sideways, and two short lines 3–4 cm above and parallel to it, are useful guide lines for this manipulation.

Since the bodice underarm has lost 5 cm in length (UP coming down 5 cm), the loss is compensated by *gaining* at least 3–4 cm *on the sleeve underarm*: this is, of course, equivalent to providing a gusset in a kimono.

Note that the small cut sections may overlap a little below the guide line, but mainly in the front, where there is often too much fullness in the hollow of the arm, and less in the back, where a flatter, less hollowed out

crown is required (the last two small sections often do not open out).

For **the new sleeve seam,** first draw straight lines from the raised point U down to the required level, i.e. for short sleeves to the lower edge (broken line), and for long sleeves to elbow level. The final seam lines are then curved to run gradually into the seam below the elbow, as shown in FIG. 6.

The seam edges U–E *must be checked* to see that they are the same length, measuring them from point U to elbow level for long sleeves, or to the top balance mark for short sleeves.

It will be noted that as a result of the whole operation the sleeve has gained not only in *underarm length* (to compensate for the lowering of the armhole), but also in

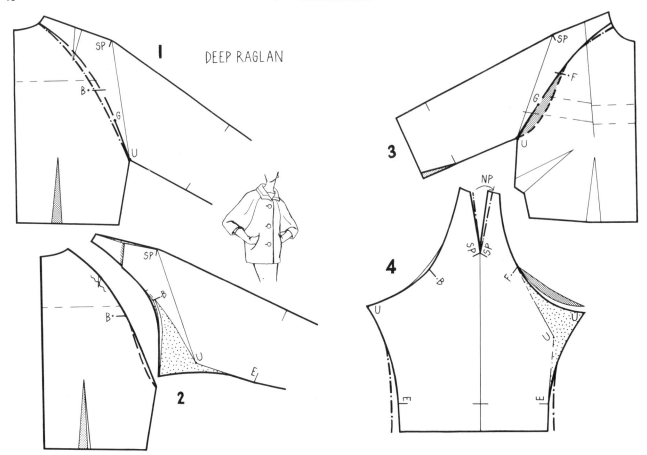

PLATE 19

width across the top, i.e. the sleeve has become wider on the DC line—an effect which is unavoidable with any definite lowering of armhole. The sleeve will thus have a more easy and draped fit over the shoulder and Top arm.

As already stated, some cutters prefer to cut this type of sleeve from a kimono foundation. This is a matter of choice: the sleeve certainly has a line and fit which justify treating it as a kimono adaptation. The raglan line facilitates the addition of a gusset: in fact it is the ideal line for a gusset extension, as will be shown in the next section—the Deep raglan adaptation—which gives the *general method* for using a Kimono block for raglan styles.

THE DEEP RAGLAN—Plate 19

This is a type of raglan which is always cut on the Kimono block. A kimono with a 7·5 cm slant automatically gives it a deep draped armhole which, moreover, is often made even deeper, e.g. for a special Dolman effect.

Plan the raglan lines in the usual way. Most of these styles follow the traditional line running from a narrow

width (4–5 cm) at NP, curving down to the low armhole, i.e. to point U. The back width at NP can be a little less than the front width, e.g. 2 and 3 cm, to allow for a slight tilting of the shoulder dart towards the front at the final stage (FIG. 4).

When the back raglan line is fairly flat (dot-dash line), the shoulderblade dart remains completely in the shoulder part where it can simply be folded out (FIG. 2).

After cutting away the sleeve with its raglan shoulder extension, introduce into the sleeve a gusset, as shown in FIG. 2. Cut away a thin strip from U up to B (where the strip remains attached to the sleeve), and pull it away sufficiently to allow for a 6–8 cm gusset extension: this method ensures that sleeve and bodice raglan lines will match perfectly (FIG. 2).

Some width is generally gained across the top of the sleeve and at point U; but the bodice part remains as it was and can even be hollowed out slightly below point B to neaten the armhole fit.

The front part is cut in the same way and the gusset is added so as to match the one in the back. However, both the lower armhole and sleeve are hollowed out more than in the back, as can be seen from FIG. 3 (the armhole) and FIG. 4 (the sleeve). The hollowing out must not affect the width at point U and at point F.

The sleeve pattern may be joined down the middle line to be cut in one, or else it may be used with a Middle seam all the way down from the shoulder dart. The pattern can be slightly sloped forward at NP by adding a little width to the back part and taking it off the front (FIG. 4).

Many deep raglan sleeves appear in coats and loose jackets which are wider than the Kimono block. Since addition of width to a kimono side seam always brings point U down, this means a further lowering of the whole armhole. A bigger gusset addition may then be necessary to make up for the bigger loss of underarm length: all this generally results in a still deeper, more draped, Dolman-like underarm which is very typical of many of these styles.

The method described can serve, of course, for a big variety of raglan styles, not all necessarily with deep or Dolman-like armholes and fit. As already mentioned, with some fashion influences, the method of cutting raglans on the Kimono block becomes popular with designers because of the softer line and more draped armhole effect it achieves.

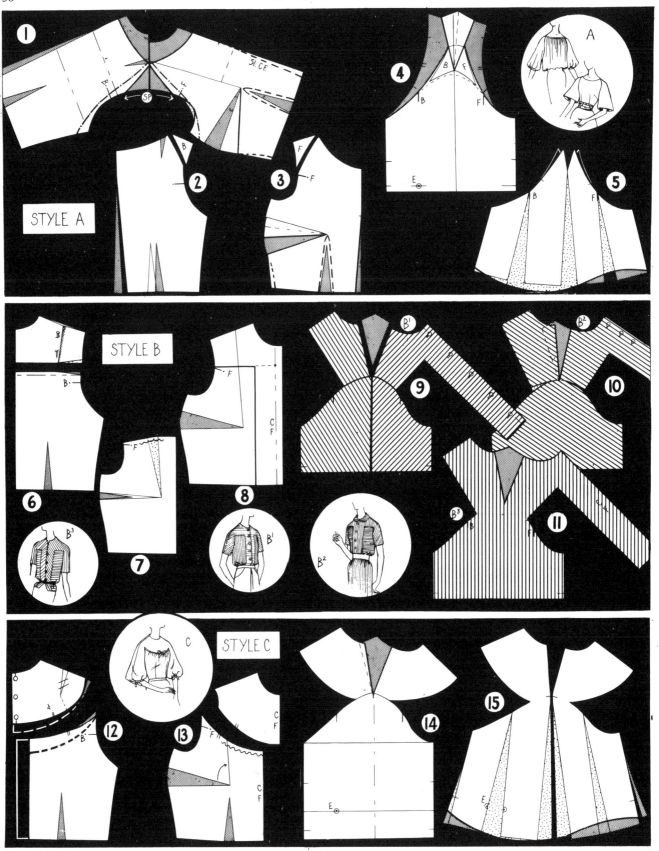

STYLE A

STYLE B

STYLE C

A

PLATE 20

PLATE 20

The examples in the Plate show the planning of more elaborate raglan styles. The first is **a Semi-raglan** which extends only half-way up the shoulder. The other two are **raglan sleeves connected with yokes,** in one case continuing into a front panel. The three designs give also a variety of sleeve styles—plain, Bell-shaped, full. Finally, in style B, the problem of **designing in striped material** is examined: as already mentioned, stripes and checks must be considered at the pattern stage as a slight adjustment of pattern is sometimes necessary.

Style A: Semi-raglan sleeves are usually pointed, though they can be of any suitable shape (e.g. square, forming a short epaulette). It is a type of sleeve which goes particularly well with a cut-out neckline, as in this style.

The bodice can be interpreted as easy-fitting or close-fitting in which case the Sl. CF would be used as well as the Sl. CB, and either the Waist darts increased (possibly also 'deepened' under the bust), or the side seams taken in to reduce the waist to Waist measurement plus 2 cm.

It must be noted that it is possible to use a High raglan for quite close-fitting styles. Whereas the Low raglan may be un-comfortable with a *tight* bust and waist fit; it is really more suitable for easy-fitting styles (see dot-dash line in FIG. 1, given as an alternative interpretation for a looser style).

Move the Bust dart lower to slope it more (FIGS. 1 and 3). Cut out neckline 6 cm down shoulder, 5 cm down CF and 4 cm down CB.

Outline **the raglan extension** half-way up the shoulder, i.e. in this case up to the cut out neckline, and measure it equally right and left from SP. Cut away and arrange above the sleeve: this of course may be the basic Raglan sleeve, i.e. a copy of the block, in which case the dart on the shoulder can be followed and un-necessary parts (beyond the points) cut away later (FIG. 4).

To add width for a Bell-shaped sleeve slash as shown in FIG. 5, and add 10–12 cm or more at the lower edge. Slashing down the middle partly closes dart on the shoulder extension: with more fullness it may close completely.

Style B is mainly an **exercise in planning stripes**. The raglan extension develops into a yoke and then continues into a front panel.

Plan the high yoke on the same level, back and front, measuring up CB and CF 32 cm from the waist. Draw the yoke lines at right angles to CB and CF. Complete the front panel 5 cm from and parallel to CF (FIG. 8).

In the back (FIG. 6) close shoulderblade dart and transfer it into the yoke seam to avoid having an obvious dart stitched across the stripes. If it is necessary to keep lower edge of yoke straight (along stripe), straighten the edge and reduce the amount added by taking it off the lower part. A shoulderblade dart can also be moved, partly or completely, into the neckline, or the two methods can be combined.

In the front the Bust dart can be left in the underarm or *part* of it moved so as to provide ease under the yoke (more becoming for some figures): transferring whole Dart might upset the run of the stripes too much (FIG. 7).

Arrange the cut-away yokes above the sleeve, as usual, if convenient using the basic raglan sleeve as a foundation.

FIGS. 9, 10 and 11 show three different arrangements of stripes giving three possible styles (sketches B¹, B², B³).

Style B/1—FIG. 9 shows horizontal stripes down CF panel and back yoke. Draw them on the pattern, at right angles to CB and CF and absolutely parallel, and continue into the sleeve: there the stripes meet in chevron pattern down the middle where *there must be a seam.* (**N.B.** It is not necessary of course to draw all the stripes as shown here, but just a few, spacing them well and keeping them *absolutely parallel.*) If the chevron does not come out perfectly, a small adjustment, shown in the next diagram (FIG. 10) may help: slash towards SP between top of sleeve and yoke and open a small gap, preferably in the back, sometimes also in the front. Adjust pattern until the stripes run better and meet correctly. This adds only a little width to the Back and possibly to the Chest.

Style B/2—FIG. 10 has stripes planned lengthwise down the CF, no join in the sleeve, which works out on the bias, and there is a seam with stripes meeting in chevron down the CB of the yoke (stripes will not meet exactly on the shoulder, but this is where it shows least). Note that the adjustment for changing the run of the stripes (already explained with the previous style) reduces the width of the dart on the shoulder, as can be clearly seen in the diagram.

Style B/3—FIG. 11 gives yet another arrangement of stripes. They meet in chevron pattern in the CB yoke seam and also down the CF. For this reason it is not advisable to have a wrap but rather an edge-to-edge opening with an invisible fastening or buttons and loops on the CF *edge*. Down the sleeve the stripes run quite straight (lengthwise) and it is *from here* that they should be planned in both directions.

Style C is an attractive but fairly simple round yoke style with an opening in the back and full sleeves.

The yoke is 12 cm deep down CF (FIG. 13) and in the back it is either the same depth, which places it on a higher level (as measured up from the waist), or it may be deeper, e.g. 15–16 cm which would make it level with the front yoke (FIG. 12).

The back has a small 1–2 cm wrap in the yoke and in the lower part some width added beyond CB (4–5 cm or more) for the fullness gathered under the yoke (this is often considerable, particularly in styles with deep yokes). The shoulderblade dart is again eliminated, either by closing it or simply by cutting it off the end of the shoulder, at SP, and lowering a little the edge of the bodice below.

The front—FIG. 13 may also have some width added beyond the CF line if the style is to be very full, but, on the whole, it is better to use *only the Bust dart*, transferring it from the underarm into the top edge to provide the fullness under the yoke: this avoids the heavy, puffed-out silhouette which addition of extra fullness to both back and front may produce.

After cutting away the yoke parts arrange them as usual above the sleeve (FIG. 14). If, when working over a Raglan block, it is found that the back yoke *overlaps into the sleeve,* the dart on the shoulder must be reduced as shown in FIG. 14, so as not to lose Back width.

Finally, separate back and front of the sleeve by cutting it down the middle, i.e. giving it a seam (FIG. 5). Then widen each part by slashing and adding at the lower edge 15–18 cm or more. Of course the middle addition partly closes the dart on the shoulder.

THE DROP-SHOULDER CUT

The Drop-shoulder cut is the reverse of the Raglan construction, with part of the **bodice extending into the sleeve.** Consequently the top of the sleeve must be cut down below the usual crown to follow and match the shape of the bodice extension. The same principle applies here as in the cutting of raglans: what is added to the bodice must correspond to what is taken from the sleeve, and the level at which the bodice crosses into the sleeve determines whether the lower armhole (below B and F) can be retained in its usual shape or not.

There exists a:

> High Drop-shoulder and a
> Low Drop-shoulder

The High Drop-shoulder, whatever its shape, always crosses into the sleeve at B and F or higher, and so retains the usual armhole in the lower part and consequently the fit of an ordinary set-in sleeve (style *a* above).

The Low Drop-shoulder crosses below B and F and is best cut on the Kimono block. It is a *kimono style with an 'armhole'* and a separately cut sleeve to which a 'gusset extension' can be added quite easily (style *b*).

Finally there are some drop-shoulder effects which are quite obviously kimono styles without any armhole in the lower part (style *c*).

THE HIGH DROP-SHOULDER—Plate 21

As already stated, a High drop-shoulder extension is always planned on or above B and F. The Centre shoulder seam must be used but the underarm seam, not being affected by the cut, generally need not be changed (though this may happen in some styles).

The longest projection is usually down the middle of the sleeve and is marked, according to style, along the Top line. This line is *moved 1 cm forward* and becomes a 'forward' Top line to match 'centred' shoulder.

Method: The basic style forms a well fitted 'cap' over the arm (see sketch in Plate 21). Outline its shape on the sleeve between points B and F—the marginal points—

and down to a point 6·5 cm from the top along the *forward* Top line (FIG. 1).

Cut away and separate the front and back parts on the *new* Top line. Take out a small dart in the front part (FIGS. 1 and 2) to eliminate the 'ease' of the sleeve crown, otherwise it will not match the armhole part to which it is later joined.

Place and pin the front and back of the bodice (already adjusted to a Centre shoulder seam) on to a sheet of paper with shoulders 1 cm apart at SP and the front NP touching the back shoulder (FIG. 2). The back NP projects beyond because of the open shoulderblade dart, which in this case can simply be ignored, as the construction does not affect the shoulder seam in this part: later the small dart will be used as usual.

The two extension pieces which have been cut away from the sleeve are now placed to the armhole (FIG. 2) with a 1 cm gap at B and with the top points 0·5 cm below SP (approximately). A gap of at least 0·5 cm, but on the average 1 cm, is always advisable in the back, but at point F one can place the extension quite close to the bodice, if a really close fit over the shoulder and top arm is desirable. Pin everything in position: the gap formed between the two sleeve extensions is of course a 'dart' which gives the cap its smooth fit over the top of the arm. This should be considered as a maximum tightness for it is seldom possible to make it tighter without making the raising of arms uncomfortable; but of course there are cases where the fit is loosened, either because of the shape of the figure or, more often, because of the looser fit of the style.

Each extension piece is now part of the front and of the back of the bodice and must be *outlined with it*. To separate the back from the front, draw the seam in a perfectly straight line from NP through the middle of the gap at SP, then follow round the two extensions, slightly curving the line below SP down to the edge of the cap to make it fit smoothly over the top of the arm. Cut on these lines. On final pattern (FIG. 3, Plate 21) clearly mark SP as a balance mark for correct assembling.

Because of the addition at point B (1 cm) which

HIGH DROP SHOULDER

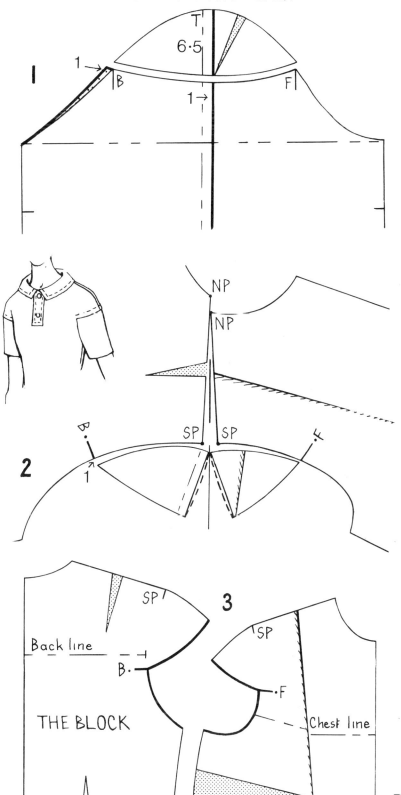

PLATE 21

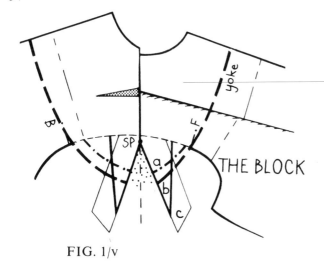

FIG. 1/v

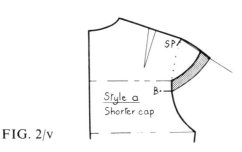

FIG. 2/v

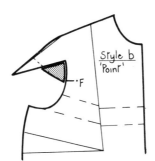

FIG. 3/v

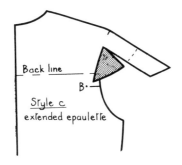

FIG. 4/v

lengthens the lower edge of the cap, the sleeve which later fits into it must also be widened a little by adding the same amount to the back of the remaining part of the crown (FIG. 1–Pl. 21). It must be noted that any bigger changes in these lines, for instance as a result of further 'loosening' of the cap (see FIG. 6) would require a widening of the sleeve, preferably through the middle, in the same way as would be done in the case of a fancy and very full sleeve set into a close fitting cap. In the case of a very full sleeve the width addition would probably be made in more than one place, i.e. down the Back and Forearm lines as well as in the middle.

The finished pattern—the cap style—FIG. 3, Plate 21, can be considered **a basic pattern** because, having once obtained the *correct slant* of the shoulder seam *below* SP and therefore the **correct tightness of the 'dart'** over the top arm, it is often possible to use it *as a block*, outlining it first, as it is, and then adjusting the drop-shoulder part to the line required by a particular style—a point or a round yoke, slightly shorter or longer—without building up the whole pattern right from the beginning.

Many simple drop-shoulder styles vary mainly in the depth or length of the cap part. A yoke, for instance, can always be added as a style line on the bodice *from the level of the cap*. Thus the possibility of simple style variation of the drop-shoulder part is a useful feature of this basic pattern, but it is of course important to note in each case whether the bodice does cross into the sleeve at the same level, i.e. at the basic points B and F or *higher*, as is often the case.

Therefore, provided the style copied has *the same tightness over the Top arm* as the basic pattern, and is neither closer-fitting (which seldom happens) or looser-fitting, the basic 'cap style' pattern can be used for many quick and simple adaptations, as shown in FIG. 1 and also in FIGS. 2, 3, 4 and 5. FIG. 2 is a very simple adaptation, i.e. just a *shorter* cap; FIG. 3 shows a pointed drop-shoulder style; FIG. 4—a style with an epaulette extended over the arm; FIG. 5—a round drop-shoulder yoke. It is quite easy to cut all these styles from the basic pattern (see shaded parts cut away).

STYLE ADAPTATIONS

In style adaptations, when planning the two armhole *crossing points* which, as in raglans, often come *above* B and F, it is necessary to consider first *the style as a whole*, in order to establish the correct level of the 'crossing points' *in relation to the whole design*. Thus a **drop-shoulder yoke** (FIG. 5) can be deeper or shallower, more curved or less curved, etc., all of which will affect the shape of the shoulder extension and particularly the *level* at which it crosses into the sleeve, i.e. higher or lower on the armhole.

FIGS. 3 and 4 are examples of drop-shoulder styles with very high crossing points, measured on the bodice preferably from SP, and reproduced on the sleeve from the forward Top line.

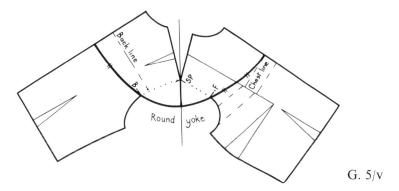

G. 5/v

It is advisable, therefore, first to plan on the bodice *the lines of the style* such as various yokes, panels, etc., then to find the 'crossing points' *if these are not actually at B and F*, and, after measuring their distance above B and F, or down from SP on the bodice pattern, to transfer these measurements on to the sleeve, marking them the same distance above B and F or from the Top line. All this is done before completing the outline of the whole shoulder extension. It is obvious that the basic pattern will not always be suitable for more complicated styles, and that there will be cases when it is simpler to reproduce the whole construction from the beginning. This is a matter of experience, and after some practice the possibility of a 'short cut' will suggest itself quite naturally.

VARIATIONS OF THE DROP-SHOULDER SILHOUETTE—FIGS. 6 and 7

Variations in the drop-shoulder silhouette are obtained either by squaring the shoulder part or by loosening it so that it does not cling so much to the top of the arm. This is not only a matter of style, but often a question of following the current fashion. Naturally, when there is a general tendency to raise (and pad) all shoulders, drop-shoulder styles are made squarer just to emphasize the fashion line. When a smoother, softer shoulder line is fashionable, there are many cases of drop-shoulder patterns being 'loosened' (i.e. flattened) on the shoulder and over the top arm so that the edge of the cap tends to stand away a little from the figure instead of moulding the top of the arm.

SQUARING OF THE DROP-SHOULDER —FIG. 6

This is achieved by slashing from SP along the armhole, both on back and front, and opening at SP a gap of 1 cm or more, according to the effect desired. A little shoulder height is added above SP (e.g. 0·5 cm each side), running off to nothing at NP but continuing over the lower part, i.e. the cap. In more exaggerated 'square' styles the addition above SP can be bigger, but is then reduced a little down the seam towards the lower edge of the cap. Squared drop-shoulders are usually padded to hold up the extra height.

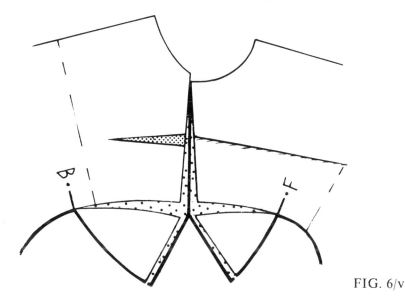

FIG. 6/v

LOOSENING OF THE DROP-SHOULDER
—FIG. 7

Here no addition is made at SP but the 'dart' is *reduced* by filling in the gap towards the lower edge, i.e. by 'letting out' there. Since this makes the cap stand away from the arm, it is usual to add a little *length* below the cap edge, otherwise the 'stand-away' effect will not be apparent and the sleeve will merely flute along the lower edge.

The cap is often lined (slightly stiffened) to emphasize the 'widening' over the arm muscle and to support the slight stand-away effect.

The widening of the sleeve over the arm muscle naturally minimizes the shoulder point (the opposite of squaring) and gives the shoulder a softer line, unless the stand-away effect is very exaggerated and stiffened.

THE LOW DROP-SHOULDER—Plate 22

When correct style interpretation demands that the **crossing points come below B and F,** the whole pattern must be cut **on a Kimono block.** Whenever bodice and sleeve are cut in one *below* the B and F level, tightness is felt when raising or moving the arms, and the problems which arise are really those of the kimono pattern. The lower the crossing points move down below B and F, the more obvious this becomes, unless suitable precautions are taken to loosen the fit in this part of the armhole.

When the crossing points are only slightly below B and F, it is sometimes possible to avoid using the kimono by leaving a bigger gap at B and F when applying the two sleeve extensions to the bodice (which naturally reduces the gap or 'dart' in the drop-shoulder part). This is really an in-between stage between a High drop-shoulder and a real kimono fit, and as a method it is sometimes useful in various other cases.

On the whole, however, it is simpler to use the Kimono block and to construct the whole pattern on it. Because of the seam under the arm (the remainder of the armhole), it is perfectly easy to add a gusset extension in these styles and they present little difficulty in this respect.

Since the shoulder and top arm fit is fairly clinging, the 7·5 cm slant block is generally used, and additional sloping (by 'squaring' at SP) improves the fit.

The style given in Plate 22 illustrates clearly the method which can be followed for other similar styles.

As in most kimono styles the main construction line for planning the armhole part is again the Gusset line, often continued upwards, even to points F/B. For many of these styles it is useful to use a Kimono block with Chest and Back lines indicated, as these are sometimes necessary for reference.

Plan the drop-shoulder line, for instance from a point 8–9 cm below SP, taking it down to Chest level, as shown in FIG. 1. It can, of course, be taken to a point above Chest level, but always below point F (which must be indicated on the block). The *final* line curves very slightly (1 cm) at the top *above the straight guide line* but would still appear as a fairly straight line on the figure. Very often extra height, say 1 cm, is added to the sleeve later, sometimes at a fitting (FIG. 2). From the point where it touches the Gusset line (some distance above G), draw the armhole part *down the Gusset line* G–U, curving it slightly.

Cut away the sleeve part (FIG. 2) and add to it **a gusset extension** in the usual way, making it 6–7 cm wide. This

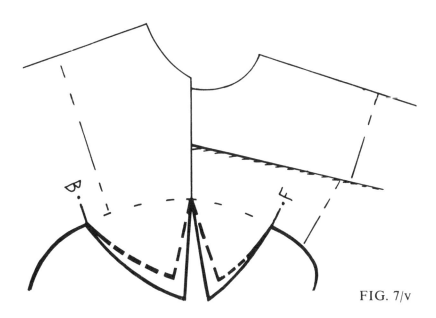

FIG. 7/v

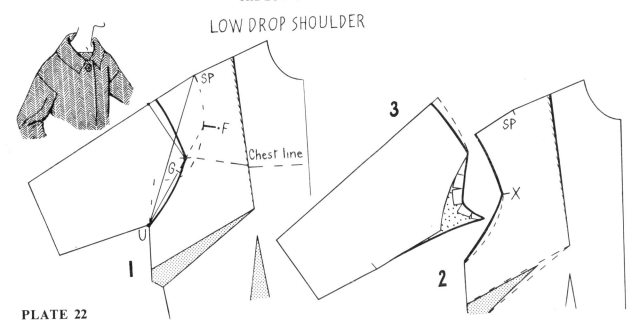

LOW DROP SHOULDER

PLATE 22

can be done of course as shown in FIG. 3, or simply by *adding* the extension, taking care however, to hollow out the top edge of the gusset where it represents the lower part of the 'flattened' sleeve crown, otherwise there may be too much fullness here when the sleeve is set into the armhole. Sometimes the armhole part can be trimmed (hollowed out) a little more in the front, below point X, but not generally in the back where both sleeve and armhole have a flatter line.

Other styles can be cut in a similar way, i.e. by treating them as kimono patterns with all their problems of fit. In all such styles, however, the *extra line provided by the separate sleeve* is naturally of considerable help, as the style can so easily be adjusted at a fitting, e.g. the sleeve can be given more slope by letting it out at the top (broken line, FIG. 3), and the armhole can be neatened by more hollowing out in the lower part (FIG. 2). The shoulder may sometimes be tightened a little, though the correct way of doing this is by using a 'squared' Kimono block.

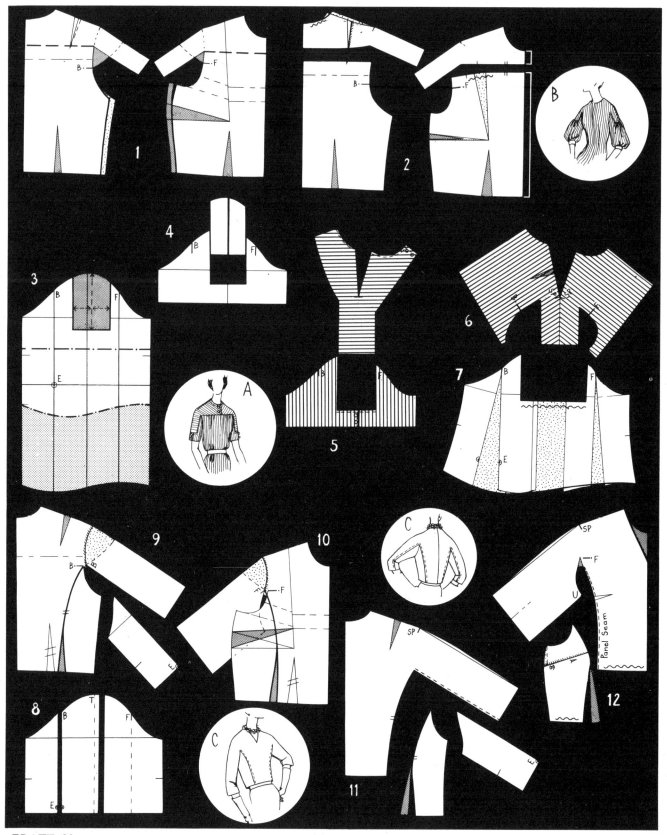

PLATE 23

PLATE 23

The three styles in this Plate follow the drop-shoulder method in a way which goes beyond simple planning of different shapes of extension.

In the first two styles, the additional problem is that of planning an extension—in itself quite simple in shape—in such a way as to achieve a special effect in a striped material. In the last style (C), the method is alternative to one already shown in the Kimono chapter and is suitable when for one reason or another one prefers not to use the Kimono block for a style which needs it only in the top part of the sleeve. This, as will be seen, can be done by treating such a style as a drop-shoulder.

Style A: Outline the **basic drop-shoulder pattern** (cap style) and plan *over it* a strip 5 cm wide and 15 cm long from SP (separately on back and front).

From the point where the 5 cm strip touches the armhole draw a straight yoke, at right angles to CB/CF. The two crossing points are above B and F: cut away the unnecessary part below the strip (shaded in FIG. 1).

Cut away the yoke. In the front, *part* of the Bust dart can be used under the yoke, but not the whole, as this would upset the stripes too noticeably. In the back also close only part of the shoulderblade dart, so as not to curve the yoke edge too much: transfer the rest of it into the neckline (FIG. 2). Place back and front yokes together and join them along the extension line (FIG. 5): the gap at the top is the 'dart' transferred from its *usual* drop-shoulder position below SP.

On the sleeve (FIG. 3) measure from the *forward* Top line 5 cm right and left to outline a 10 cm wide and 15 cm long 'square' shoulder extension. Cut it away (FIG. 4). Shorten sleeve to the required length, i.e. 8–10 cm down the underarm.

Plan the stripes on the pattern of the yoke, starting from the lower edge of the extension (FIG. 5) which has *no seam in the middle* (see sketch), and continuing the lines absolutely parallel to see how they work out on CB, where there must be a join (though not below the yoke) and on the CF, where there is a small wrap and opening.

Style B is **a variant** of style A, which has no yoke, a ¾-length sleeve with fullness gathered under the shoulder extension, and a different arrangement of stripes.

Plan the drop-shoulder section in the same way but without a yoke. In this case there is a seam both on the shoulder and in the middle of the extension (FIG. 6) where the stripes should come together in chevron pattern. Test stripes on pattern by planning them from CB and CF.

If there is some difficulty in getting the stripes to meet correctly in the middle of the extension, the *angle* of one extension may have to be altered very slightly, i.e. back or front part straightened a little by a slash from the angle towards SP (opening the angle a little).

After cutting away the extension part from the sleeve pattern and adjusting it to the correct length (dot-dash line FIG. 3), add width to the sleeve as shown in FIG. 7, to double (approximately) the length gathered under the extension.

Style C appears as a style with a kimono sleeve at the top and an ordinary set-in sleeve in the lower part. This type of sleeve has already been discussed in the Kimono chapter, but it can also be treated as a drop-shoulder and this is sometimes more convenient. There must always be **a separate underarm section**—a sidebody—for although no building-up of 'gusset extension' is involved here, a sleeve cannot be laid flat against the armhole without overlapping into the bodice and so part of the bodice underarm must be removed (FIG. 10).

Three versions are possible: with extra sleeve seams on both back and front (along Back and Forearm lines), as style C; with no extra sleeve seams as sketch D; with *one* extra sleeve seam, back or front, as in the version described here. The method will serve for all three cases. In the pattern dealt with here the back of the sleeve is in *two parts*, and the front in one.

The sleeve (FIG. 8) is first divided in two along the forward Top line; the back part is then cut again along the Back line.

In the Back, using the **basic drop-shoulder pattern**, first outline the underarm section, taking it from point B, and moving the Waist dart into the seam. Place the top part of the back sleeve to the 'armhole' (always useful to indicate it on a drop-shoulder block), *following the slope of the drop-shoulder extension* (FIG. 9), i.e. the sleeve is placed over the cap which gives it the correct slant. Outline the whole together.

In the front the Panel seam must be drawn sufficiently far in to enable the whole front sleeve to be applied *without overlapping into the bodice* (FIG. 10), after the underarm section has been removed. There must also be a good allowance for turnings, i.e. a gap between point U and the Panel seam (FIG. 12). The sleeve is applied, as in the back, and outlined together with bodice, following the slope of the drop-shoulder cap extension. The separate cut-away pieces of the pattern are shown in FIGS. 11 and 12. They are assembled in the usual way. Armhole parts must match the edges of the undersleeve, and a slight adjustment may sometimes be necessary.

The front Bust dart is eliminated in the separate underarm section with only a small end of it projecting beyond the Panel seam. Its position is slightly changed, as can be seen in FIG. 10.

N.B. Turnings must be handled with care in the angles at B and F (in the main bodice part).

The same method would be applied to the other two versions.

This chapter deals with sleeves and armholes which are of unusual shape, which do not follow the usual method of construction or which are a *combination* of different types of sleeve and methods of cutting. They form an important group in advanced pattern designing.

Two additional sleeve blocks are also given here.

ADDITIONAL SLEEVE BLOCKS

These are:

The Forearm seam sleeve and
The Two-piece sleeve

Both are mentioned in the basic chapter on sleeves as **types of Shaped sleeve** which have the shape controlling dart running *down the arm*. Of these the Two-piece sleeve is used mainly in tailoring, while the other pattern, though not often used nowadays, gives the *basis of the method* and must therefore be described before the Two-piece sleeve construction is explained.

Both sleeves are adapted from the Straight sleeve block.

THE FOREARM SEAM SLEEVE
—FIGS. 1, 2, 3, 4, 5, 6, 7

As already stated, in its simple shape this sleeve is not much used in modern pattern designing, but it represents a basic method—that of shaping a straight sleeve to the curve of the arm by dart and seam, or by two seams, which actually *follow the natural curve of the arm*. In the past this was the main block for all shaped sleeves, whether tight fitting or loose.

Method: Outline a Straight sleeve block, the same width right through. Fold the pattern lengthwise along the Back line and again along the Forearm line, so that the edges meet *down the middle* (FIG. 1) and there are *two* folds. Secure the edges: the pattern is now a *tube*, and new seams can be planned *in any position*, ignoring completely the underarm seam of the block.

At the wrist measure from the Forearm fold 1 cm and mark point X. Then measure from X half of the Wrist measurement X–Y = 8·5 cm (half of 17). The remainder beyond Y is the depth or width of the **Back line dart**. Draw a straight line from Y up to E (Elbow point): the part outside this line will be cut away (FIG. 2).

From E, at right angles to E–Y, measure half Elbow width ($\frac{1}{2}$ of 30 = 15 cm) and mark Z. Draw the **Forearm seam** from F through Z down to X which can be raised $\frac{1}{2}''$ to shorten the seam. Cut away the parts beyond the Back dart and Forearm lines (shaded in FIG. 2), curving the lines as shown in the diagram, and cutting through the two thicknesses of paper (FIG. 3). Opened out, the pattern appears as in FIG. 4. Cut down a little at F on both edges. The sleeve head may be hollowed out more.

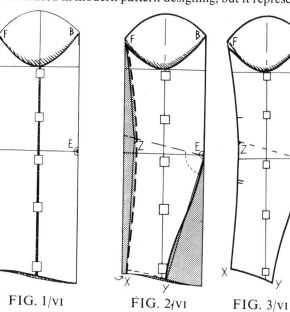

FIG. 1/VI   FIG. 2/VI   FIG. 3/VI

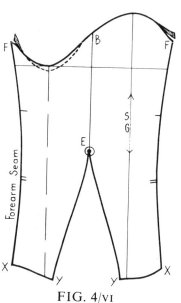

FIG. 4/VI

FIG. 5/VI

This pattern was much used before as a Tight fitting sleeve. It has a smooth fit along the Forearm, following the curve of the arm. The Back line, however, with the well defined elbow angle, though fitting well to the curve when the arm is bent, tends to appear overshaped (point of dart 'poking out' and loose) when the arm is straightened, more so than the modern Tight fitting (French) sleeve which, with its *shaping dart across the elbow*, adjusts itself more easily to either position of the arm.

There are, however, some styles for which this sleeve block can still be used. One of these, a Bell-shaped sleeve, is shown in FIGS. 5 and 6. It has a Forearm seam.

It is obvious from this example that the special feature of this pattern, i.e. its curving Forearm, can be just as useful in a loose fitting style which does not involve any overshaping of the elbow. A Bishop sleeve with a cuff can be cut in the same way and this is how these sleeves were actually cut at the beginning of the century.

Finally, by closing the Back line dart up to the Elbow point and transferring its fullness into a slash above, various Leg o' Mutton styles can be obtained (FIG. 7), usually with some additional height of crown. This is therefore the pattern of the Edwardian period, and its occasional re-appearance in modern times is generally

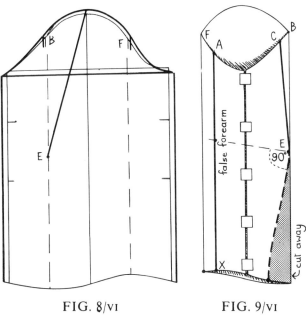

FIG. 8/VI   FIG. 9/VI   FIG. 10/VI   FIG. 11/VI

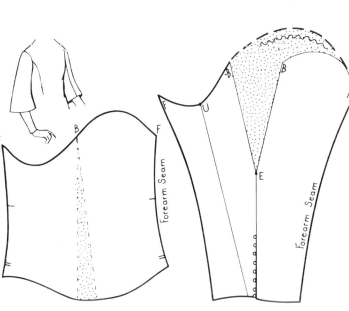

FIG. 6/VI   FIG. 7/VI

due to an Edwardian influence on dress designers.

To make the Forearm seam less conspicuous, it is possible to move it further in under the arm, usually 2–3 cm from the Forearm line: this is known as the 'false Forearm' and is explained in the Two-piece sleeve pattern, where it is generally used.

THE TWO-PIECE SLEEVE—FIGS. 8, 9, 10, 11

As this sleeve is used mainly for jackets and sometimes for coats, the Straight sleeve block must first be adjusted to the correct fit. This adjustment would, of course, not be necessary in the case of dresses or blouses.

For a jacket: make the Straight sleeve block 2–2·5 cm wider, adding 1 cm on each side of the pattern (FIG. 8). Move points B and F 0·5 cm *out* to make the four lengthwise sections of the pattern equal. Deepen the crown by going up 0·5 cm on the Middle line and down at UP, i.e. hollowing it out below the basic DC line (1 + cm down if the sleeve crown originally was flatter than 13 cm). For a coat or heavy long jacket the addition will be bigger (see chapter on coats).

Fold the pattern, as described for the Forearm seam block, along Back and Forearm lines, to make a 'tube'.

Then measure 2·5 cm in from the Forearm fold and draw line A–X parallel to it: this is **the false Forearm** position.

At the wrist measure, this time from the original Forearm fold, towards the Back line, half Wrist width, e.g. 14 cm for a 28 cm finished jacket wrist. From here draw a line up to Elbow point E for the dart, which in this case is also the lower part of the Back line seam. Curve it very slightly, as shown in FIG. 9.

To complete the Back seam, measure at the top from B 2 cm down the curve to point C, and from here rule a line down to point E to meet the lower part of the seam.

Cut away the Back line dart up to point E (FIG. 9), cutting through *two layers*. Then *roll the pattern over* so that the false Forearm–line A–X–comes to the left edge and becomes a *fold* (FIG. 10). At the elbow level measure from the *back fold* half Elbow measurement + 1 cm and through this last point (Z) shape the Forearm seam A–Z–X curving it as shown in FIG. 10. Cut along this line *through the two layers of paper*. Draw balance marks 5 cm above and 7 cm below the elbow level, which is again marked on the Forearm seam by a line from E, at right angles (or almost) to the Back line dart.

Finally cut on the line C–E through *one layer only*, to separate the Top sleeve from the Under-sleeve.

FIG. 11 shows the two parts of the final pattern. It is usual to trim away a little above the Forearm seam.

The Two-piece sleeve is given here in its more modern version which is a little looser and straighter than the classical Jacket Two-piece sleeve (Chapter Ten).

The pattern is placed on the material with top and bottom points of Forearm seam (A and X) to the straight grain.

ARMHOLE SHAPE VARIATIONS

Variations in the shape of the basic armhole are usually connected with **the way the sleeve is fitted on the shoulder.** This is mainly a feature of fashion—**the fashion 'shoulder line'**—e.g. the fashion for high fitting sleeves, low fitting sleeves, etc. It affects the shape of the armhole and of the sleeve head, though at times only very slightly. There are of course long periods when the 'natural shoulder line' is followed.

Variations in armhole shape may also be produced by the special fit which some clothes demand, mainly extra *allowance for unrestricted arm movement*. This is essential in most clothes worn for sport, dancing (i.e. ballet) and for various kinds of work.

In most cases, therefore, the fit of the sleeve and consequently the *shape* of the armhole and sleeve head are a compromise between what is comfortable and fashionable, with the *basic armhole*, which follows closely the natural arm 'scye', taken for general guidance.

In all changes of armhole the main point to remember is **the armhole's connection with the sleeve:** they are complementary, and what is lost in one must be gained in

the other to retain the correct, comfortable length between CB (CF) and elbow. A change in armhole shape usually affects the sleeve crown, and while some of these changes are well established and known (e.g. in sportswear or some industrial clothing), others have to be discovered by experience and by careful observation of the 'fashion shoulder line'.

Generally speaking, **when sleeves are fitted low,** an **off-the-shoulder armhole,** with more width across back and chest and a lower underarm UP, requires a sleeve head which is shorter down the Middle line and narrower across the top, between B and F, but more hollowed out under the arm. Yet, in some cases, for special effect or comfort, the crown height can be retained or the sleeve underarm can be kept high for greater ease in raising arm.

When sleeves are fitted high, the **armhole is well raised on to the shoulder,** with its front part (below SP) hollowed out over the shoulder bone and its back part less straight; while the bodice UP is generally higher, i.e. kept closer to the arm. The sleeve head compensates for the 'loss' in the armhole by being raised more (particularly to the front of the middle, i.e. of point T). Often this is done in the exaggerated way with which the fashion for 'Raised' crowns, with considerable extra fullness (in the shape of darts, tucks, gathers, etc.) has made us familiar.

It is therefore impossible to establish a shape of armhole and sleeve head which would be correct for all times and purposes.

All these changes, however, are technical changes which must be accepted as part of the technique of pattern designing, i.e. of the art and skill of adapting basic principles, shapes and methods to the never-ending flow of changing fashion ideas. Among these the 'shoulder line' effect is very important.

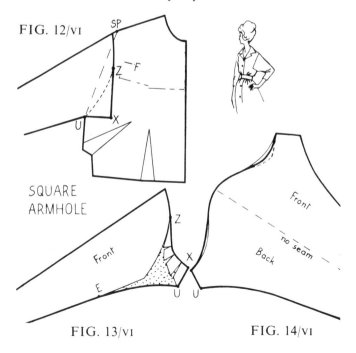

FIG. 12/VI

SQUARE ARMHOLE

FIG. 13/VI   FIG. 14/VI

Apart from these constant fashion variations there are, however, a few special *styles* of armhole, notably the **Square armhole** and the **Deep armhole,** for which there exist quite definite methods of adaptation and of sleeve adjustment.

SQUARE ARMHOLE—FIGS. 12, 13, 14

This armhole has a 'draped' fit under the arm and, since this is typical of the kimono cut, styles with square armholes are usually cut on the Kimono block. Although it is possible to use an ordinary bodice block (as with the second method for Deep Armhole), it is more practical, whenever possible, to treat it as a kimono adaptation.

After outlining a 7·5 cm slant Kimono block, draw the armhole from a point 1 cm outside SP straight down to point X, 5 cm inside point U (FIG. 12). Cut away the sleeve part and slash into it from U up to point Z (dotted line FIG. 12). Then cut across and swing up to obtain a 'gusset' extension on the underarm (FIG. 13). Line X–Z curves as on a sleeve head (though flatter). The underarm E–U is lengthened by the value of the 'gusset', i.e. by 6–7 cm.

Back and front parts of sleeve are cut in the same way (gussets must match) and then usually joined along the top into one whole sleeve (FIG. 14). The front of the crown is hollowed out more to neaten it by removing excess fullness in the hollow of the arm, while the back is kept higher, sometimes raised. A final adjustment can always be made at a fitting.

DEEP ARMHOLE

This is a style of armhole which may be used either with a Kimono or a standard Bodice block.

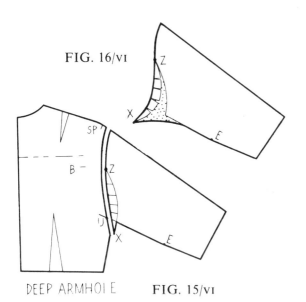

FIG. 16/VI

DEEP ARMHOLE   FIG. 15/VI

DEEP ARMHOLE ON A KIMONO BLOCK
—FIGS. 15, 16

An 'armhole' is sometimes used in a kimono as a *feature of style*. It is naturally a *deep* armhole since point U of a Kimono is *below* the UP of an ordinary Bodice block.

An armhole in a kimono pattern may also be used in styles with Combined sleeves (see later in this chapter). Thus there exist **Kimono styles with armholes,** either partial (back or front part only) or complete.

Method: Outline the armhole on the Kimono block from a point just outside SP, curving slightly down to 3–4 cm below U. For a really 'deep' effect it is better to come down below U, though point U may also be used.

Cut away the sleeve part (FIG. 15). Then outline on it a small section to half-way up the 'sleeve crown', i.e. to point Z, opposite B, and separate it from the sleeve but without cutting it away completely. Slash it across from the inner edge 3–4 times and move it away, curving to allow for a gusset extension on the sleeve underarm. As in the case of the Square armhole, this changes the kimono sleeve into one approaching a *set-in sleeve* in shape and fit. Complete as shown in FIG. 16. Front and back parts may be joined along the Top line into one whole sleeve, or used separately, according to style.

DEEP ARMHOLE ON A STANDARD BLOCK

An increase in size of armhole, achieved by lowering UP, is generally followed by a hollowing out of the sleeve, i.e. a corresponding lowering of sleeve point U, to adjust the sleeve crown to the bigger armhole. This change, however, is usually a small one, seldom more than 1–2 cm (except in some coat patterns), as the lowering of both UP on bodice and U on the sleeve shortens *the total underarm length* and is in any case *possible only in loose fitting style.*

Further cutting down of armhole and sleeve underarm soon brings in the trouble of *excessive loss of underarm length* so well known in kimono cutting.

When, therefore, a Deep armhole is a feature of a style, a special adjustment to compensate for loss of underarm length has to be made on the sleeve, just as in a Kimono or a Low raglan. The method is, in fact, similar to the one used for Low raglans and consists in building up, i.e. extending the length of the sleeve underarm. If necessary, the method could be adapted to a Square armhole used with an ordinary bodice block.

Method; A Deep armhole is generally slightly off the shoulder and ends at least 4–5 cm below the normal UP. A Centre shoulder seam and a more forward side seam are used.

In the back (FIG. 17, left) draw armhole from 1 cm outside SP, through point B (or just outside) down to lowered underarm point (U), in this case 6 cm below normal UP.

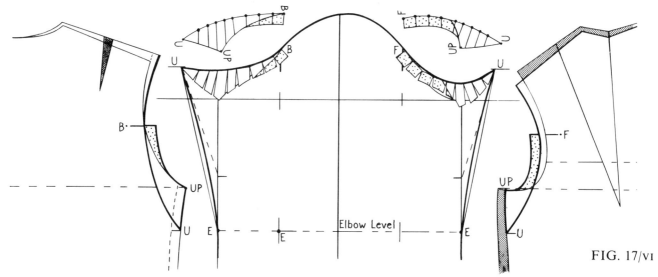

FIG. 17/VI

In the front (FIG. 17, right) the armhole line begins from the same point, passes 0·5–1 cm outside F and down to the new underarm point (U), matching the back. In both cases a little width is added, *in the pattern only* (not garment) from B and F downwards (shaded), to make it easier to cut into the lower parts of the armhole which are *detached from the bodice and added to the sleeve*.

After cutting away these parts (see small FIGS. above the sleeve), divide them into small sections, cutting *from the armhole edge*, and arrange each part, as shown in the middle, first matching points B and F. As with the Low raglan, some overlapping is permissible in the front.

The two points U of the sleeve are taken 4–5 cm up above the usual DC level to lengthen the sleeve underarm and to compensate for the loss of 6 cm on the bodice underarm. Extending DC line of sleeve right and left of pattern and drawing short lines, parallel to it and 5 cm higher, makes it easier to do this more accurately. Length U–E must be the same on both edges. It should be checked and made to match if unequal. For short sleeves the checking is done on the actual sleeve length level (broken lines); in long sleeves — at elbow level. The final seam is slightly curved.

COMBINED SLEEVES

These sleeves are a combination of Set-in, Kimono or Raglan sleeves, so that in each case the back and front parts of the sleeve are different. Several combinations are possible and examples of the most usual ones are given here to explain the method.

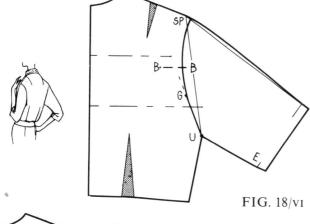

FIG. 18/VI

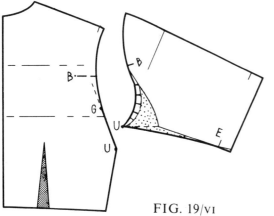

FIG. 19/VI

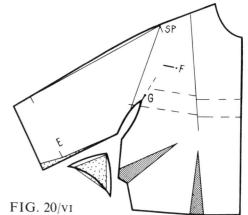

FIG. 20/VI

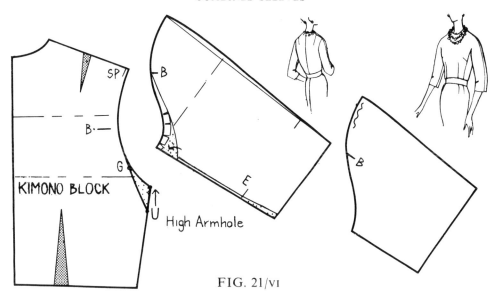

FIG. 21/VI

KIMONO AND SET-IN SLEEVE
with deep armhole – FIGS. 18, 19, 20

This is the most usual combination, cut on the Kimono block and having therefore a deep armhole. The sleeve may be an ordinary set-in sleeve in the back and kimono in the front, as shown here, or vice versa.

After outlining a Kimono block with a 7·5 cm slant, draw the armhole line from 1 cm below SP, down to point U, curving it 2–2·5 cm from the straight 'Armhole line' SP–U.

After marking on it point B, cut away the sleeve part and slash into it from U up to B, as already explained for the Deep armhole (FIGS. 15, 16). Cut across several times and curve up (to point U) to obtain a 6–7 cm gusset extension. The 'sleeve' acquires a shape resembling that of an ordinary set-in sleeve and gains in underarm length.

In the front, where the kimono cut is retained, a simple standard (set-in) gusset is used, which must match the gusset extension of the back sleeve.

The back sleeve may be joined to the kimono front along the Top line and be cut in one with it: this depends of course on the style, but is very usual.

KIMONO AND SET-IN SLEEVE
with high armhole – FIGS. 21, 22

This cut is possible only in styles where the kimono part can be *built up to a high underarm level*. As will be remembered from the Kimono Chapter Three, high fitting or 'built-up' gusset extensions can be used in styles which have a separate underarm section – a sidebody – usually outlined by an armhole Panel seam. Such a style is given here.

The back armhole is drawn as for the style above. After cutting away the sleeve part, slashing into it and allowing for the gusset extension, the underarm is simply

built up 4 cm and the same is done to the bodice part (FIG. 21). The sleeve will be *less wide* at the top than in the first case, and a small part of the projecting piece will be cut away (once the method is understood the building-up of the sleeve can be done directly, without the preliminary slashing, etc.). The final shape of the sleeve is like that of an ordinary set-in sleeve.

In the front, the underarm section (sidebody) is outlined and cut away, and its underarm line, as well as that of the sleeve part is built up, exactly as explained in the method given in Chapter Three (Plates 10 and 14). In both cases the building-up is 4 cm (not 5) to allow for a slightly lower UP and looser armhole. The extensions on front and back must naturally match.

The method can of course be applied in the same way to a style with kimono back and set-in sleeve in the front.

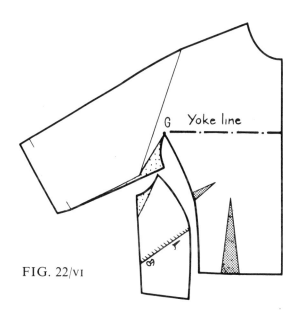

FIG. 22/VI

KIMONO AND RAGLAN COMBINED
SLEEVE—FIGS. 23, 24, 25, 26

The Kimono may be combined with a Raglan sleeve, using the latter either in the front or in the back.

After outlining the kimono, the raglan line is drawn as shown in FIG. 23 (in this case it is in the front), following the Gusset line in the lower part. The sleeve part is cut away and a gusset is added to it in the usual way (FIG. 24). In order not to spoil the raglan line, it is better not to add the gusset to the bodice part (though theoretically this, or even a divided gusset, is possible).

In the back, which retains its kimono sleeve, either an ordinary set-in gusset is used (FIG. 25) or, if the style has an underarm section, a gusset extension is made on the sleeve part of the kimono after the sidebody has been cut away (FIG. 26).

This, of course, is not a case where the underarm can be built up to a higher level because the front has a *Low raglan sleeve* which must be retained as a *feature of the style*.

The raglan part of the sleeve is joined to the kimono along the Top line and cut in one with it. This is very usual in these styles, but of course not essential.

The raglan shoulder dart is shown in two different positions: in its usual place—FIG. 25, and transferred to the front—FIG. 26.

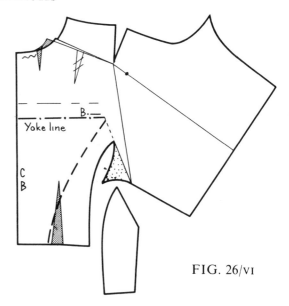

FIG. 26/VI

Other style variations are possible (see dot-dash and broken lines in FIG. 26), but whatever the shape of the sleeve combination, the general methods used in kimono and raglan cutting would apply to most designs of this type.

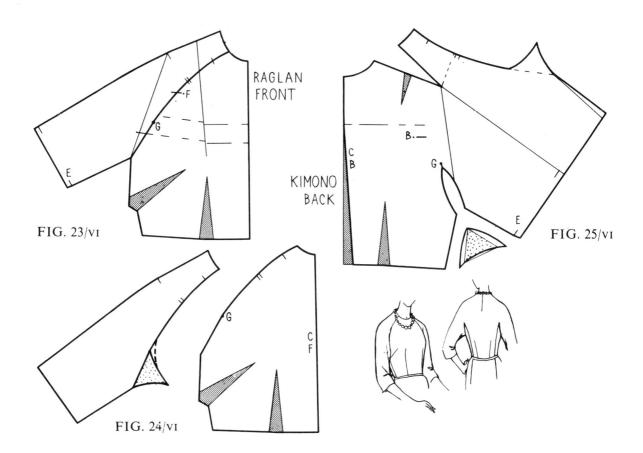

FIG. 23/VI

RAGLAN FRONT

KIMONO BACK

FIG. 24/VI

FIG. 25/VI

DRAPED STYLES

In no other styles does modelling play such an important part as in draped designs, and many cutters prefer to model these patterns entirely on the stand or figure, or even to drape the fabric itself. To a designer this can certainly be the quickest way of developing a new idea or of getting the general effect of his new design.

But in one way or another all cutters, even those who prefer cutting on the flat, use some modelling when dealing with draped styles, if only *to discover* a new way of draping, *to check* a draped effect on the figure or *to test* the draping qualities of a fabric.

It need not go beyond that, however, and many well-known and popular 'draperies', often referred to as classical, can be reproduced on the flat quite correctly, provided the details of the draped folds are carefully analysed and understood, and some 'experimenting' is allowed for. Even if all patterns of draped styles cut on the flat have to be tested on stand or figure, to see that the *amount of fullness* is right and to check *the set of the folds*, the actual planning and cutting of the pattern can often be done more accurately and quickly by following well-established methods of block adaptation.

DRAPED FOLDS—VARIOUS TYPES

In draped styles we deal with a variety of folds:
(a) **Loosely hanging folds,** attached at one end only, such as pleats, round pleats or folds, flares, cascades;
(b) **Folds caught at both ends.** These can be either:
   (i) stretched tightly on the figure—swathed effects;
   (ii) draped easily but set in a certain direction;
   (iii) hanging in festoons, as in various 'cowl' effects;
(c) **Graduated or tapering folds** which run off to nothing at one end. They may run in different directions, radiating from one point, meeting, or intersecting, producing a big variety of interesting effects.

When cutting draped styles on the flat, the main problem is to judge correctly the **character of the folds** (tight, loose, soft, etc.), their **position,** particularly in relation to the figure-shaping darts, and their **depth** for which correct extra width has to be allowed in the pattern. It is, in fact, usual to estimate the extra width required and, if possible, to test it with the fabric, before beginning to plan and design the pattern.

DEPTH OF DRAPED FOLDS

When **judging the depth of draped folds,** it must be borne in mind that an average, clearly defined fold, even when not particularly deep, requires 6–8 cm extra material (i.e. 3–4 cm on the double). For two folds, for instance, 12–16 cm will usually be added between the cut up sections of the pattern. Shallow and *short* folds need less—about 4–5 cm. Deep, and particularly *long* folds need more, 10–12 cm and sometimes much more—up to 20–25 cm.

The length of the fold, as judged from the sketch, particularly in the case of graduated folds, is therefore quite important and must be taken into consideration. Long folds are generally deeper than short ones: they cannot continue to their full length if there is not enough width or depth at their 'base'. This can be easily established by draping on the stand folds of different depth.

Finally the texture and thickness of the fabric influence the fold allowance, increasing it for soft (limp) and thin materials, such as silk crepes, chiffon, etc. and reducing it for heavy, bulky fabrics.

When folds are small (shallow) but numerous and very close together (gathered), as for instance down a draped CF line (Plate 24, style A), it is easier to estimate the necessary allowance on the principle of deep gathers. An average gathered effect is obtained by *doubling* the length over which the fullness appears, while for closely draped small folds, just as for closer gathers (e.g. smocking), $2\frac{1}{2}$ and 3 times the length, sometimes even more, would be used. A length of chiffon can be gathered or draped into a quarter of its original length, while for wool or brocade this would be either too bulky or simply impossible.

The only practical way of acquiring experience in judging fullness for different draped effects is to experiment with a variety of draped styles and different fabrics and to remember the effect of the allowances made.

THE FIT OF DRAPED STYLES

There are many draped styles in which *the set of the folds* depends entirely on a sufficiently close fit of the garment. Without this close fit the extra material added *will not drape effectively* and the fullness introduced for the folds will simply look untidy and heavy.

It is particularly important in these styles—many of them evening dresses—to ensure the correct 'line' and fit, i.e. tightness of the dress before planning the position and depth of the draped folds.

BASIC METHODS

The principal or standard method of introducing extra width for draped folds is **by cutting and opening gaps in the pattern.** This can be described as the Cutting-up method.

Method 1 has two important variants:
(*a*) cutting right through as for pleats, folds, gathers;
(*b*) cutting up to a point, as for flares.

Method 2, though less used, is essential for achieving certain draped effects. It provides for the folds **by adding width from outside** the outline of the draped part, and *adjusts the shape* of the pattern at the same time.

Other methods – simpler and more experimental – may be used in some cases, when Method 1 is thought to be too slow and complicated and Method 2 unsuitable. These may include a certain amount of *guessing* at the final shape of pattern, adjusting details 'by the eye' and also some **modelling,** e.g. 'modelling on the flat' which consists in setting folds into shape over a flat pattern.

The very important **testing and adjusting on the stand of all 'draped' patterns cut on the flat** is, of course, a form of modelling and is complementary to all these methods.

METHOD 1—THE CUTTING-UP METHOD

The cutting is usually done on a line or lines drawn *in the direction of the folds*, as shown by the sketch. It is not always necessary to reproduce every single fold, i.e. to make a slash for each separately: this depends on the details of the design, the number, size and arrangement of the folds, and one slash is often made for two or more small folds. The main thing is to produce a gap running in the right direction, through which sufficient width for one or more folds can be introduced. However, when the folds are few, well set apart and very definite in character, depth and length, it is usual to make a separate slash for each fold.

When cutting right through, whether for loose-hanging folds (round pleats) or folds caught at both ends, the amount added may be the same or bigger at one end than at the other. Care must be taken to join the pattern pieces again correctly, and the usual precaution of 'balancing' the separate parts against each other by **folding out the additions like pleats** is generally observed.

When cutting up to a point for folds which run off to nothing at one end, the slash must be made either **to the edge of the pattern** or **to the point of a dart.** There are therefore two ways of obtaining width for graduated folds: by introducing it *additionally*, or by *taking it from*

darts, either the figure-shaping darts of the block or darts made additionally for this purpose (see skirts). The darts are usually closed in the process and *their width* goes into the draped folds. The darts are thus 'draped', though not necessarily in their original position (examples of simple draped darts were already given in the basic course as one of the ways of using the dart fullness).

The Bust and Waist darts therefore play a very important part in patterns of draped styles. They can be: (*a*) used to obtain draped folds; (*b*) used to increase the depth of draped folds obtained by additional slashing; (*c*) not used at all and moved out of the way, e.g. into the underarm. The last usually happens when it is not possible to join them to other folds because they are in the wrong position for the folds, i.e. they will not run in the right direction (see style D, Plate 31).

In each case, when using the bodice darts for draping, one may be dealing either with the standard (usual depth) darts or with *increased* darts, when a specially close fit is required. This happens mainly with the Waist dart, though in the really moulded styles, tight on and above the bust line (e.g. with a strapless top), the Bust dart would be increased to produce the correct close fit as well as give more *depth* to the draped folds.

In some cases the two basic Darts of the block have to be re-distributed, e.g. equalized *to provide the same width*, before they can be used, either draped independently or added to folds obtained by slashing.

When studying draped styles it is necessary to understand which folds come from the Darts and which from additional slashing, i.e. from cutting to edge of pattern. Darts are always connected with the outlining of the shape of the figure and generally with a closer fit, and so are the *draped folds obtained from Darts*. Both are the result of moulding the fabric to the curves and hollows of the figure, and the closer fit, the more there is to go into the Darts and into draped folds obtained from them.

The only way to learn to design patterns of draped styles on the flat is to work through a number of suitable examples illustrating the standard methods, the variety of ways in which they can be applied, the important details which have to be considered and the many problems which arise. In modelling the final results are often so quickly arrived at that problems are not always recognized, reasoned and understood, as they must be when cutting the same pattern on the flat. The ideal for all patterns of draped styles is a practical combination of flat cutting and modelling.

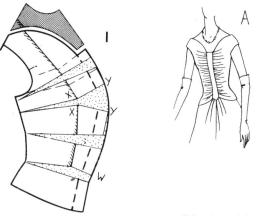

PLATE 24

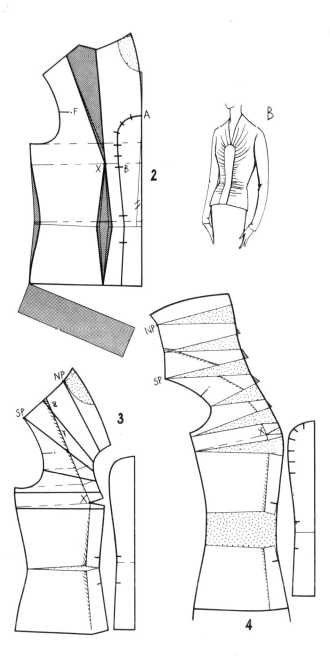

PLATE 24—DRAPED BODICES

Style A: This well known draped style, shown here as an evening dress bodice (may be a blouse), is a good **illustration of the standard Cutting-up method.** The back is plain and well-darted. The extension below the waist may be added later.

Both Darts contribute to the draped fullness and, since the fit is fairly close, particularly at the waist, the Waist dart is increased by the addition of the Sl. CF and the side seam shaping (as shown in FIG. 2). Both darts are lengthened to meet at point X and, after making a slash from CF, i.e. from Y to X, the Darts are closed: this gives only 8–10 cm fullness on CF. It must be increased.

Cut through the open CF dart from X to the side seam opening 2–3 cm at X: considerably more is thus added to CF length. Make two more slashes, one above and one below, opening 4 cm or more to produce a total length which at least *doubles the length* of the draped part of the CF. Make the fullness additions according to weight and texture of fabric (after some preliminary testing of the effect). Open more at X, if necessary. For fullness at the waist leave a gap when adding extension, or slash if pattern is already cut below the waist.

Complete the pattern to style, cutting out the neckline well at the sides. The CF band may be quite separate, laid on over the gathered CF seam; or the gathers may be set *into* it, when it becomes of course part of the bodice which must then be reduced accordingly down the CF (broken line). Half width of band = 2–3 cm.

Style B: This is another useful example of Method I. The distinctive feature of the style is a narrow CF panel, into which the draped fullness of the top part is gathered from every direction— from shoulder, armhole and side seam. As will be seen, the Darts here add very little to the draped fullness, which is produced mainly by *slashing to edge of pattern.*

After increasing Waist dart by 1–2 cm, outline panel from 2 cm above the Chest line, making it wider at the top. Around its curved edge, mark from CF, at 2·5 cm intervals, the position of 6 slash lines (to just below true Bust line). Length of curve A–B = 15 cm. Add the raised neckline of the style.

After cutting away the panel, slash from the front to X and close both Darts to X. Note the gap at the waist which must be cut to enable the Waist dart of a *long bodice* to be closed and the pattern *to lie flat.*

Plan the lines of the slashes: from shoulder (SP, NP and halfway between), from armhole (Chest level) and two from the side seam. Draw the lines and cut on them. Open the slashes, as shown in FIG. 4, adding 4–5 cm in each slash, according to fabric: this more than doubles the length A–B.

If the fullness is to be gathered to produce small but fairly closely packed folds (as sketch), this should be sufficient. But if the fullness is to go into *separate* well-set folds, more may be needed to give *each* fold a 6–8 cm depth (3–4 cm on the double).

Cut *right through the waist* to add 8–10 cm for the draped fullness there. These folds go right through and are caught in the side seam, as well as under the front panel.

PLATE 25—SKIRTS WITH SOFT DRAPED FOLDS: PEG TOP STYLE

All the styles here have **softly draping folds** and all the fullness is produced *by slashing from the waist*, though the folds are set and arranged in different ways.

In all cases the hem width of the Standard block (e.g. 120 cm) is tightened by 15–20 cm, often to the 'minimum hem width' which is equal to the Hip width in very short skirts or 5–6 cm more in slightly longer ones. The resulting silhouette—widening towards the hips and then again narrowing towards the hem—is known as **the Peg Top line**. In most of these styles the back is plain, but tightened at the hem (on the seam).

The slashes go either to the edge of the pattern, as in FIGS. 4 and 5, for folds set definitely sideways or, for straight or only slightly sloping folds, as well as for the cowl effect (style D), the slashes are made from the waist down to the top of a *dart pinned from the hem*. **Hem width** can always be **transferred into the top** (as shown by modelling): that is the **basis of the Peg Top cut**.

Since the hem cannot be reduced beyond a certain limit (hem loss in Standard block can be up to 8–10 cm on half-pattern), additional fullness at the waist can be obtained along the edges of the half-pattern, the CF and side (FIG. 3). In more exaggerated styles (barrel-shaped, etc.), slashing from the top may be done down to the hemline, which will then curve and not be straightened out, as shown here (FIG. 3).

Style A—FIGS. 1 and 2—is the simplest case. The slash is made down the middle to a point half-way down the length: the gap at the top is thus as wide as the dart pinned out below (5 cm). More width can be gained by including the Side dart (4 cm) or even by sloping seam beyond it, with or without further loss of hem width at the side. The 8–10 or 12 cm thus obtained are sufficient for one deep fold, or a deep and a small one, or simply gathers.

Style B: By bringing point X down to Knee line (FIG. 3) more width (10–12 cm) is gained above. This may be increased further by going beyond the side seam and the CF. The fullness here is set into deep 'box-pleat' folds.

Style C: A somewhat different effect is obtained by making the slashes from the waist *to the side seam* (FIG. 4) and opening each to a different width: the longest 8–10 or even 12 cm; the middle to 6–8 cm; the shortest to 4–5 cm (FIG. 5).

Style D: Here the Peg Top effect is achieved by 'cowl' drapery at the side, set into plain back and front panels.

On a Standard block outline the panels a little straighter than usual, cut them away. Make a tracing of the side down to Hip line, to use under the draped part (FIG. 6).

On the middle section (FIG. 7) *which has no side seam*, mark position of the top loop and measure its length along curve A–Z–B (Z is 2–3 cm above Yoke line). This is the length (40–42 cm) to which the pattern must be extended at the top, along A–X–B. At the hem mark a 5 cm dart.

Slash pattern to Knee line level, pin out the 5 cm dart below. The gap which opens must make A–X–X–B long enough for the top loop (about 40 cm). Move end of slash lower or higher to increase or decrease this length, as required.

A little extra height at the top (3–4 cm) allows for the second loop to be *folded* over and caught under the panels (this is optional). Allow for the facing of the cowl when cutting out.

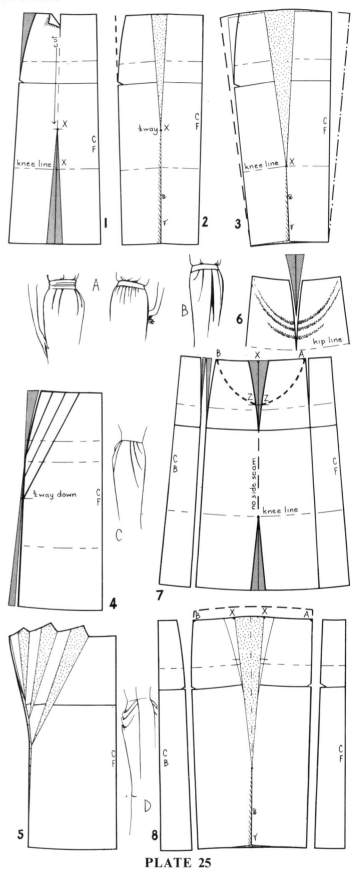

PLATE 25

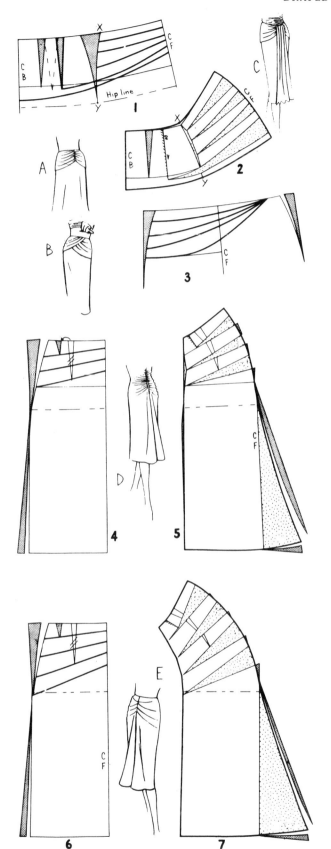

PLATE 26

PLATE 26—SKIRTS DRAPED ON THE HIPS: SWATHED EFFECTS

These are examples of swathed effects, with the draped folds stretched almost tightly on the hips. The first two styles are yokes which may be part of different skirt styles, straight or full. The other styles are complete skirts, draped in the same way on the hips. These are always straight down the sides but have extra, often considerable, hem fullness concentrated in the CF (modelling shows how this effect is achieved).

Style A—a yoke draped down CF—has no side seams and is cut in one with the back (plain or darted). Outline it on the Standard block, 18–20 cm deep on CB, 12 cm on CF; then plan four slash lines, all to be connected with Waist darts *to achieve the close fit*. There is no slashing to edge of pattern: the Waist darts provide all the fullness needed. Place top slash 2–3 cm below the waist, the lowest 2–3 cm above the lower edge, the other two spaced between them.

The three top slashes connect with the big Side dart, as shown in FIG. 1 (the spacing along the Side dart is wider than on CF). The lowest slash connects with a smaller back Waist dart (2–3 cm deep) which comes out of the total WR of the back.

First cut along the Side dart (along X–Y) and then from CF along the slash lines. Closing the whole Side dart (curving X–Y), open the gaps on CF more or less equally. The lowest slash is taken to the back dart, also pinned out. 15–18 cm are added to the 12 cm CF which is thus more than doubled. For more fullness, if required by style or fabric, the second back dart can be used in the same way, (making a single deeper dart), or some width can be added from below.

Style B is a cross-over front yoke, coming *from side seams*. The method is similar, but only the Side dart can be used here (not necessarily the whole of it). Slashes going across the front are longer and open more; fullness drapes into one 'point' (i.e. smallest space possible).

Style C—sketch—shows the effect of a *straight* piece of fabric draped round the hips. Note in sketch waist dipping on CF.

Style D is cut on a Straight block, already 10–12 cm tighter in the hem, and is further reduced, 2–3 cm on each seam edge, to a *minimum width* (100–106 cm). The lowest slash line is 10 cm down CF and 15 cm down the Side dart, which is cut away. Move front dart further out, shorten it to level of the top slash.

Cut on the lines from CF, the top one only to the small dart which is *closed to produce the top gap*. Other gaps are opened *as required* by the style, in this case only moderately full in the draped part, so that 14–15 cm extra will a little more than double it.

Draw a new CF line through the slashed section, losing and gaining, as usual (FIG. 5). Straighten side seam, losing a little on the hips and below. If necessary, further tightening of the draped part can be done later on the figure or stand.

Finally add **extra hem width at CF** for the deep flared folds below hip level. As draping on the stand shows, such folds appear quite naturally when CF is gathered *upwards*. The deeper the drapery at the top, the deeper are usually the folds at the hem, e.g. 12–13 cm (see next style).

Style E is cut in the same way, but with a deeper draped effect. The lowest slash line is 14–15 cm down CF and below the Hip line at the side. Four slashes are made, and about 25 cm extra added to the CF, almost trebling the length of the draped part. A bigger addition is also made at the CF hem (15–18 cm).

Fullness may be set into 4–5 *definite folds* instead of being *gathered* into small, tight folds.

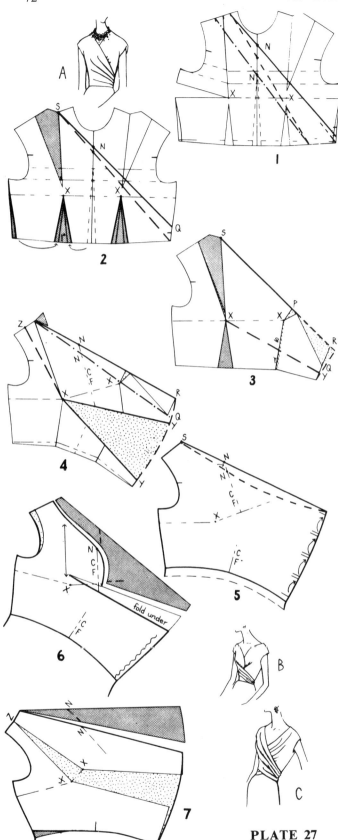

PLATE 27

PLATE 27—DRAPED CROSS-OVER BLOUSE

The pattern of this classical draped style has many interesting features. It shows, for instance, how shorter folds are obtained from the Darts, while longer folds require additional slashing. The former run off to nothing near the highest point of the bust, the latter go over and beyond it.

A special problem is also the depth of the neckline, i.e. point N down CF: it tends to work out too high with certain positions and slants of the crossing edges. FIG. 1 shows three different positions and others are possible. Sloping lines begin from different points at the top, ending either at the waist (12–13 cm from CF), or a side, or up the side seam. In each case point N on CF is on a different level. This point must be noted at an early stage.

The line chosen here to demonstrate the general method runs from the Shoulder dart, 5 cm from NP, to 5 cm up the side—a difficult and 'tight' cross-over, giving a very high neckline on CF, so that the problem of how to deal with it can be examined (in some cross-overs it does not exist).

Style A gives the basis of the method. The folds are short and it is obvious, even from the sketch, that they come from the Bust dart to which the Waist darts are added, as the waist is close-fitting (modelling proves this).

Using a *whole bodice front*, draw the cross-over line S–Q, as shown in FIG. 2. Increase the depth of both Waist darts by 2+ cm adding value of Sl. CF and side shaping. Cut away pattern beyond cross-over line. The waist is lengthened for style in final stage—FIG. 5.

From the left Waist dart draw a line at right angles to S–Q and cut it to X (FIG. 3). Close the Waist dart. The gap which opens at P breaks the edge S–Q. Straighten it, continuing to point R: this already gives some width for the folds (Q–R = about 6 cm) which comes *from the closed left Waist dart*.

From Y, half-way between waist and Q, draw a line to right side X, cut on it and then close *right* Shoulder and Waist darts, meeting at X (FIG. 4): a big gap opens on the opposite side, giving 15–18 cm extra width (the total here is now about 33 cm). All the darts, except left Shoulder dart, are now collected in *one big draped dart* in the left side seam.

The part played by the left Shoulder dart must be explained: it remains open to *lengthen* the cross-over edge and help to bring point N down. This point will not be as high on the figure as on the pattern if the edge is left slack (i.e. slightly curving). For a really *tight* edge the Dart should have been closed and the fullness added to the folds, which in this case would have been excessive.

For further lowering of point N: (a) cross-over edge can be further *eased* by lengthening (FIG. 3); (b) edge can be lowered on side seam (dot-dash, FIG. 4) losing some width there *and on bust line*; (c) edge can be curved slightly (through N 2–3 cm lower) losing little on bust and nothing in the folds (FIG. 5); (d) edge can be curved the other way, retaining full width on bust but losing some at the base (like original 'break' of line—FIG. 3). The choice depends on details of style, fabric and shape of figure: for some bulky fabrics less width in folds is an advantage; for some shapes of figure loss of width (e.g. on bust) is not advisable, etc.

Style B is another version of the style with the top part tucked under the draped folds (FIG. 6 shows the adaptation).

Style C is a very **important variant** of the style, with **higher folds,** going over the bust and up towards shoulder. Cut from middle of side to X, and from there to Z on the shoulder. Open 5 cm at X: this makes a considerable addition to folds on the side: an equivalent amount is taken off the top (less, if draped fullness is to be increased). Edge lengthens, folds become looser (slacker) and point N comes down. This is usually a softer draped effect.

The draped cross-over may be set into side seam or continued to the back, sometimes looped over as a sash.

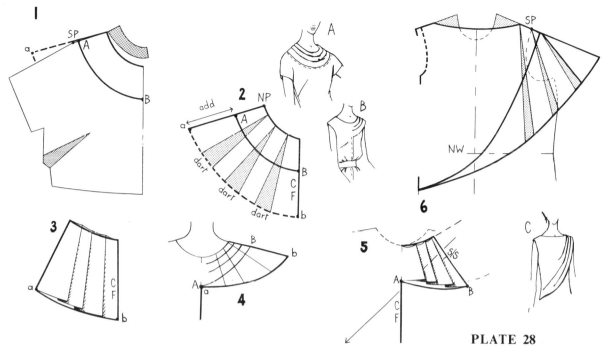

PLATE 28

METHOD 2—OUTSIDE ADDITION FOR THE FOLDS

This method is best explained on simple examples, and draped yokes are very suitable styles for this.

PLATE 28—EXAMPLES OF METHOD 2

Style A is a **Round draped yoke** set into a plain bodice.

After cutting out the neckline, 2–3 cm down CF and 4 cm on the shoulder, outline the yoke part, 8 cm deep, and cut it away on line A–B (FIG. 1). Measure its lower edge A–B and make a note of it. Then add beyond it 15–18 cm *for two folds* (FIG. 2). Measure *new* outer edge, a–b, compare with original, and *reduce it* by darting (FIGS. 2 and 3) *to the original length A–B*, to fit into the bodice. Note that **this changes the shape of the yoke**—*straightens it*. This change is very important and without it the added width will not set correctly into folds.

N.B. It is not correct to slash through the yoke to expand it in depth only: in this type of 'cowl' drapery there is a definite proportion between depth and *width,* achieved only by such a *change of shape*.

Theoretically, the addition could also be made at the top edge, which would then have to be slashed and *opened to regain its original length* (as style A, Plate 29). In this case, however, it would not be convenient because lines projected above NP and CF soon meet and intersect.

Style B also follows this method. Draped asymmetrically, on one shoulder only, the **loose draped yoke or 'scarf'** (2 versions) is an extension beyond the CF of the right (plain) side of the bodice and is cut with it. Folds are either set into the shoulder seam (one version), or draped over the shoulder to hang down as a loose end (scarf) in the back: in both cases they run off to nothing on the CF. The addition is therefore made on a direct extension of the shoulder and is gradually reduced towards CF (FIG. 4).

After measuring the two curves, the outer edge is reduced to the original length A–B by darting (FIG. 5), all the darts going into the neckline edge.

Style C—FIG. 6—has a **draped loose front**, detached at one side and at the lower edge, and draping from one shoulder only. It is possible to cut it either by method 1 or 2.

The addition of width for 2–3 folds (Method 2) lying close together (overlapping) on the shoulder, is made as in style B. The darting to reduce the lower edge to the original length (the difference here is not big) is made entirely into the shoulder, avoiding the neckline so as not to spoil its boat-shaped style.

The folds can also be produced by slashing from the shoulder (Method 1). The short top fold may be connected with Bust dart, the long ones cut to the lower edge and side.

PLATE 29—EXAMPLES OF METHOD 2

In this Plate are given further examples of Method 2, used in 'cowl neckline' draperies, for which this method is particularly suitable. Although a method for simple cowls was given in the basic course, this is the systematic way of arriving at any style and depth of cowl drapery. **Style A** is **a deep cowl drapery** in the back of a dress— usually a plain, close-fitting sheath style, cut higher in the front and with a plunging neckline in the back, over which the drapery is placed.

Outline the shape of the draped part (FIG. 1) on the block, cut away and add to it depth for two folds, above the top curve, going 15 cm up the CB but adding nothing on the shoulder. In this style there are no folds on the shoulder, though there may be in other cases (FIG. 2).

Since the new top curve a–b is shorter than the original A–B length, it must be slashed and expanded *to regain the original length* (FIG. 3): this increases the top width across as well as *straightens* the whole curve of the original pattern. The length of the top edge corresponds of course to the 'depth' of the highest loop of the cowl. Extra width for facing (turn-back of the top edge) is added when cutting out. It is cut on the true bias.

For a style with folds on the shoulder, the short line B–SP would be extended to allow for them: this can be done below the lower edge, gradually running into it.

Style B is yet another type of neckline drapery—a **draped plastron** (bib), covering a plain bodice front. It has folds on the shoulder where it therefore requires more extra width than down the CF (modelling shows this clearly).

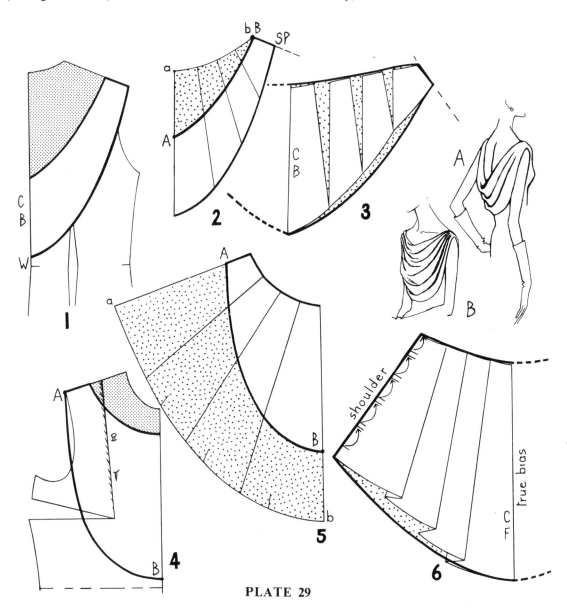

PLATE 29

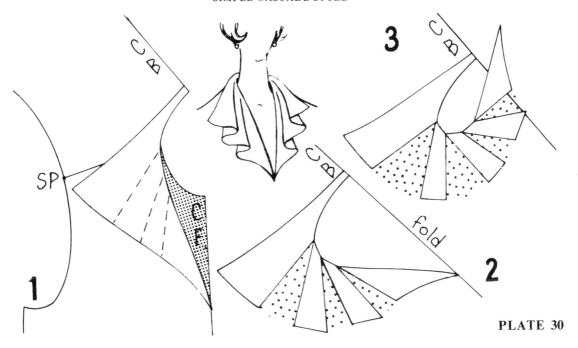

PLATE 30

After cutting out the neckline, as shown in FIG. 4, make an outline of the draped part, taking it down nearly to the waist. Add twice as much (25 cm) along the shoulder than down the CF, i.e. below point B. Measure the two curves, as usual, and reduce the lower to the length of the original A–B by darting (FIG. 6).

On the final pattern plan the folds very close along the shoulder (small spaces). It would not be convenient to cut this pattern by adding depth above the neckline, as was done for style A, for reasons already mentioned.

The whole draped part would be cut on the true bias.

OTHER METHODS

Theoretically, it is possible to cut all 'draped' patterns by the two methods described. In practice, it is found that this is often a slow and tedious way of arriving at *some simple patterns*, the shape of which is quite well known. There exist therefore useful 'short cuts' which most pattern designers would accept as practical. Some of these consist in *guessing* the final shape and then testing and adjusting it to the details of the style. Other simpler methods are connected with modelling.

Modelling is not only important for testing patterns, 'draping' them on the stand both at the final stage and throughout the work, to avoid accumulating errors of judgement; it can also be used to cut more quickly a *part* of a draped style, the rest of which is more conveniently cut from the block. It is also possible sometimes to 'model on the flat', over a pattern, by actually *shaping the paper into folds* or flares.

This is not the place to describe methods of direct modelling, but those who can model have the advantage of being able to cut patterns on the flat with more confidence and often with greater speed.

A few examples will be given of such simpler methods which often include a certain amount of guessing and always much testing. They are more experimental than the systematic methods described above. The best examples are found in patterns of draperies usually described as 'cascades', i.e. *overlapping folds*, draping over each other. They appear in collars, jabots and various loose panels.

PLATE 30–SIMPLE CASCADE STYLE

This style of flared collar is an example of a **cascade drapery** in which the folds *overlap*, i.e. fall over each other.

To cut it by the standard Cutting-up method, the outline of the *final* (already draped) collar would have to be made with every fold outlined and then slashed to insert the width.

By treating it as a simple flared pattern, making a simple basic outline (back edge straight, not curved round the neck, as in sketch), and then making three slashes (two might make the inner curve too angular), the whole operation is considerably simplified and speeded up.

Some guidance as to the width to be allowed in the gaps can be obtained from the length of the original outline (FIG. 1) which can be *doubled*, or increased less (FIG. 2) or more (FIG. 3). It is also helpful to note and remember how the pattern *curves*, approaching a half-circle (FIG. 2) or going beyond it (FIG. 3). In the first case the collar can be cut 'to the fold' (effect rather skimpy), in the second it must have a join in the back.

The *effect can be tested*, not only on the stand, but already on the flat, by folding out the additions (the extra paper) between the slashes (i.e. bringing slashes together) and, if necessary, correcting the width at once, before checking the 'hang' of the folds on the stand.

Another cascade style which lends itself well to a simpler and more experimental way of cutting is shown in FIGS. 1 and 2. This type of loose panel which drapes along its loose edge (the other is caught in the side seam) may appear in both bodices and skirts. The draped part is *known to be an extension* of the loose edge and so can simply be added to it in the pattern. What must be established, however, is the width of the projection X–a at the top which is equal to the *length of the top fold* X–b; the amount of fullness needed for the number of folds shown; and the final shape of the edge.

If the length of the fold X–b is more than ⅓ of the total skirt length, say 30 cm, make X–a 30 cm. At the bottom there is a flat part from side seam to point Z from where approximately the outer edge of the extension begins, curving slightly up to point a at the top. Fold the cascade—in this case two overlapping folds—to see the effect: if not deep enough, length will have to be added between Z and point a by cutting up to point X (as in FIG. 2). With more experience, measuring on the pattern the length a–Z will show already if there is enough for two very deep folds (20–25 cm each).

Again the experimental way of arriving at the pattern is quicker and simpler than the systematic Cutting-up method when applied to this particular draped style.

The second style, in FIG. 2, is another version of this type of cascade, fuller and forming more than two overlapping folds, coming down nearly to hem level. It is obvious, if only from the previous example, that the natural edge of the extension would not give enough to achieve this effect and that it would have to be lengthened by slashing. All slash lines must go up to point X.

Note different shape of outer edge. This shape can always be arrived at correctly by setting the folds into their correct final position, i.e. *draping them on the flat*, and then trimming the graduated length of their hemline, cutting hem of each fold in turn until the correct effect of the sketch is reproduced. This, in fact, is what is usually done when modelling this pattern on the stand.

PLATE 31—DRAPED NECKLINES

These draped necklines are all well known classical styles. They are examples of styles to which either standard method—I or II —could be applied with the same result in the end. The standard Cutting-up method is used here.

Style A is a built-up draped neckline, high at the sides as well as in the front, with one or two deep folds at the base of the neck and going into a V in the back.

In all cases of draped necklines it is usually more convenient to move the Shoulder dart into the underarm, sometimes folding the pinned out Dart the other way (see FIG. 5). For all styles with built-up necklines the Centre shoulder seam should be used.

Measure **the basic neckline** curve NP–N (front) to use later as **a controlling measurement** (11 cm in this size).

Method: Build up a Raised neckline at the side (FIG. 1) extending the shoulder seam 3–4 cm beyond NP and raising the line slightly to O to make the line drawn from O down to CF point N equal to the controlling measurement of basic neckline (11 cm), otherwise the top edge will be too tight.

Draw two slash lines from N: the first to NP and the second to point Y, 4 cm farther down the shoulder. Cut on these lines from point N, separating two small sections.

From a point on the neckline (P), 4 cm from CF, draw a line to point X, to connect neckline with Bust dart (FIG. 1).

Decide on the height to be added above CF neckline (N) to drape back into two folds at the base of the neck, eg. 10–12 cm. Swing up the two detached pieces until the top edge is the required distance from neckline, i.e. 10–12 cm. The top edge O–N, which is equal to the controlling measurement 11 cm, projects *beyond* the upward continuation of the CF line: this would make the raised edge *too tight*.

To remedy this, cut from P to X (Fig. 2) and close part of the Underarm dart. Open the gap until the extended CF line just touches the line O–N at the top, so that the two small sections no longer project beyond it and the neckline thus *regains its correct size*.

The rest of the Bust dart is used according to style.

Back neckline—V-shaped, high at the side. Extend shoulder beyond the NP to O (as front). Mark depth of neck down CB (V). NP–V is the controlling measurement. Compare with O–V: if too short, *raise point O* (as in the front) until line O–V is correct.

N.B. If **using Method II** for this style, draped height would be added above point N and the shoulder extended: this would give a very narrow top edge, to be widened by cutting down to point X and *closing part of Dart*. Unnecessary width round base of neck would have to be reduced by hollowing out (curving) the shoulder seam, to achieve correct shape.

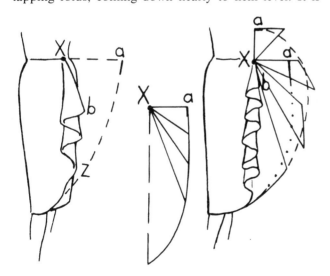

FIG. 1/VII   FIG. 2/VII

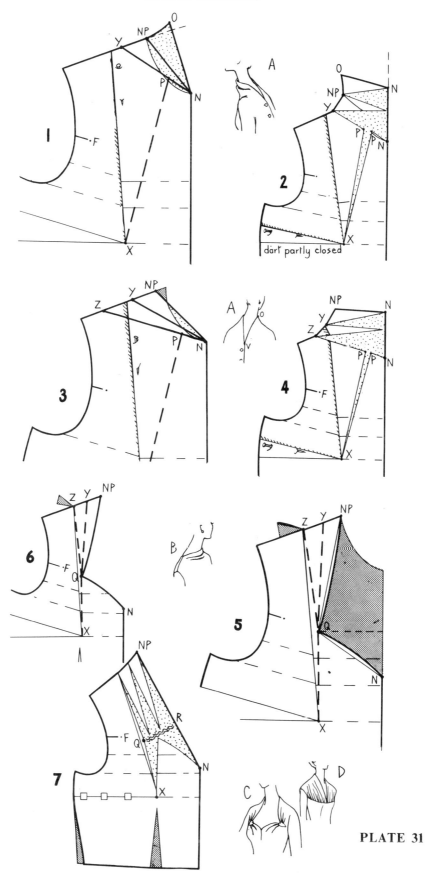

PLATE 31

Style B—FIGS. 3 and 4—is another version of draped neckline with the folds at the base going further *across* and into shoulder, with no height at the side. In these styles the neckline is usually cut away at the side, at least 2–3 cm or more (boat-shaped), to help the folds to set correctly.

The top edge here runs from 2–3 cm inside NP down to N and two slash lines are drawn—one to Y, near the closed Dart, and the other to Z, 4 cm further out. All lines meet at N.

Cut from N to swing up the two small sections for CF height (10–12 cm). Cut from P to X and close part of Dart *to prevent any overlapping* beyond CF line.

Style C—FIGS. 5, 6, 7—shows a different type of draped effect, achieved by making a long V loose enough to be pulled back into a 'heart-shaped' neckline, with the draped folds at the corners caught by gathering or under a clip.

After closing Dart (folding it the other way—FIG. 5), outline shape of *finished neckline*, placing Q—widest part near the closed Dart—on a level 9 cm down CF or 3–4 cm above Chest line. Measure neckline from NP to Q and Q to N and use this as a controlling measurement, i.e. 16·5 + 11·5 = 28 cm.

Cut out neckline (Fig. 6) cutting away the shaded part. Draw slash lines from Q to points Y and Z on the shoulder, point Y half-way between Z and NP. A third line from Q goes to X—the Dart. Slash from Q to all these points.

Close Dart completely when a gap will open at Q (FIG. 7). Move out the two small sections at the top, giving shoulder a *slight upward curve*, to lengthen final outer edge. Connect NP and N by a line which must be equal (or nearly) to the controlling measurement 28 cm. It can be curved more, to increase fullness Q–R available for draped folds.

When the width Q–R is gathered and pulled up, the neckline will assume its correct shape (heart-shaped).

The width Q–R (9–10 cm) could be increased by adding part of the Waist dart. This would increase the draped effect of the style, but would also widen the neckline.

Style D is an example of draped fullness which cannot include the Bust dart because of the position of its folds. The Dart must therefore be moved elsewhere before cutting for the folds.

LINGERIE PATTERNS
Part 1—Petticoats, Brassieres, Nightdresses

All the standard blocks—Bodice, Sleeve and Skirt—are used for cutting underwear and nightwear patterns, as are also some of the additional foundations such as the One-piece dress, the Kimono and the Raglan. It is also convenient to have a special block for petticoats, and of course for the knicker patterns (Chapter IX).

The Petticoat foundation is used for patterns of slips or petticoats from the shoulder, for cami-knickers and also brassieres. As it is tighter than the ordinary One-piece block it can sometimes be used for closer-fitting dresses without sleeves (e.g. evening dresses).

The Bodice and Sleeve blocks are used mainly for nightdresses, pyjama tops, dressing gowns and dressing jackets; the Skirt block—for short waist-petticoats and for nightdresses and dressing gowns with a join at the waist. Finally, various combined garments, such as cami-knickers, pyjamas, sleeping suits, etc. require both a bodice and knicker foundation. All the blocks, therefore, play their part in lingerie cutting according to the type and the style of the garment.

THE PETTICOAT BLOCK—FIG. 1

This is really the One-piece dress foundation with the following modifications:

(*a*) It is tighter round the bust, since it is not used for garments with sleeves.

(*b*) The Waist is slightly raised.

(*c*) The True Bust line is on the same level, back and front, and is usually referred to as the Basic line.

(*d*) The Shoulder dart is increased to tighten the top edge and give it a more clinging, semi-brassiere fit.

(*e*) The Waist Reduction (WR) is planned differently.

Method—FIG. 1.

Outline the bodice block as usual, and continue the CB and CF lines to the required length which is usually 5 cm less than the dress length or, nowadays, even shorter.

Reduce the Width of the top at the side, taking off on the Bust line 1 + cm in the back and 1 cm in the front. At the waist use the *inner side seam* and run the new side seam into it.

Retain the full width round the hips at least in the block. Continue the side seam through the usual H point.

Placing the yard stick on Waist and Hip points, rule the lower part of the side seam, below the hips, running the line smoothly into side seam above. This gives the *width of the hem* which is completed, as usual, curving up

slightly at the sides, a little shorter than CB and CF.

An alternative method is to fix the hem width according to the hem measured on the One-piece dress and only then to complete the side seam. The first method may give a little more hem width which is generally quite useful.

Draw a new Waist line 1 cm higher, to ensure that all waist shaping, by seams or darts, has a slightly *high-waisted* character, suitable for most petticoat styles.

FIG. 1/VIII

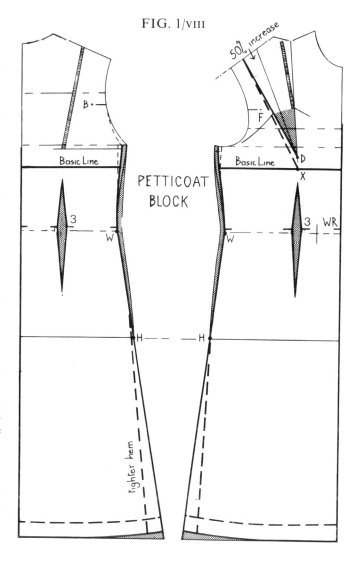

Mark the True Bust line on the same level back and front, preferably in its basic position, 4 cm below the Bust line. It is an important line in this block and the **Basic line** for the planning of all brassiere or 'bra' styles.

Increase the Bust dart by 50%, adding half as much again to the Dart width across the top.

The Waist Reduction (WR) is influenced by the consideration that most petticoats are made *without openings and plackets*. The finished waist width must therefore be big enough to go over bust and shoulders. In smaller sizes (waist 70 cm and below) an addition of 10–15 cm to the waist measurement is usually safe, giving an **average 80–85 cm finished waist**. In the larger sizes it may be sufficient to add 10–12 cm as the Waist measurement itself is already bigger in proportion to the Bust. But much depends on how *pliable* the figure is and also how '*stretchy*' the style and the fabric. An actual test is the only safe way of finding the *minimum* waist a figure can 'squeeze' into, and a block can give only a safe *average*, not allowing for very square stiff shoulders or over-developed bust.

Measure the waist as usual from CB towards CF, allowing 41–42 cm in the smaller sizes and ½ waist + 5–7 cm in the larger sizes. What remains beyond that point is the WR which is divided equally between back and front. The *whole* WR is thus conveniently indicated on the block by a single back and front dart. Other methods of waist shaping need not be shown on the block, but in style designing they will generally be used in preference to waist darting (e.g. shaping in CF and CB seams).

The above measurements and proportions are given for *general guidance* and will vary in practical pattern designing. Not only will this depend on style or type of petticoat but also, considerably, on the fabric and on the sewing and finishing technique used. Nowadays many, if not most, petticoats are machine-made garments, often made in stretchy fabrics (locknit, etc.) or, in the case of woven fabrics, cut on the true bias, not so much for style effect or better hang, as for greater 'stretch' and size adaptability.

All this is part of the wholesale manufacturing technique which has brought in many changes. Under its influence petticoat styles are now designed to avoid various complications of finish such as openings, darts, or anything requiring hand-work, while full use is made of trimming easily done by machine—flounces, frills, pintucks, lace appliqué and edging, etc. Styles have accordingly become more standardized and the fit of the petticoat often depends not only on cut, but also on the use of various devices which make it possible to put it on easily without an opening, even when the style appears to be quite well shaped to the figure. The popular 'brassiere top' style with 'points' in the front and a *low-cut* back, made in locknit fabric, is a good example of this technique: here everything is combined to ease the putting-on of the garment while retaining a good shape and reasonable tightness round the bust.

Reliance upon **stretchy fabrics** often makes it possible to **reduce the proportions given above** without risk of the petticoat tearing or not standing up to much laundering. In woven fabrics, however, greater care must be taken not to lose size unless an opening can be used, and to make allowance for possible shrinking and tearing of seams.

Practical details of size and fit are given in connection with the various style adaptations, but the following few **remarks on size adjustment** are of *general* interest.

The Bust width of the block can be reduced for a closer fit, using the full 1 + cm reduction on the front and even more than 1 cm on the back, provided there is enough 'stretch' *in the style* (as in the 'brassiere top' example mentioned above), or/and if a stretchy (or bias) fabric is used. A slip worn under a tight (evening) dress could also be reduced, but it would usually have a placket. For some styles the bust width may have to be *increased* if there is difficulty in putting on the garment, e.g. styles with built-up tops or with a tight, straight top edge.

The Hip width is sometimes reduced for slips worn under tight dresses or in the case of stretchy fabrics. But generally the *hip allowance should be reasonable* (5–6 cm) to allow for the shrinking of fabric in the wash and also for **correct bias cutting**. Tight bias petticoats by expanding round the hips, particularly when one is sitting, tend to get shorter and to 'work up' on the figure: this is a frequent defect caused by skimped hip width.

The Waist width is reduced to the *standard* fit (as the block), more often by shaping in Sl. CB/CF, in Panel seams or more curved side seams than by darting. If a *tighter* waist fit than that is required, then a placket is essential. In some cases one need not be concerned with the actual waist width as, for example, in high waisted, Empire-line petticoats, where the tightest fit is below the bust line.

SIMPLE PETTICOAT
(straight or built-up top)—FIG. 2.

This is the simplest petticoat, consisting of a plain back and front. There are two main versions: with shoulder straps and a straight top edge or with the whole top built-up to the shoulders (mainly in larger sizes).

Though less shaped than the average modern petticoat, it is a useful style when a looser-fitting garment is required. Its plain top also provides space for an effective display of every kind of decorative work, embroidery, etc.

For waist shaping use the darts of the block, but for a looser fit waist darts can be omitted. On the other hand when used as a slip under a close fitting dress, the darts are increased, making it necessary to have a placket.

The fit at the top is generally fairly loose, with less

FIG. 2/VIII   FIG. 3/VIII   FIG. 4/VIII

width reduction and usually just the *ordinary* (not increased) Bust dart. Excessive tightening round bust and waist may make this petticoat difficult to put on unless an opening is provided or the top is finished off with 'points' or a fold of more stretchy fabric—net, chiffon, lace.

Transfer Bust dart into underarm, making it a little smaller than on the block. Then draw the top edge 2·5 cm above the Chest line, coming down to 1 cm below the armhole from where it continues into the back, still 1 cm below the Bust line. **Hem width** can be added only by sloping out the side seams.

The shape of a *built-up top* (detail inside FIG. 1) varies with round, V-shaped or other simple neckline.

FOUR-GORE PETTICOAT
(Pointed top)—FIGS. 3 and 4

This is another simple style but with the advantage of extra seams (CF/CB) to help with the waist shaping. The top finishes with 'points' and is shown in **two versions,** the second with a semi-fitting brassiere front. A 'pointed' top *expands* when the petticoat is put on (a 'stretchy' style) and so can be made closer fitting.

After outlining the block, draw CB and CF seams following the usual Sl. CB/CF of bodice block, and continue the lines W–H straight down, thus adding width to the hem. This may be reduced later, if preferred, on all seams or at the sides only.

The waist shaping is in the seams, therefore darts can be avoided. Curve the side seam 1·5 cm more in the back and 1 cm more in the front: this disposes of the remaining WR. Total width lost is now equal to the block Waist darts.

The height of the front point can be measured 12 cm above D, 14 cm above X or 5–6 cm above Chest line. Make YD = ZD, so that Y and Z come together when Dart is stitched. Draw a line from Y down to CF Bust level (or just below) and from Z down to 1 cm below armhole level, curving it slightly (FIG. 4). The back point, if used, is 5 cm above the Bust line.

In the **second version** the separate 'brassiere' front is outlined as shown in FIG. 4, and the *end of the Waist dart* is included in it. This makes the top more clinging to the figure and, with the help of the *increased Shoulder dart* of the block, gives more shape to the petticoat. Since no corresponding dart is used in the lower part, its top edge is slightly reduced at the seams (dotted lines, FIG. 4).

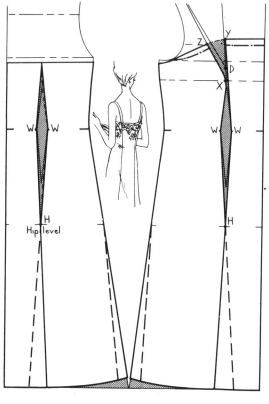

FIG. 5/VIII   FIG. 6/VIII

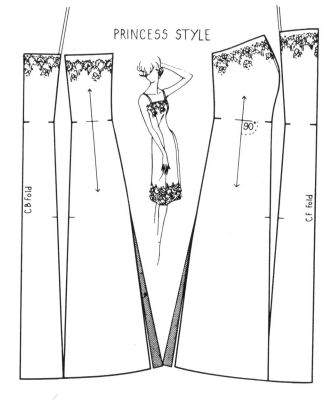

FIG. 7/VIII   FIG. 8/VIII

PRINCESS PETTICOAT

Straight top—FIGS. 5. 6. 7. 8

The style is based on the classical Panel cut, always popular, particularly for machine-made petticoats. Panels follow the Waist darts of the petticoat block.

The Back: The width of the half-Panel, in this case 7–8 cm, is fixed by the waist dart and is 1 + cm more at the top and on hip level (FIG. 5). Continue line W–H straight down, adding to the hem: hem width can be reduced at the sides or retained, as preferred. FIG. 7 shows finished pattern.

The Front: Determine the level or height of the top edge. In this case it is taken 1·5 cm above the Chest line, but it may also follow it (dot-dash line) or be higher. From the top edge draw the Panel seam, following first the Shoulder and then the Waist dart, and keeping line smooth and well shaped (FIG. 6). Allow 1·5 cm more at the hip than at the waist. Continue seam straight down. The side front, as usual, encloses both darts. FIG. 8 shows finished pattern.

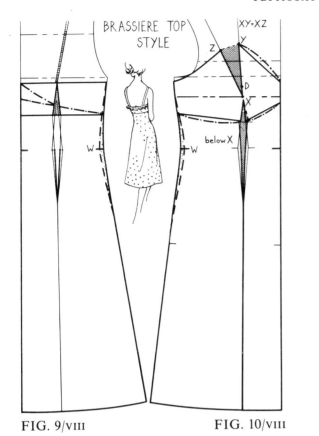

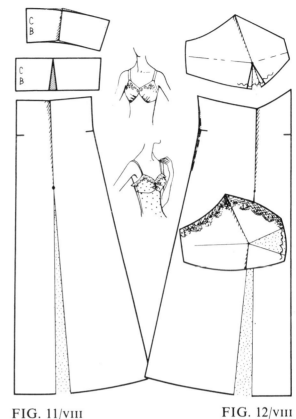

FIG. 9/VIII FIG. 10/VIII FIG. 11/VIII FIG. 12/VIII

BRASSIERE TOP PETTICOAT

(Empire line) – FIGS. 9, 10, 11, 12

The style has a raised waistline, the join between the top and skirt being under the bust, i.e. well above the natural waist. The top is well shaped to the figure, emphasizing the 'Empire line' effect. The skirt part, once detached from the top, *can be widened by flaring*, thus avoiding excessive sloping out of side seams which so often spoils the hang of a petticoat. The style may be cut on the straight grain, but is more often cut on the bias, for which extra skirt width is useful. It may also have a bias skirt and a straight grain top part.

Waist shaping is achieved by closing *part of the Waist dart*, overlapping or darting it *in the pattern*. The reason for using only *part* of the dart becomes obvious if one realizes that in the pattern the dart can be eliminated only by taking it to the top *in a straight line*, so that instead of reducing itself above the waist it continues to increase and may lose too much width on the top edge.

The Back: after outlining the block, reduce the Waist dart to half its depth (or just over) and continue the two dart lines *straight up* for some distance (FIG. 9). To compensate, reduce the waist a little at the side seam.

Outline the top which, in the back, is just a straight band, 8 cm deep. Re-draw the Waist dart in it, making it wider to match the *increased* dart below, and taking it to the top edge which is, as usual, 1 cm below the Bust line. Sometimes in these styles the skirt part is taken higher on CB, often right to the top edge, to form a 'point' (dot-dash lines). This of course reduces the top part, often to just two small sections which, however, must retain the dart.

After cutting away the top (FIG. 11), slash from the hem up to the point of the Waist dart and fold out the dart above: this opens the slash and widens the hem.

In the top part close the dart: this will give it a slightly curved shape (see details above, FIG. 11).

The Front: after reducing the Waist dart and curving the side seam more instead outline the brassiere top as shown in FIG. 10. Y–Z is 12 cm above X, or 4 cm above Chest line. The CF dips to 3 cm above, and skirt 'point' goes up to 2 cm below the basic line. The 8 cm depth at the side is equally divided, and the depth below point X is 6–7 cm. All these proportions may vary, of course, and the lines may be straight or curved, according to style.

Bring the Shoulder dart down to point X and raise the Waist dart to the same point, increasing its depth to match the dart in the skirt part. After cutting away the top, close the Shoulder dart and transfer it into the 'waist' or move both darts into the CF (see other version).

The skirt part is completed as in the back (FIG. 12).

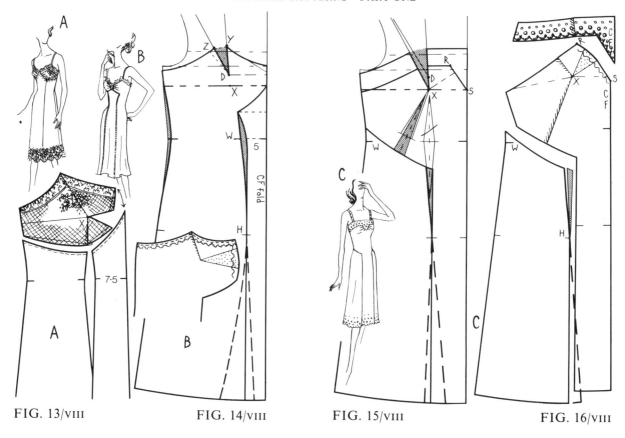

FIG. 13/VIII   FIG. 14/VIII   FIG. 15/VIII   FIG. 16/VIII

MORE ELABORATE PETTICOAT STYLES—
FIGS. 13, 14, 15, 16

These are variations of the basic styles already given.
Style A is a **Princess style with a brassiere top,** front and
back, or front only. The back may be plain or with a
CB seam. Outline brassiere and plan Panel line before
cutting. The Panel goes to the top and ends in a point,
16 cm above the waist, with the dart fullness set into folds
or gathers each side of the point.

Style B is also a Princess (Panel) petticoat, again with
a pointed front Panel and the **top cut in one with the Side
front.** The Panel does not go to the top edge, only to the
basic line (flatter point). Back is plain or with CB seam.

Plan the front panel, which is quite narrow, 5 cm at the
waist and widening to 8 cm half-way up to Basic line.
Below the waist continue the panel straight down, later
adding width from hip level (5–6 cm at the hem). Outline
the top of the petticoat as shown in FIG. 14. The point YZ
is shorter, only 2–2·5 cm above Chest line. The front top
edge is slightly curved to provide more fullness for the
gathers. The Shoulder dart may be further increased
to provide still more fullness when *transferred into the
CF*, where it is either set into folds or gathered.

The Panel (Side front) seam is shaped to include the
greater part of the Waist dart (2 cm): the remainder is
taken off the side seam by curving it a little more.

Style C is yet another style based on the **Panel cut,** this
time with the whole **front top cut in one with the Panel,**
and the Side front joining on a low level, the seam slanting from just above the waist down to 6–7 cm below it.
The back may be plain or with a CB seam, and with a
band at the top (5 cm wide) to match the front; or else
with a slanting 'waist' join continuing that of the front
to a CB point well above the waist.

THE QUARTER-CIRCLE PETTICOAT—Plate 32

The style is cut from a Quarter-Circle pattern and either from
the top of a petticoat block or just the ordinary Bodice block.
Its main features are a clinging, high-waisted effect with a close
fitting brassiere top and a fairly full skirt, flaring well in the front
(on the bias) though rather flat in the back. It has only *one seam,*
in the CB. In spite of the good hem width (about 1·5 + m) it does
not cut into much material, provided a SG (selvedge) join is used,
as in most circle patterns.

The Skirt part—FIG. 1

Take a full Quarter-circle pattern with a standard 70 cm waist and *lower the waist to increase its size* to at least 80 (82) cm—the minimum petticoat waist width. Coming down 4 cm below the top increases the waist by 7–8 cm. *From the new waist* measure the length required, e.g. 60 + 4 = 64 cm. The extra length enables the skirt part to be fitted to the top on a *raised line*, 4 cm above the NW. Divide the pattern lengthwise by folding it into 4 equal sections. Build up the CF to a point 13 cm above the waist (point N). Since the skirt has *no side seams*, the position of the 'bodice' side seams must be found on the skirt waistline. Mark this position (points S) 1·5–2 cm to the back of the quarter creases (broken lines). Connect points S with N, curving the lines 2–3 cm below straight construction lines. Measure the length N–S and make a note of it: the front of the top must fit into it.

The Top of the petticoat—FIGS. 2, 3, 4, 5, 6, 7

The top has its waist raised 4 cm. Outline **the back** (FIG. 2) following the Sl. CB, taking it in on the side seam 1 cm at the top (more if this is the Bodice block), and enough at the waist to reduce waist sufficiently, without use of dart if possible, to match the skirt waist beyond point S. Draw a "point" 5 cm *high* above the Bust line, where the shoulder strap begins. **Other versions** are given lower—one well cut down on CB and one with a downward CB point below the waist. These may be used instead of the higher back (FIG. 4).

In **the front** (FIG. 3) point YZ is usually fairly high—14 cm above X or 5–6 cm above Chest line. The lines from Y and Z come down to 1 cm below the bust line level (as in the back). After taking in a little at the side seam, to reduce length of lower edge and generally *tighten the top*, draw a well-curved line up to CF point N. After measuring it, compare with line N–S on the skirt pattern to establish the amount of fullness to be gathered, darted, or simply folded into skirt waist.

The Shoulder dart may be stitched in its original position (under the shoulder strap—FIG. 5), or, in other versions—style B —moved into the lower edge and darted (deep dart under the bust) or gathered (FIG. 6). Yet another version—style C—shows a fancy seam from the underarm (FIG. 7).

The top of the petticoat is generally cut with SG down the CB which is usually placed to the fold; but it may have a seam if a placket is required, or simply for economy in the lay. In the front, the SG is usually along the front V-edge.

As with all circular patterns which do not fit into an average single width material, it is necessary to have a SG join along one selvedge to increase width of fabric in order to accommodate the pattern (FIG. 1). On the figure this join will come about 20 cm above the hem in the CB. Occasionally, when the high waist works out too tight, a short placket is used in the CB seam.

The style is not very suitable for larger figures because it does tend to get tight *under the bust*. Lowering CF 'point' (8–10 cm up only) helps with this defect, and a CB placket may also be used.

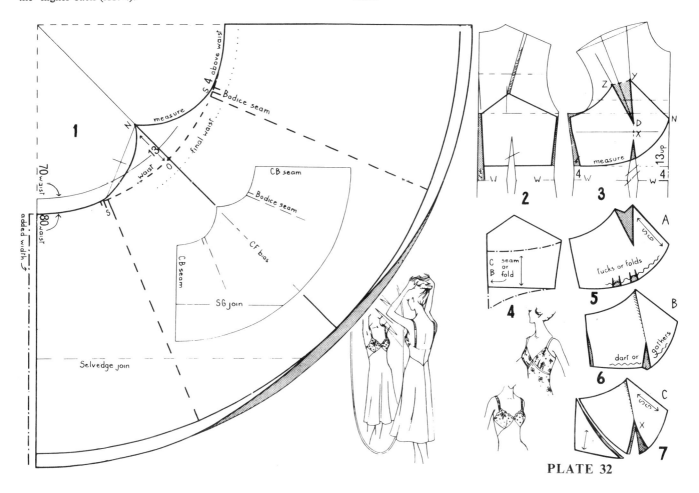

PLATE 32

The Brassiere, or 'bra' as it is now called, is a garment which does not usually come up to the shoulders or down to the waist and so, to ensure its correct position on the figure, some other guide line must be found from which it can be correctly 'balanced'. The True Bust line is an obvious choice as a **Basic line**. As already stated, it is drawn on the same level across the pattern, i.e. parallel to Bust and Waist lines.

The Basic line thus ensures the correct balance of the pattern. Theoretically, it represents a line on the figure which passes over the highest part of the bust, then about 4 (5) cm under the arm and well under the shoulder-blades in the back. It thus misses the second curve of the figure which, if included, would reduce the possibilities of *tightening*, so essential for this pattern. This is, of course, just a convenient *construction line*: the finished brassiere, as will be seen, tends to dip in the back, as it would naturally do if modelled on the stand.

The proportions above and below the Basic line may be equal (for some simple styles), but generally vary according to the type and style of the brassiere and also according to fashion which influences considerably the shape of foundation garments.

An important point in brassiere cutting is the *doubling of the principal darts* to ensure a very close fit above and below the bust (FIG. 1, Plate 33). Sometimes, to follow the shape of an individual figure, additional tightening and shaping is necessary (e.g. in the seams or by an extra CF dart): this is best done at a fitting.

Apart from tightness (close fit), there are other features of fit which may have to be considered: extra support in the lower part or special control of the shape of the bust, etc. To achieve the necessary results there exist various devices which belong to a special manufacturing technique and are outside the scope of pattern construction. These devices, such as padding and reinforcing in different ways, tightening of edges, wiring, etc., may sometimes affect pattern proportions, and certainly result in a big variety of brassiere styles.

STANDARD BRASSIERE STYLE
and five variants – Plate 33

Outline the top of a Petticoat block joined at the underarm point, using *ordinary Bodice block darts*. **Double the darts,** increasing them equally right and left at the waist, but making the addition to the Bust dart $\frac{3}{4}$ on the left). It is easier to measure this on the shoulder, adding, e.g. 5·5 cm outside and 2 cm inside the original dart for B 92 cm. Take the new front darts to point X. In the back raise the new Waist dart to the top edge after the outline is completed. Use Sl. CB and CF to reduce further the width of the pattern.

Plan the proportions above and below the Basic line as shown in FIG. 1. On the CF divide the 5 cm depth either equally or allowing a little less above than below. Over the bust prominence measure from X 9 cm up and 8 cm down (or 10 and 9 cm). On the underarm – 3 (4) up and 4·5 (5) cm down. Some styles are deeper. On CB allow 1·5–2 cm above and below. Connect all these points and complete outline as shown in FIG. 1. The width, along the Basic line, should not exceed the Bust measurement, and may even be a little less if an elastic is used in the back.

Cut out the shape outlined (FIG. 2). The side seam may be left in its usual position, as in the examples in FIGS. 4 and 5 (the smaller and generally less shaped type of 'bra'), or it may be moved closer to the bust and placed the same distance from X as the CF (SX = XF). This makes it possible to fit the front much closer to the shape of the bust.

In the back close the Waist dart to the top edge which breaks here, forming a small point: this is sometimes omitted or, on the contrary, further increased by raising it 1 cm and completing top edge as shown in FIG. 6 (dot-dash lines).

When a forward side seam is used, the underarm gap is *folded out as a dart* (see FIG. 3). If it is thought necessary, further width reduction is made here as shown in FIG. 1. Cut away the front part, shaping the seam as in FIG. 3 to obtain further tightening of the top and bottom edges.

The Bust dart can be **used in many different ways.** It can be left where it is, as a small seam above the Waist dart (FIG. 4, sketch B) or joined to Waist dart in a complete vertical seam (FIG. 4, style D), sometimes with gathers on CF *to increase the bust shaping* (the CF is widened for this purpose as if to allow for an *extra 'dart'*); or it may be moved into the Waist dart (FIG. 5, style E) or into the CF. But the most usual is to cut the pattern on line F–X–S and separate it into two parts joined by a horizontal seam into which the Darts move. The top edge of the lower part can then be raised slightly (1–1·5 cm) for further shaping. Further raising of this edge, i.e. deepening of the lower part gives still more pronounced shaping (deeper cup), while its 'flattening' has the opposite effect. It is a popular variation much used in modern brassiere designing.

To provide extra support and tightness under the bust a separate section is often added below the front (FIG. 7). It varies in shape and may be either a narrow strip, hollowed out under the bust curve, joined to the other side by a wide elastic in the middle (style F) or a wider piece, like a corselet, completely filling the middle (style C) and sometimes coming down almost to the waist (diaphragm control). These additional parts, however, seldom present any difficulty in cutting and fitting if the main part of the brassiere has been shaped correctly.

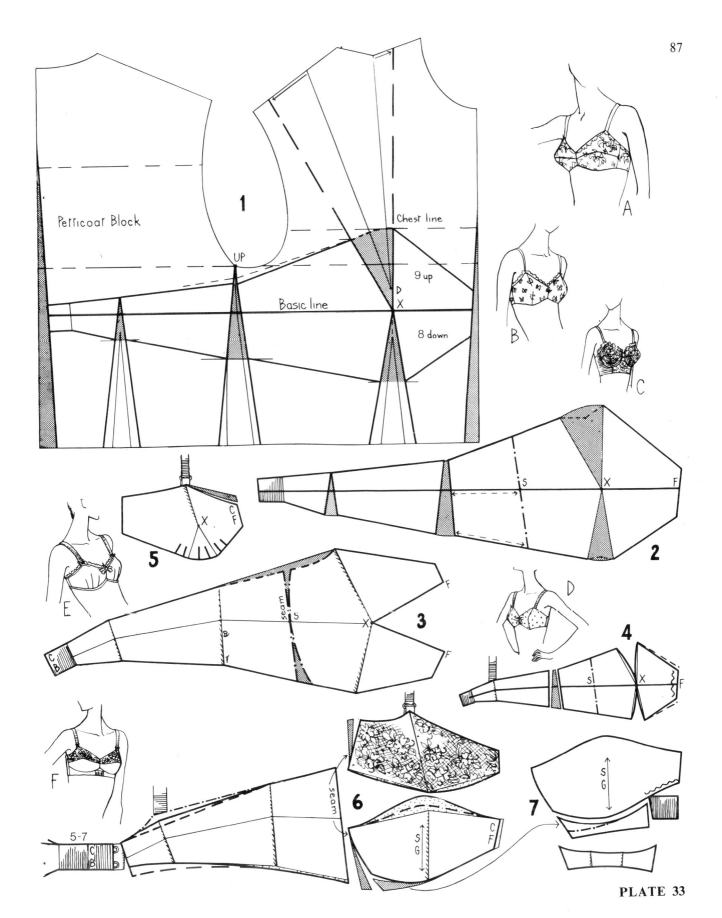

Petticoat Block

Chest line

UP

9 up

Basic line

8 down

1

A

B

C

2

3

4

5

6

7

E

D

F

seam

S

X

F

C

F

S
G

C
F

S
G

5-7

C
B

PLATE 33

WAIST PETTICOATS

The short petticoat from the waist presents no difficulty in cutting and requires no special block. It is simply an *under-skirt*, nowadays used largely to protect or support the outer skirt, or sometimes to achieve a special effect in the hang of a dress. It is, in fact, a 'lining' for the skirt rather than a lingerie garment. It is cut just like a skirt from one of the Skirt blocks.

There are three main types:

(*a*) **The tight petticoat** worn under straight skirts to prevent them losing their shape: it is usually made in a firm fabric.

(*b*) **The average petticoat**, often with a flounce, worn under a skirt or a dress *to prevent the hem falling in*. This is usually cut on the Standard block or on the Fully shaped or Quarter-circle block (for evening dresses), often with a flared or gathered flounce of varying depth. Most evening dresses, even of average width, need such a petticoat, though many of these are joined to a top to make a full length slip.

(*c*) **The very full and stiff or specially shaped petticoat** intended *to hold out a dress* skirt, sometimes in a special or very exaggerated way. The effect of these petticoats does not depend entirely on cut, but also on the fabric used (stiff net, etc.), on methods of joining the various parts and finishing them (mounting of flounces, wiring of hem, etc.). Though much in fashion recently, even for ordinary wear, they are mainly an *addition* to a dress style, emphasizing a special *stand-away effect* of the design, all round or in one part only (e.g. petticoats supporting skirts with 'crinoline' or 'bustle' effect). No standard styles can be given they follow the line of the dress.
(see sketches on page 93).

NIGHTDRESS PATTERNS

Nightdresses are cut from the ordinary Bodice block or the One-piece dress foundation. Skirt blocks, including the Circle pattern, as well as Sleeve blocks are also used for some styles. No special nightdress block is therefore necessary and the cutting of nightdress patterns is mainly a question of correct style interpretation.

It may be useful to make a note of the following few practical points:

(*a*) Most nightdresses are easy fitting garments: addition of *extra ease round bust and hips* is therefore usual.

(*b*) A more *forward underarm seam* (reducing difference between back and front) is generally preferred.

(*c*) Extra ease is thus often added to back only. In styles with sleeves *more back width* is essential for comfort.

(*d*) The *Centre shoulder seam* is much used.

(*e*) The armhole is generally cut down 2–3 cm.

(*f*) The Bust dart is used according to the style, but is not often increased. On the contrary, sometimes it is *reduced* and partly 'lost' in the armhole.

(*g*) The *minimum hem width* for comfortable wear must be known and kept in mind.

(*h*) The *arrangement of seams* may be influenced by the **width of the material**; therefore the width to be used must be considered when planning the pattern.

Although there is no special block for nightdresses because the styles are so varied that they require the use of all the blocks, it is, nevertheless, convenient to have a simple *straight* one-piece nightdress to use as a *basic pattern* for the simple loose styles now fashionable.

BASIC ONE-PIECE NIGHTDRESS — FIG. 17

Extra width of 2–3 cm is added to bust and hips of Bodice block *in the back only* (front unchanged). For the *sloping out of seams* add on the hip level 2 cm in the front and 4 cm in the back: this gives the minimum hem width.

The Hem width, obtained by sloping out the side seams as described above, is under 150 cm. Only a further 6–8 cm can be added on each seam edge if the pattern is to fit into the half-width of a 90–100 cm fabric. These additions would make the nightdress just under 200 cm round the hem, which is a very usual width for many styles cut with CF and CB to the fold of the fabric. Styles with more hem width have to be planned differently (Plates 34, 35).

The Shoulder seam is raised in the back and cut down in the front to become a Centre shoulder which is more convenient for styles well cut out at the top (narrow shoulders). Some 'tailored' styles with sleeves, however, may be cut with an ordinary shoulder seam.

The average length for long nightdresses is 140 cm and up to 148 cm down CB; for the ¾-length styles 100 cm down CB and for short styles 40–46 cm below NW.

The Bust dart can be left in its usual position, as on the Bodice block. It may be useful, however, to indicate its reduction (broken lines) to ⅔ or even half of its width. This may sometimes be necessary in very simple styles, without sleeves: the 'lost' dart fullness then simply 'drapes' in the armhole, as in a Kimono pattern.

THE PATTERN — FIG. 17

Outline the Bodice block as usual. In **the Back** draw a Centre shoulder seam and continue CB line down to 100 cm below the waist. Add 2 cm on the Bust level and 4 cm on the Hip level. Rule a straight seam through these points. Complete hem as usual and measure it. Lower UP 2–3 cm. Widen Back and draw armhole more or less curved, as required by style (e.g. with or without sleeves).

In the Front lower shoulder to centre position. Continue CF seam down to the same level as the back. Add 2 cm only on the hip level and draw side seam as shown in diagram. Complete hem. Lower armhole 2–3 cm to match back. Widen Chest and re-draw armhole flatter.

The basic pattern can now be used as a foundation for other simple styles, as shown in Plates 34 and 35.

THE SIMPLE KIMONO NIGHTDRESS

FIG. 18

This is yet another basic nightdress which it is possible to cut very quickly and simply without the use of a Kimono block. Since there are quite a few kimono-cut nightdresses and most of them are uncomplicated in

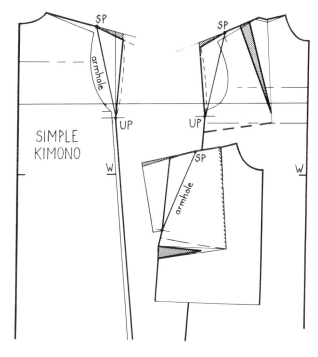

FIG. 18/VIII

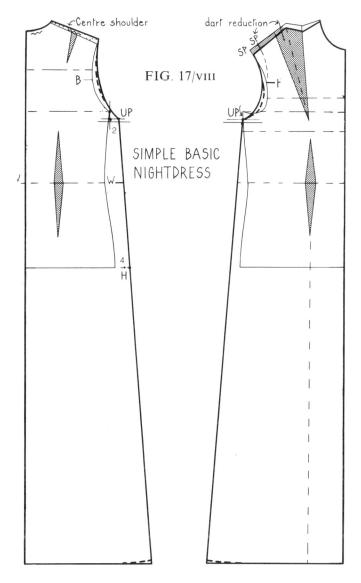

FIG. 17/VIII

SIMPLE BASIC NIGHTDRESS

design, it is useful to know this simple adaptation.

Outline the Basic nightdress (explained above), sometimes with extra fullness down CF and CB (for style).

In the Back add 1 cm to side seam and lower the armhole another 1–2 cm to adjust it to the lower kimono UP. Raise SP 1+ cm and rule a new shoulder seam through this point continuing it another 6–8 cm beyond (or as required by style). Break this line from SP (1 cm). This is already a very short 'sleeve' just covering the top of the arm—such as one sees in many nightdresses. Join it to UP by a straight line which may be curved out slightly to cover the back of the top arm.

In the Front raise SP 0·5 cm only and take it 2·5 cm up the shoulder line, reducing the depth of the Shoulder dart by the same amount (the Dart is now only 5 cm wide). Complete the sleeve part as in the back, hollowing the edge a little if desired (dotted line). Transfer the remaining Dart into the underarm where it will give quite a small dart (3–3·5 cm) placed just below the True Bust line or on it. If the style suggests it, the Dart may be transferred into the hem and lost in the hem width, giving extra fullness in the front.

If a short real kimono sleeve is wanted, the shoulder line can be continued further until a line at right angles to it will give a small (3–4 cm) sleeve extension *under the arm*.

A little *extra* fullness (5–8 cm) is often added down CF and used in some fancy way in the neckline, e.g. in pin tucks, gathers, under a yoke, etc. or moved into the shoulder.

PLATE 34

The four simple styles in this Plate are all cut from the basic nightdress and illustrate different ways of using the Bust dart, methods of providing and using extra fullness and ways of solving problems of fabric width.

Style A—FIG. 1—is a design in which the Shoulder dart provides extra fullness for the hem. When moved into the hem (through point X) it gives fullness exactly where needed. A sash or ribbon pulled through a front slot at the waist holds the fullness in correct position for the style.

According to width and texture of fabric and effect desired, either the whole or only part of the Dart is used (to avoid too much hem width); the rest can be 'lost' in the armhole by ignoring the rest of the Dart and redrawing the armhole higher on the shoulder.

If it is essential that the pattern should fit into a usual width of fabric, the slope at the side can be reduced until the hem is not more than 40–45 cm across on the half-pattern. More hem width is possible, however, if the addition of a wedge-shaped piece at the side is acceptable (FIG. 1). The alternative is to have a more forward side seam, as shown in Pl. 35 FIG. 7, and to use more material. The problem does not arise, of course, with the wider fabrics often used in the trade.

Style B—FIG. 2—is a more 'tailored' design and moving Dart into hem would not suit it. It needs *some* extra fullness *all the way down*, not mainly in the hem. The Bust dart is moved into the underarm leaving the top quite plain and on the straight grain, suitable for pin tucks for instance. The Dart may again be reduced a little thus giving a smaller dart under the arm. If this loosens the neckline, there are ways of tightening it by facing, binding, etc. Suitable finish should thus be considered at the pattern stage. Extra width added on CF must be just sufficient for the trimming (e.g. pin tucks) without increasing the hem width too much for this style.

Style C—FIGS. 3, 4 and 5: a popular modern style which can be full or three-quarter length, or short. The pattern is almost a straight piece, gathered above the bust. Wide shoulder straps for a very open top complete the design.

After outlining the basic nightdress to the required length, plan the top as shown in FIGS. 3 and 4. In **the Back** the top edge is placed fairly high, but may be lower if preferred. The end of the shoulder strap, drawn in its correct position, dips slightly towards the new armhole. The width beyond CB almost doubles the length of the gathered top edge (8–10 cm for 11–12 cm top edge). **The Front** goes up to 3 cm above the Chest line and down to 3 cm below it on the CF. 8–10 cm are allowed beyond CF for the gathers in which the Shoulder dart is also incorporated.

Since adding down CF and CB may widen hem too much for width of fabric, the slope at the side is reduced.

Style D is similar in cut to style C but has a different neckline— round in the back (higher) and in the front.

The straps for styles C and D are either plain straight bands, trimmed with lace or frills, or *ruched* bands for which, according to tightness of ruching and type of fabric, at least double the length must be allowed.

PLATE 35

These are further styles which can be cut from the simple night-dress. The cut is based on the standard method for yoke patterns. The wide, cut-out neckline presents a special problem: it must be dealt with either by increase of original Dart or by darting edge later.

Style A is a very popular design, with a narrow 'yoke' in the shape of a curved band (6–7 cm wide).

Back—FIGS. 1, 2: plan the curved band like a yoke. Make it 6 cm wide and on the shoulder take 2·5 cm of this width beyond SP (even for an 'off-the-shoulder' effect it is advisable to leave some of the width *on* the shoulder). The CB neckline depth may vary and the band may be drawn higher (dot-dash line, 10 cm below the nape) or lower, giving a deeper curve, 15 cm down—a popular neckline for the style.

Point Y is 2 cm inside the basic armhole. The part of the band above it remains loose to fit over the top of the arm. Y–Z (4 cm) is a space without any gathers below; the part beyond Z covers the gathered part. After cutting away the yoke (FIG. 2), the lower part is extended beyond CB sufficiently to double (or almost) the length from Z to CB. Correct the top edge to a smoother, flatter curve. If the hem is excessive, reduce the slope of the side seam.

Front—FIGS. 3, 4: move the Shoulder dart into the underarm (temporary dart) to plan the 'yoke' part more easily. Here the curve is fairly shallow (higher neckline), measuring 6–7 cm down CF. Its width is 6 cm, as in the back. On the shoulder the band is again 2·5 cm beyond SP. Point Y is 2 cm inside the armhole and Z is 4 cm further (the flat part). Beyond the CF add 12–13 cm all the way down (FIG. 4). If necessary, reduce the side seam slope. After cutting away yoke, move the Bust dart into the top edge, where it adds to the gathered fullness.

The top edge of the band can be tightened by a small dart across, as shown in the back (some distance from CB) or by *additional* overlapping of closed Dart (front). In this style it is easier to do the tightening in this way. As the weight of the garment will tend to stretch the band, it can also be tightened in the shoulder seam to fit closer over the top of the arm.

Style B (2 versions) is a similar pattern but with the yoke in the shape of a square (4 cm wide). To tighten the top edge it is advisable to plan the square over the Shoulder dart increased by 50%, as in petticoats (FIGS. 5 and 7). The back neckline is usually round but, if square, it can be planned over a closed neckline dart. Darting the finished band, as in style A, would spoil the shape of the square. Plan yoke and then complete pattern, as shown in FIGS. 5 and 6.

The second version (sketch C) has a straight band under the arms (dot-dash line, FIG. 5) joined to shoulder straps of the same width, producing a similar effect of a square.

N.B. A nightdress with more fullness and a wider hem can be obtained in this and other styles by a re-arrangement of seams. Move side seam forward, as shown in FIG. 7. The front can thus fit into a double width, leaving the back much wider, so that *two* widths, joined by a seam in the CB, have to be used. This gives an attractive back line.

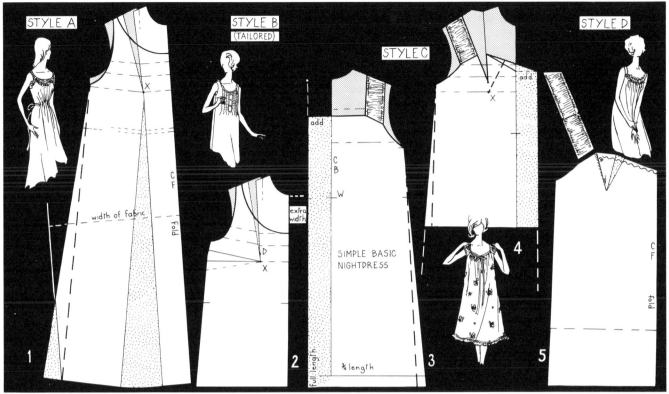

STYLE A

STYLE B
(TAILORED)

STYLE C

STYLE D

X

width of fabric

fold

CF

add

C
B

W

SIMPLE BASIC
NIGHTDRESS

¾ length

full length

extra
width

D

X

add

X

4

C
F

fold

1

2

3

5

PLATE 34

STYLE A

STYLE B

SP

Z

Z

C
B

2

add

Y

Z

Z

Y

Z

D

X

W

C
F

3

4

Y

Z

5

CF

increased dart

6

7

UP

Z

CB seam

CF fold

1

further possible addition

CB seam

CB fold

add

reduce hem

cut away

cut away

reduce hem

CF fold

usual side seam

W

new side seam

H

CF fold

PLATE 35

PLATE 36

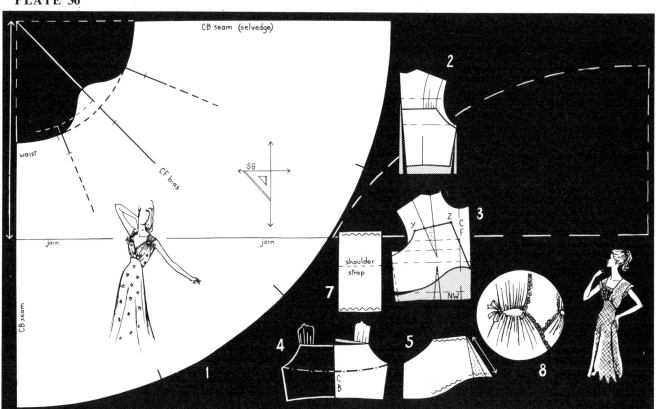

PLATE 37

PLATE 36

These styles are fitted a little closer to the figure.

Style A is a simple Princess design in 4 gores, with CF and CB seams, no join at the back waist but a separate front top. It is most conveniently cut from **the One-piece block.**

Back—FIG. 1: outline the One-piece dress using a *centre shoulder seam.* Raise shoulder 1 cm above SP and extend it 2 cm. Add 1 cm width at bust and hip level, re-draw seam without continuing it below the hips. Lower the armhole (UP) 3 cm. Re-draw armhole to a flatter shape adding width to back. Cut out neckline, as shown in the diagram.

Add the nightdress length down CB, another 25–30 cm below the dress length. On this level draw a straight hemline extending it right and left for hem width addition. Later complete it, curving as shown in FIG. 2.

The hem width of the **lengthened** foundation, in this case just about 1½ m, is even less than the minimum hem of a simple nightdress. The style suggests a fairly full hem. To increase it by another metre add 12–13 cm on each of the 8 seam edges (less on CF if preferred).

Reduce the waist using Sl. CB and taking in the side seam 1–2 cm to obtain a 18–20 cm quarter waist. Draw the side and CB seams straight up to these points.

Front—FIG. 2: proceed as for the back, adding 1 cm above and 2–3 cm beyond SP, lowering armhole, redrawing it with chest width addition. Then plan the top as shown in FIG. 2.

After increasing Waist dart by 2 cm (allowed for at the side), draw the lower edge from 1 cm above the NW up to the True Bust line level as shown in FIG. 2. Complete neckline from there up to the shoulder, cutting it out to match back. Cut away the top, close both Darts to point X and transfer them into the CF (detail inside FIG. 2).

Proceed with the skirt part as in the back. Correct the top edge (broken line) and reduce waist 1+ cm at CF and enough at the side to achieve a 20–22 cm width. The *total waist width* should be as loose as a petticoat waist.

Style B is loose but has a fairly shaped front, pulled in by a sash from the side which ties in the back.

The back—FIG. 3—is cut from the simple basic nightdress with little change except for slight shaping of the side seam. The straight top has shoulder straps, and another version (dotted line) is given with a deep V-neckline and wider shoulders. The length is shortened to allow for a 13–15 cm gathered flounce.

The front—FIG. 4—is more conveniently cut from an ordinary Bodice block, with shoulder centred and armhole lowered to match the back. It is a 'corselet' style with a yoke of lace or net at the top. Dart fullness is used in the middle part, above the corselet. The sash pulling in the corselet is set into the side seams.

Plan the corselet above and below the Waistline, shortening it from the side (3 cm *in* from inner shaped seam). After *increasing* Shoulder dart by 3 cm and *closing* it, outline a 9 cm deep yoke, 9 cm below shoulder and neckline. It goes up into a small point on the Shoulder dart, up to 9–10 cm below the shoulder (the front length of the strap).

Cut away corselet (FIG. 5) separating skirt from bodice and yoke. Close Shoulder dart to X and slash below X: this concentrates all dart fullness in the lower edge of the middle part. The amount, which is small, can be increased by side addition.

Complete skirt, adding 10 cm extra down CF for the fullness gathered *under* the corselet. Shorten to allow for flounce.

The corselet which still contains an *unused* Waist dart can be further shaped by closing this dart. In order to do this without reducing top and bottom edges, slash pattern lengthwise along waistline, but without cutting right through, and fold out the dart correctly, as shown in detail inside FIG. 5. Extra width which accrues is the 'fold' which always appears when a straight piece is *tightened horizontally* on the figure (a simple test will prove this). The CF can be straightened (with a small loss) in order to place pattern to the fold.

N.B. This **method of eliminating the Waist dart in a pattern** is also used for dress styles, when the design makes it difficult to lose the Dart in any other way.

PLATE 37

This is a nightdress similar in cut to the petticoat in Plate 32, with a Quarter-circle skirt and a seam down the CB. It has an attractive high-waisted line, well fitted under the bust, and gently flaring out towards the hem. Because of the full length, it has a good width round the hem, yet it cuts into a reasonable amount of material. The top can be in a variety of styles and one popular version is given here.

The Skirt—FIG. 1: lower the standard waistline of a Quarter-circle skirt 4–5 cm to obtain at least 80–82 cm waistline (more for larger sizes). From the *new* waistline measure down CB the full length plus 4 cm (to allow for raised waist effect). Outline the raised top 10 cm above CF waist: the shape is a curve, but a point can also be used. Complete pattern as described for petticoat. The SG join will come quite high on the pattern.

The Top part is cut on the **Bodice block.**

The Back is plain, either built up fairly high (FIG. 2) or cut lower (dot-dash line, FIG. 4). It is tightened at the waist to fit the corresponding skirt part, raised 4 cm above NW and has wide shoulder straps draping on the shoulder and long enough to join the front above the Chest line.

The Front—FIG. 3—is drawn from a line 4 cm above NW, to follow the outline of the skirt top (10 cm up on CF). It crosses over the CF (4 cm wrap). At the top measure 12–13 cm down *both* sides of the Dart and rule a line 15 cm long *through these two points.* Place point Y 3 cm inside the armhole and point Z 15 cm from Y. From Z complete the slanting front, i.e. the cross-over. After cutting out the front, add 5 cm fullness to lower edge, as shown in FIG. 5.

The shoulder strap (FIG. 6) is cut to the width Y–Z or slightly more (15–18 cm) and its *front end* is joined to Y–Z edge by a ribbon slotted both through the strap and the edge Y–Z; this is tied together, pulling the ends into the shape of a small circle (FIG. 8). The other end of the strap is gathered and stitched to the top edge of the back.

Style B—sketch—shows another (kimono) version of the top.

LINGERIE
Part 2—Knicker patterns

The comfortable fit, good appearance and wear of knicker garments depend considerably on a **correct total crutch length**. Yet this is seldom taken as a direct measurement and is usually arrived at in the pattern by finding the correct 'Depth of crutch', i.e. the level on which the CF and CB seams jut out or 'fork out'. The Depth of crutch is therefore *the main proportion* which must be established in every case.

There are various methods for finding the required **Depth of crutch**: some are based on the height of the figure (or length to knee); some on the 'bodyrise'—a measurement taken down the side of the figure, from waist to the seat of a chair on which the person is sitting; some on the Hip measurement, *as in this pattern*. As each of these measurements is based on one controlling factor only, while actually all three—height, hip girth and length of legs—may affect the final total crutch length needed for a comfortable fit, it is obvious that no one method can guarantee a perfect result when used alone and without a fitting.

A controlling (front-to-back) measurement, taken between the legs from CF to CB waist could be useful in many cases but is seldom taken in practice. It is given sometimes in Trade Size charts for checking the minimum size to which a knicker garment must conform. It is not a measurement necessary for *drafting* the pattern, but only for *checking* the final result, in the same way as the armhole of a bodice is checked additionally.

KNICKER BLOCKS

There are two Knicker Foundations:
        the Standard knicker block and
        the Skirt-knicker block.
The main difference between the two blocks is that the **Standard knicker pattern** with its CB-to-CF crutch seam can more easily be made to fit the shape of the figure and is therefore particularly suitable for styles which are more figure-fitting, e.g. all close-fitting knickers, trunks, and also pyjama trousers.

The Skirt-knicker pattern, more often without a CB-to-CF seam, generally hangs away from the figure like a skirt and is therefore primarily a foundation for styles which must achieve this effect, e.g. all kinds of loose panties. When close fitting, as it sometimes is, it remains nevertheless more *shapeless* than the other pattern (e.g. as the pilch knicker). Moreover it represents an im-portant *basic method* of cutting applied not only to lingerie but also to other garments which *combine* skirt and knicker cut, such as various garments used in sports-wear, divided skirts, etc.

In actual practice the dividing line between the two foundations is not very rigid and it is possible (though not often practicable) to pass, by various adaptations, from one to the other, making, for instance, the Stan-dard knickers so very loose in the leg as to be almost like a skirt, and vice versa. It is, therefore, mainly a matter of which block is nearest to the fit and line of the style to be cut.

Both foundations are developed from the Skirt Block which must be the Standard block with the hem equal to $1\frac{1}{5}$ Hip width, and *not wider*.

THE STANDARD KNICKER BLOCK –
FIGS. 1, 2, 3, 4

Measurements
  Hips—taken as for skirt. For Knicker block use 94 (or 98) cm.
  Length—down the side, varies. For block—40–42 cm.
Basic proportions used in the knicker draft:
  Basic line (widest part) = $\frac{3}{4}$ Hips.* For H 94 = 70 cm (H 98 = 73/74 cm).
  Crutch depth = $\frac{3}{8}$ H or *half* of Basic line minus 2 cm (33/35 cm).

It is the Hip measurement, therefore, on which the construction of the pattern is based and·from which the two *controlling proportions*—the Basic width and the Depth of crutch—are derived. The side length is of little importance and any convenient length can be used with-out affecting the *fit* of the block, which is generally drafted in the shape of loose fitting 'French knickers' with a straight hemline—a convenient shape for use in further style adaptations.

N.B. The **Basic width** (widest part of the pattern) must not be confused with the **Hip width**, which is measured higher on the skirt Hip line.

Outline the Standard skirt block to just above the knee line level leaving some paper to the right and left (FIG. 1). Mark the Yoke line, the Hip line and the beginning of the centre seam of the skirt, but not the darts. For future use, however, make a note of the *total WR*, as shown by the darts.

* See Table p. 104.

Work out the **Basic line** (leg width) = $\frac{3}{4}$ Hips, and make a note of it. For H 94 it is 70 cm (H 98 – 73 or 74).

From the waist, from point 0, measure down the CF the **Crutch depth** = 33 (35) cm and mark point X.

From point X draw a short line at right angles to CF and on it measure from X $\frac{1}{10}$ of Hips minus 1 cm, i.e. 9·4 = 9 minus 1 = 8 cm (for H 98 = 9·8 = 9·5 minus 1 = 8·5 cm). Mark **point F**: this is the **front Fork point** – the most forward point of the pattern.

Place a metre stick along this short line and rule a line *back* across the whole skirt and beyond it. This is the **Basic line** of the pattern on which the basic leg width = $\frac{3}{4}$ Hips is measured from F to the **back Fork point** B. In this case it is 70 cm (73 cm). Thus B–F = 70 cm; O–X = 33 cm.

Fold pattern in half lengthwise, so that point F comes exactly over point B and the Basic line is bisected. The lengthwise crease produced by this folding is the **Middle line** or Side line on which the length is measured and which is always *at right angles to the Basic line*. It does not follow the side seam of the skirt, which crosses it.

The **front and back seams** are drawn by joining points O and F and points S and B by curved lines, as shown in FIG. 2.

Down the side, i.e. the Middle line, measure **the length from the waist** (40–42 cm). This should come below the Basic line. Draw the hem parallel to it. Shorten the hem line 2–3 cm at each end.

Complete the leg part by joining the ends of the hem line with points F and B by straight or slightly curved lines – **the inner leg seams**.

The **waist** of the block is usually left big enough for an elastic finish, i.e. $\frac{1}{2}$ hips + 2 cm minimum. Measure it and, if too small, point S can be moved farther out and the seam redrawn. When a flat finish (darts and placket) is

used, the back seam can come in a little (dot-dash line, FIG. 2).

FIG. 3 shows a version of the block with a *shaped waist*, i.e. a suitable **arrangement of darts** (for WR = 13 cm), a **placket** which follows the *skirt* seam, further waist reduction on CB and a little on CF – all this to achieve a smooth fit at the top without any gathers. A combination of waist darts (in the front) and elasticated gathers (in the back) is also possible, usually requiring one longer or two shorter plackets. It also shows the correct way of **shortening the length** down the side, without interfering with the crutch depth and the *fit* of the knickers. All these practical details are planned according to style, fashion and, in the wholesale manufacturing trade, according to the accepted production technique.

The back seam S–B is longer than the front seam O–F and the difference can be seen clearly when the pattern is folded as in FIG. 4. This difference (3–4 cm or slightly more) can be reduced a little by simply bringing point S 1 cm down and re-drawing the waist; or, vice versa, occasionally increased. More definite changes in this length, however, are explained in ·the section 'Fitting adjustments'.

N.B. It must be remembered that on the figure the waistline – back and front – will of course be on the same level, as also will the Hip line, so that the extra back length (appearing as extra height in FIG. 4) will, on the figure, be really *below* the Hip level.

The total Crutch length can be checked by measuring the front and back seams, O–F and S–B, and comparing the *combined* length with the checking measurement if taken. It will be found to be slightly longer than necessary, as the block has quite a loose crutch fit. There is no inconvenience in leaving it like this since it can be changed quite easily in adaptations to suit any style and

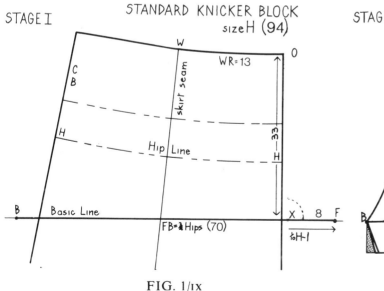

FIG. 1/IX

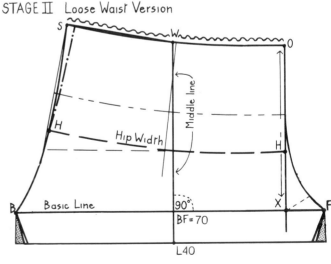

FIG. 2/IX

Shaped Waist Version

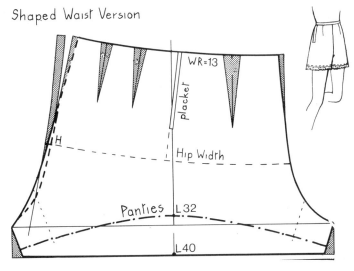

WR=13

placker

H

Hip Width

Panties L 32

L 40

FIG. 3/IX

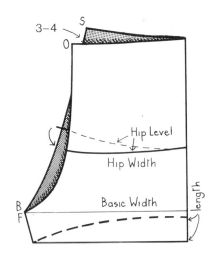

3–4 ⟶ S
O

Hip Level

Hip Width

Basic Width

B
F

length

FIG. 4/IX

fit. If preferred, however, the total crutch length can be reduced by *reducing the Depth of crutch*, as shown in FIGS. 5 and 6.

Depth of crutch can be reduced either by making a horizontal tuck across the pattern, as shown in FIGS. 5 and 6, or by lowering the waist (e.g. at a fitting). The opposite would be done to increase the depth, slashing the pattern and inserting extra length or, more frequently, simply adding height above the waist.

Adjusting the width of the pattern, often required in style adaptations, is quite simple. A lengthwise tuck is made down the side, i.e. the Middle line, to reduce the width (FIGS. 5 and 6) and a slash, with width inserted, to increase it. In some cases some increase and decrease must also be made at points B and F.

ADJUSTMENTS OF LINE AND FIT—
FIGS. 5, 6, 7

The Standard knicker block, as drafted, represents an average fit of quite loose knickers on a figure of average proportions. In adaptations it undergoes various changes and it is useful to understand the effect of some of the adjustments used and the circumstances in which they have to be made.

Variation in the Depth of crutch is probably the most important and frequently used adjustment. Generally speaking, the greater the Depth of crutch and consequently the *total* crutch length, the less the knicker garment clings to the figure and vice versa, the shorter the crutch—the closer the fit. When it is necessary that a style should have a closer fit or even mould the figure, the total crutch length is reduced by shortening the Depth of crutch, as explained above (FIGS. 5 and 6). This happens in closer-fitting knickers, trunks, briefs and of course also in tailored shorts and slacks. When, on the other hand, the line must be more 'draped' and the hang more like that of a skirt, the crutch length is increased to enable the garment to stand away from the figure.

Because of the big variety of garments to which this basic principle applies—from close fitting panties and trunks to the very loose 'divided skirts'—it is difficult to

FIG. 5/IX

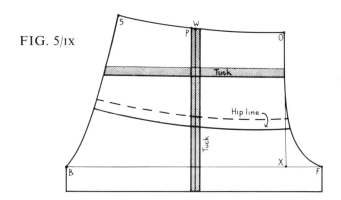

S   P W   O

Tuck

Hip line

Tuck

B   X   F

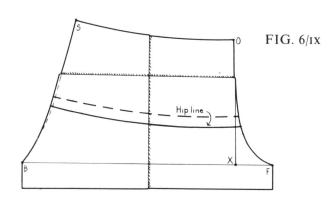

S   O

Hip line

B   X   F

FIG. 6/IX

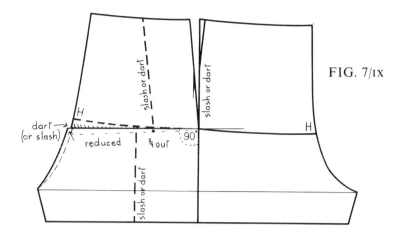

FIG. 7/ix

give a definite ruling on what the Depth of crutch in a *Knicker block* should be. The only way to deal with the problem is to know, by experience, how loose the *crutch fit* of the block is and to regulate it accordingly in the various adaptations. Where the range of adaptations is narrow, i.e. when the block is used, for instance, mainly for close fitting knickers, or shorts or slacks, it may be convenient to shorten the crutch permanently to avoid the constant repetition of this adjustment. The block given here has a loose crutch fit and adaptation methods must be planned with this in view.

In connection with **individual fitting** it must be remembered that a stout figure needs a longer crutch than a slim one *of the same height* and that adding more width, beyond what the average pattern for that size requires, is not the way to deal with the problem of the stout figure: it is the crutch length which *must be sufficiently long for the big Hip size*. That is why a *tall* but slim figure will often have a shorter Depth of crutch than a short but stout figure. In this connection proportions based on the Hip measurement are more practical for knickers, though length of legs (bodyrise) is an additional important factor (e.g. in patterns of slacks).

Difference in length between back and front seams is yet another detail which sometimes has to be adjusted for various reasons. The block has 3–4 cm more length

on the CB seam, projecting above CF waist in FIG. 4. In most cases this can be reduced or occasionally increased *a little* at the top. But, since on the figure this extra length actually comes below the Hip line, it is here that it is more correct to make the adjustment in all but the simplest cases. The excess length depends on the *slope* of the CB in relation to the vertical CF ('seat angle' in slacks): the greater the slope, the greater the length (see slacks in Chapter Twelve). Therefore by reducing the back seam length, as shown in Fig. 7, the back seam is also *straightened*, and vice versa. This is the way to correct a *baggy* back seam or, sometimes, on the contrary, to provide more length and ease for bending. The correction is usually small and often supplemented by a slight adjustment at the top.

A horizontal 'dart' (1–2 cm) is taken out below the Hip level as far as the middle of the pattern (sometimes only ⅔ out), where it meets the end of a slash from the waist. This reduces back seam length and also the slope. The reverse is done to increase the back length and slope of the back seam. In some cases the slash or 'dart' is taken into the hem, thus either tightening or 'flaring' the back part, i.e. fitting it closer to or away from the figure.

It is not difficult to realize that this straightening or sloping of back seam corresponds to a more shaped or straighter skirt block.

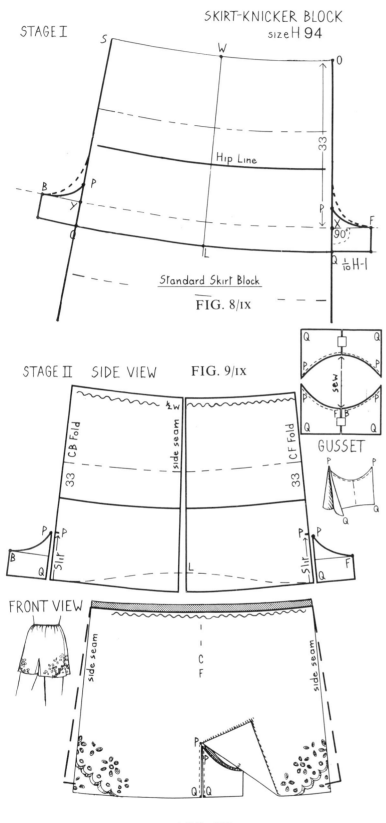

STAGE I

SKIRT-KNICKER BLOCK
size H 94

Standard Skirt Block

FIG. 8/IX

STAGE II   SIDE VIEW   **FIG. 9/IX**

GUSSET

FRONT VIEW

FIG. 10/IX

THE SKIRT-KNICKER BLOCK —
FIGS. 8, 9, 10

This pattern can be used with or *without* a *CF/CB seam* and in this latter version its usefulness goes well beyond lingerie cutting. Not only are various panties and cami-knickers cut by this method, but also many garments used for sportswear, e.g. various types of 'divided skirt'.

It is, in fact, a basic method for changing a skirt into a semi-knicker garment and as such it must be considered among the important methods in pattern designing. When used without a centre seam it must have a side seam like a skirt. The CF and CB are then placed to the fold, (often on the true bias) and **the crutch piece is cut separately** and then added by setting it into a CF and CB slit.

Measurements and proportions

Depth of crutch — as for the Standard block.

Length — 5–6 cm more than the crutch depth.

Outline the skirt block, measure down the CF the Depth of crutch (X) and on this level draw a short line at right angles to the CF. Measure on it $\frac{1}{10}$ of Hips minus 1 cm, i.e. 8 (8·5) cm. This is the front Fork point F.

Repeat the whole in the back, i.e. on the CB line measure the Depth of crutch (same as front) and *on this level* draw a short line *at right angles* to CB, on which the same measurement ($\frac{1}{10}$ H − 1 cm) is taken for point B. Add 1 cm above CB waist and redraw waistline.

N.B. In this type of pattern the same Depth of crutch (33/35) should be considered as a *minimum* rather than a loose proportion. It may be increased in some cases to achieve a more skirt-like effect.

Draw the front and back seams B–P and F–P only 4–5 cm up if no centre seam is to be used; but if the pattern is to be used with a CF/CB seam, then these lines are taken a little higher (broken line).

Complete the crutch pieces making them 5–6 cm deep: this is their most usual shape and size. They are then cut away for styles without a CB/CF seam (FIG. 9). Each piece is *cut double* (see detail above FIG. 9) and the two are set into CF and CB *slits* cut 10 cm up from the hem, and are stitched together along the curve.

The side seam, in this case, follows the seam of the skirt. The length, taken down the side, though it may vary, is usually made to come in line with the crutch part, so that the hem is an even curve, parallel to the curved lines of the skirt. If a shorter side length is wanted, this must not affect the crutch part: the hem will then go up at the side and lose its even curve.

For styles cut with a CF/CB seam the crutch pieces remain *attached to the main pattern* which is then treated like an ordinary knicker pattern.

FIG. 10 gives the *whole* front of the pattern (without CF/CB seam) showing the 10 cm slit at the bottom, also a simple method of widening the hem by sloping out the side seam.

STANDARD KNICKER BLOCK
ADAPTATIONS

French Knickers and shorter panties—FIG. 3.
The Standard block is already a pattern of so-called 'French knickers', with loose leg and straight hemline which makes them very suitable for a certain type of trimming (e.g. drawn-thread work). Keeping the hem straight, however, makes the pattern rather long, though it could be shortened a little by a tuck across (1–2 cm): the crutch depth of the block, being loose, would allow this.

For **shorter panties** the length can be reduced at the side only, *without reducing Crutch depth* any further, which will of course make the hemline curve up at the side (FIG. 3).

The top can be gathered on to an elastic (the most usual) and must be big enough to go easily over the hips. However, in **stretchy fabrics**, so much used nowadays, this is of less importance and ½ Hips, may be quite sufficient for the waist, while the hip width itself may also be reduced (by lengthwise tuck—FIG. 5). The top likewise may be darted (as FIG. 3), all round or front only, or have a small half-yoke (front only).

Directoire knickers—FIG. 11

These are also very much like the Standard block, but with a closer-fitting leg, which is either gathered on to an elastic (like bloomers) or eased into a band (a cuff) fitting tightly round the thigh. In its *modern version* (and in stretchy fabric) this type of knicker is often made closer fitting so that both *width and crutch depth can be reduced*. Often a side seam is used as well, as shown in Trunks (FIG. 12), though less shaped. In fact, in their tightest and shortest version they often take the place of real trunks (e.g. for sportswear).

An important point to note is that for comfortable fit between the legs the *inner leg seams must be lengthened* 4–5 cm below the straight edge of the block. The side length can be as short as desired, increasing considerably the curve of the lower edge, but the *crutch depth must not be further reduced*.

Gussets and reinforcing pieces are very usual in this type of knicker to strengthen the part between the legs (closer-fitting styles need it more than loose panties), or sometimes to expand it, i.e. to increase the 'inner span', and sometimes to economize material. The best type is always the one which follows the shape of the pattern and is planned on it (as shown in FIG. 11). This may be just a shaped *lining piece* (the best for good wear), or a part detached from the pattern and used as a separate, faced, gusset (for further details see children's knickers—Chapter Fourteen).

The familiar square gusset is rather clumsy and less satisfactory in prolonging the wear of knickers.

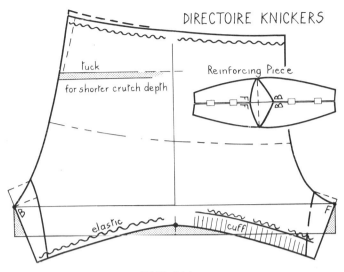

FIG. 11/IX

Trunks—FIG. 12

These are usually very close fitting, quite short at the side and therefore with a very curved lower edge. Much of the adaptation consists in losing size—both width and length—even in the crutch part. A lengthwise tuck can be made *in the block before outlining*, so that the pattern is already tighter (as in FIG. 12). The crutch depth is then reduced from the top, i.e. by lowering the waist 3 cm. To shorten crutch further 1 (2) cm is taken off B and F: this reduces *total crutch length* by at least 5–6 cm.

Draw a side seam, shaping it at the top and lower edge as shown in the diagram, but without losing on the hips, which *are already tighter* (additional shaping is possible

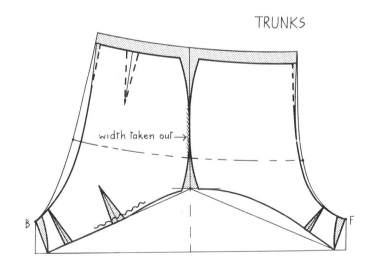

FIG. 12/IX

at a fitting). Curve the front and back seams *more*, to fit them *closer to the figure*. Finally, tighten the lower edge until it fits the thigh, by darting and easing, as shown in FIG. 12. Curve the lower edge coming down in the back and hollowing out well in the front. The top is darted for a close waist fit and has a placket. If necessary, a little final tightening can be done at a fitting, mainly by pulling up at the waist and by tighter darting.

Pyjama trousers—FIG. 13

There are many different styles of pyjama trousers, and although the general rule is to provide *more ease in a sleeping garment*, it is not always applied in present day cutting, as some styles are extra full while others may be almost close fitting.

The Standard block has a sufficiently loose fit for nightwear, and thus for many pyjama styles it can be used as it is, and for some even be reduced (e.g. when using stretchy fabrics). Nevertheless, as a general approach to nightwear cutting, the question of correct *increase*, in both width and crutch depth, must be considered.

Thus the pattern in FIG. 13 is shown with an addition

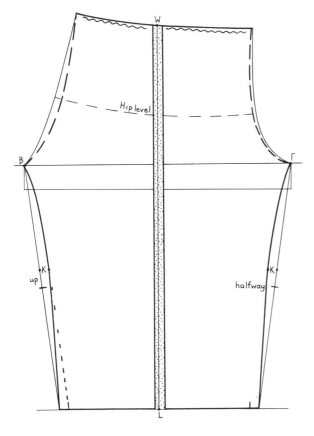

PYJAMA TROUSERS

FIG. 13/IX

of 3 cm of width down the side, which is quite usual for average or classical style pyjama trousers. For some styles—very loose, and hanging in folds, or gathered round the ankle—the addition would of course be more than that.

The total crutch length is often increased by 1–2 cm for greater comfort. This can be done by adding from the top, i.e. by raising the whole waistline, without changing *the relative length* of back and front seams. It can also be done by increasing the back seam length only, which provides more ease for bending but tends to make the back seam 'baggy'.

A method used in some styles to provide the necessary ease without causing the back seam to sag, is to increase the Crutch depth substantially (3–4 cm), either by slashing or from the top, and at the same time to *reduce the difference* between the two seams by *shortening the back seam* as shown in FIG. 7. Although back and front are now almost alike, the *total* crutch length is not reduced, sometimes even increased. This increase in depth is particularly suitable for certain 'draped' styles with much fullness, hanging in folds almost like a skirt.

To complete the pattern continue to the full length required down the side, and at the bottom measure the hem equally to the right and left of the Middle line. Complete the inner leg seams by curving them 2–3 cm from a straight line on *Knee level*, which is marked 5 cm above the half-way point. Bottom leg width = 50–56 cm.

SKIRT-KNICKER BLOCK ADAPTATIONS

This block is used mainly for various types and styles of panties, i.e. short and more or less loose knickers which in present day wear take the place of 'French knickers'.

The block itself, as shown in FIG. 10, is already a pattern of simple panties which can be widened a little in the hem by sloping out the side seams and, if preferred, shortened a little in the crutch by lowering the waistline. The hem is of course slightly curved being parallel to the curved lines of the Skirt block.

Flared panties—FIGS. 14, 15

These panties (with side seams and no CF and CB seams) have a fuller hemline than average and appear like a short, slightly flared skirt. Since the waist is usually *quite tight—without darts or gathers*—it is necessary to have one long or two shorter plackets in the seams. At the time when these panties were much used they were generally cut on the bias and were described as 'evening dress panties' because of their smooth fit under a clinging dress, with neither darts, front or back seams nor gathers to show through.

Fold the pattern lengthwise twice, to obtain 4 equal sections and three crease lines. This may be done more conveniently after detaching the crutch pieces, or by simply outlining the pattern *without* them.

Draw three darts from the waist, one along each crease, down to 2 cm below the Yoke level to reduce the waist to a tight fit. For a WR of 12–13 cm this will give three 4 cm darts. 1–2 cm may be left in the waist to allow the side seams to be curved very slightly at the top. After making three slashes from the hem, one on each crease, fold out the darts above, transferring all the waist fullness into the hem which will now be fuller, more curved and flaring. Draw the side seam through the centre of the middle slash.

The crutch part or 'gusset' is cut separately, as usual, and set into 10 cm CF and CB slits.

Panties — modern version — FIGS. 16, 17

This style, though cut from the Skirt-knicker block, appears in its final stage like the pattern of ordinary short knickers with a CF and CB seam, i.e. as if cut from the Standard knicker block. The example shows how easy it is to convert the Skirt-knicker block into an ordinary Standard knicker pattern. The crutch is a *separate piece* which, however, is not set into slits, but simply joined to the CF and CB. This is done mainly for economy in cutting and because of the easy finish of the crutch part.

Place the crutch pieces of the Skirt-knicker block as shown in FIG. 16, with a 3 cm gap between P and CF/CB. Outline the whole together, curving the CF and CB seams. Shorten the side length by 4–5 cm or more (e.g. to a 35 cm length). The width may also be reduced, if desired, by a lengthwise tuck along the side: this would depend on the fabric used. The pattern then appears as in FIG. 17, very similar in outline to the Standard knicker pattern.

Detach the crutch pieces along their long edges P–Q (broken lines in FIG. 17), join the F and B parts as usual, and in the material allow for a facing to double each piece (this, of course, is not essential, but usual in trade cutting), so that the lower edge is *a fold*. This double gusset is then stitched to the main part exactly *where it was cut away* and its curved edge P–FB–P becomes part of the CF and CB seams, i.e. part of the total crutch seam.

Pilch knickers — basic — FIG. 18

This is a popular pattern, now used mainly in its shortest, close fitting version, known as 'briefs' (see below). It is given here in its basic (not reduced) shape which is adaptable to a few other styles.

First *measure the front and back seams*, i.e. the crutch length from O to F and from S to B (1·5 cm difference). Then cut away the crutch pieces and apply the two lengths straight down CF and CB respectively, going deep enough below point X for the pattern *to retain the full crutch length*. In this case the lowest point comes 5 cm below X. CF and CB are now quite straight and can be placed 'to the fold' when cutting out in material.

From the lowest points draw short lines, 5–7 cm long,

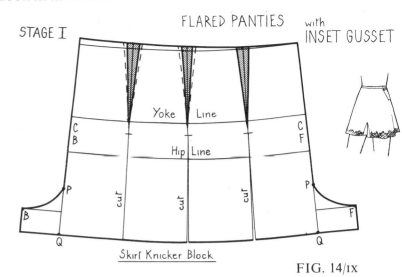

STAGE I — FLARED PANTIES with INSET GUSSET

Skirt Knicker Block

FIG. 14/IX

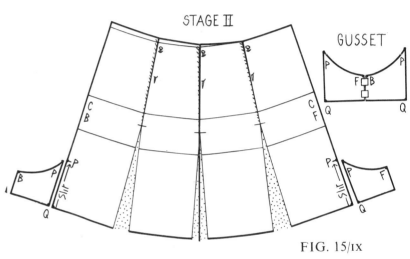

STAGE II — GUSSET

FIG. 15/IX

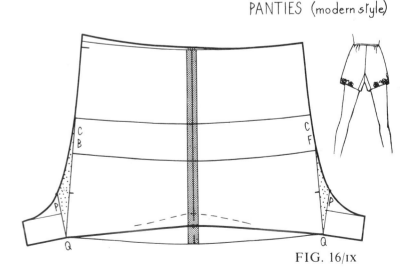

PANTIES (modern style)

FIG. 16/IX

FIG. 17/ix

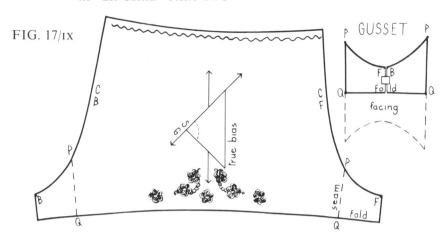

PILCH KNICKERS (basic)

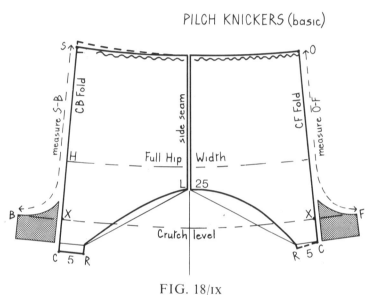

FIG. 18/ix

at right angles to CB/CF: this is the *width of the crutch* C–R. This may be a seam, straight or curved, (broken line) or the line may go 'to the fold'. In the case of a crutch seam it is usual to allow an extra 1 cm depth in the back so that the seam comes a little forward (i.e. well in the middle between the legs).

The side seam is usually short, 25–28 cm, and the lower edge of the pattern is therefore shaped accordingly, curving up from R towards the side seam. The back curve is made flatter than the front which is well hollowed out.

Since this is now more often a close fitting knicker pattern, the back seam (point S) can be raised a little to make it a full 3–4 cm *above* the front waist.

In some adaptations, e.g. short *gathered* styles for which the pilch knicker can be used *as a foundation*, the pattern is widened down the side to provide the fullness. In this case both the lower edge and the waist are gathered.

BRIEFS

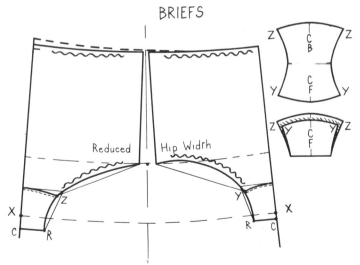

FIG. 19/ix

Briefs — FIG. 19

This is a closer-fitting version of the pilch knicker pattern. Reduce the *width* of the pattern by 3–4 cm as shown in FIG. 19.

The *total crutch length*, which in the basic pattern (above) is as long as in the Standard knicker block and thus gives the pattern a loose crutch fit, must be reduced by 5–6 cm for a *close* fit. In this pattern this is simply done by *adding less below the crutch level* than in the basic version. Add only 1 cm below on the CF and 2–3 cm on the CB or reduce the basic pattern by losing a total of 5–6 cm.

Make the crutch width just 9 cm, i.e. R–C = 4·5 cm, and complete the lower edge curving it up to a still *shorter side seam*, 20–22 cm long on an average. This lower edge is usually well shaped i.e. hollowed out in the front, and fits the top of the leg well, often with the help of elasticated gathers. It must not be too tight, of course, and an *average thigh measurement* is often used in the wholesale manufacturing trade to check its size.

The crutch part of this pattern is generally cut away along a slightly curved line, 8–9 cm above the lowest level, cut out separately, made double (faced) and then joined to the main part to form a re-enforced crutch part in the garment.

Details of style and finish will vary, of course, but this general outline would apply to most up-to-date patterns of briefs.

Cami-knickers — FIG. 20

Cami-knickers are usually adapted from the petticoat block by adding the crutch part in the same way as it is done in the Skirt-knicker pattern. In the garment the crutch part is set in as a gusset into slits a few inches long up the CF and CB.

The crutch pieces are added to the pattern *after measuring the required Depth of crutch from the waist level* which should be indicated, even if not actually used for the style. The usual Crutch depth of knickers is increased for cami-knickers by 2–3 cm (sometimes more at a fitting), so that the crutch pieces are placed lower than they would be in a knicker pattern (e.g. 35 cm down instead of 33 cm).

There is more strain than usual on the crutch part in most *combination* garments, whether the lower part is actually *attached* to the top, or the garment is simply cut all in one, as most cami-knickers. Extra crutch ease is therefore needed. **Lowering the depth of the crutch,** to gain total crutch length and ease, is a better way of dealing with this problem than increasing the back length only, as is sometimes done in combination sleeping garments (where the trouser back seam is lengthened). It is in any case more suitable for cami-knickers for it does not spoil the hang of the garment, as a 'baggy' line in the back would do.

Apart from the extra crutch ease required, it is also important that cami-knickers should hang away from the figure without being pulled in between the legs like real

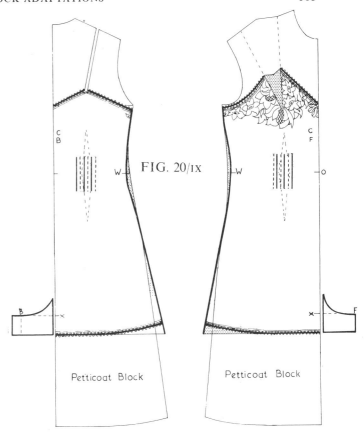

FIG. 20/IX

Petticoat Block

Petticoat Block

knickers: a deeper crutch produces that effect. But it must be remembered that there were styles in the past, and there may be some now or in the future, where this particular effect of an easy-fitting 'petticoat', hanging away from the figure, may not be required: crutch depth must be regulated according to style and fashion line as well as comfort in wear.

As cami-knickers are usually fastened (buttoned) between the legs, to bring the placket into a better position, well in the middle, and to provide an underlap for the buttons, it is necessary to make the back crutch piece longer than the front, by at least 2–3 cm. To avoid having the crutch part too long between the legs, one can reduce the basic length a little before adding the extra 2 cm or more on the back part.

Cami-knickers may sometimes be cut with a CF and CB seam (such styles existed in the past). The crutch can then be added as shown in FIGS. 16 and 17, and the whole cut in one without a gusset.

Some styles of cami-knickers could also be designed on the principle of a pilch knicker attached to a top (or simply cut in one with it). This would be quite a suitable way of cutting a *closer-fitting combination garment*, but would not be correct for the loose cami-knickers which must hang and look like a short slip or petticoat.

The crutch part or gusset is sometimes *simplified* and a simpler version is shown below (FIG. 21).

Simple crutch gusset — FIG. 21

This gusset can be used both for cami-knickers and ordinary Skirt-knickers. It is an adaptation of the standard gusset made to avoid an extra seam. The curved seam which usually joins the two parts is here eliminated.

Place the crutch pieces as shown in FIG. 21, with the two points P touching and the inner edges below F and B overlapping enough to make the length between the outer, lower points equal to 9–12 cm, the usual width of crutch in a loose fitting style.

Outline this as a complete section which can be set in, as usual, into a slit along P-Q, one in the back and one in the front of the garment. For cami-knickers the back piece is made longer. For ordinary knickers, the two parts are joined to form one continuous strip with a point at each end: the points go into the two slits.

A still simpler way of dealing with the crutch part of cami-knickers is to cut a straight strip, 8–10 cm wide, without points at the end, make it double and fit it to the 'hem' of the garment in such a way that back and front are joined between the legs (in cami-knickers it consists of course of two shorter strips, buttoned in the middle). It is the most primitive version of a crutch gusset, much used in the past when it was desirable to avoid *Cutting into* the garment, but also to give the cami-knickers a still more skirt-like appearance. The strip was attached invisibly on the *inside* of the garment, usually a little above hem level, not set into a slit. Such a gusset does not really require a pattern, but its length would still have to be based on a correctly planned crutch depth.

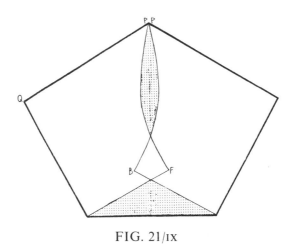

FIG. 21/IX

TABLE OF ¾ HIPS PROPORTIONS

HIP measurement	H 78	H 82	H 86	H 90	H 94	H 98	H 102	H 106	H 110	H 114	H 118	H 122
¾ HIPS	58·5	61·5	64·5	67·5	70·5	73·5	76·5	79·5	82·5	85·5	88·5	91·5

The 0·5 cm can be increased or decreased to the next *whole* centimetre, as convenient.

TAILORING PATTERNS
Part 1—Jackets

The basic cut of tailored garments differs little from that of dresses, particularly when the style of the dress is of the shaped, close fitting variety. It is therefore possible to use the Bodice block, with some adjustments, to reproduce the cut and fit of jackets and coats.

Simple though these adjustments are, it is most important to understand their purpose, for such understanding gives considerable control over various difficult points of cut and fit connected with tailored garments, such as fronts falling away, lapels and collar setting badly, various defects of waist shaping, etc. A 'Tailoring block' must allow for these special problems as well as provide the extra ease necessary for an overgarment.

Tailoring deals largely with styles which are well established and which can be described as **classical styles.** The Lounge jacket, the Panel jacket, the Chesterfield, the straight 'boxy' coat, the full swing-back or 'swagger coat' — all these are styles which, with seasonal variations, are seldom completely out of fashion. A study of these styles, and particularly of the details of their cut, is essential when learning tailoring, for without some reference to their well established lines and proportions there is always danger of missing the correct final effect of a classical tailored suit or coat. These remarks do not necessarily apply to so-called 'dressmaker suits' and fancy coats, but even the most fancy styles borrow much from classical tailoring

It is also important, when dealing with tailoring, to bear in mind the **close relationship** which exists **between the pattern and the tailoring technique** as a whole. The making-up and finishing of a tailored garment includes a considerable amount of shaping by means of pressing, shrinking and stretching with the iron, and the use of various interlinings, stay-pieces, padding, etc., to provide and improve the shape of the garment and to preserve it in wear.

The shape and fit of a jacket, therefore, depends not only on the 'cut', i.e. the pattern, but also on special manipulation during the various stages of making-up. This work — the hallmark of high class tailoring — represents craftsmanship based on long training and experience. It naturally influences the pattern, for since extra shaping can be given to a tailored garment by skilled stretching, shrinking and other detailed manipulation, it is not necessary, nor always desirable, to have so much shaping, i.e. darts, extra seams, etc. in the pattern itself.

While in dressmaking, because of the type of fabric used (silk, rayon, light woollens, cotton, linen, etc.) one has to rely almost entirely on seams and darts for any close fit to the figure, in tailoring there are other means of obtaining this effect. With a good tailoring cloth it is possible to stretch the material to provide extra ease over the bust or the front of the shoulder bone, to shrink it to fit the hollow of the waist, and so on. This reduces the depth of any necessary darts and sometimes does away with them completely. The padding of shoulders (and armhole) which was used in tailoring even before it became later so fashionable in dressmaking, works in the same direction. Hence there are jacket styles which show few darts of any importance (sometimes no darts at all), yet seem to be sufficiently shaped and well fitting.

On the other hand it must be borne in mind that every kind of manipulation in tailoring is highly skilled work, slow work, and as such, expensive work. Because of this, in mass production it must be reduced and replaced by machine work wherever possible. The growth of mass production methods in tailoring has naturally affected the patterns, one of the effects being the appearance of more darts, and deeper darts, than were used before. It is obviously quicker and therefore cheaper to sew up a dart or additional fancy seam than to stretch and shrink with the utmost care and skill various parts of the jacket.

This trend tends to be reversed again with the appearance of special pressing apparatus, capable, for instance, of moulding in one operation the complete front (foreparts) of a jacket. This naturally affects the details of patterns used in highly mechanized (factory) tailoring.

At all stages, therefore, the close relationship of pattern, i.e. cut, and tailoring technique is most important. The very details of a jacket pattern cannot be properly understood unless reference is made to the manipulation required to achieve the *final* result, e.g. the manipulation of a tailored collar. There are many such examples where only correct workmanship ensures the good fit which cut alone cannot achieve.

Before proceeding to the adaptation of the block there is one other important point which must be stressed. The classical method of producing patterns for tailored garments is **drafting**, often done directly on the cloth. In practice, experienced tailors may resort to quicker methods, including various 'adaptations' of their blocks. But whatever 'short cuts' they may use, the fact remains that their pattern designing technique is *based on direct* *drafting skill.* This skill includes the ability to draw well-shaped, well-balanced lines and this, no less than the manipulation technique, plays an important part in producing the precise, clean lines which are the hallmark of a good tailored suit.

It is essential to appreciate this fact and to understand why a learner specializing in tailoring must aim at acquiring and developing this skill, and why for some purposes (including examination work) drafting is essential. In following a method like the one described in these chapters (itself originally based both on Modelling and Tailor-drafting), it is necessary to appreciate the effect of precise, well-drawn lines in a tailoring pattern, and to recognize the importance of knowing *the established details and proportions* of classical tailoring.

All this is not a feature of pattern designing for dresses. In dressmaking, line and style details are more fluid and much more subject to fashion. Too much precision of line or rigidity in detail is even a disadvantage and makes the garment heavy and often noticeably out of touch with the *finer points* of fashion. In tailoring fashion influence is more tempered by tradition, and whatever exaggerations some modern designers may introduce into a tailored coat or suit, something always remains of the true classical cut and fit.

TAILORING BLOCKS

Just as the Bodice block is not a replica of the figure but the pattern of a dress bodice, with an average allowance for fit, so the Tailoring block is the pattern of a simple jacket with sufficient ease to be worn over another garment, such as a blouse or light dress. This block has all the characteristic features of a jacket: a wrap, lapels marked by a 'Crease line', suitable shaping of waist, adjustment of neckline for a tailored collar, additional ease in the shoulder part and a bigger armhole.

This simple basic jacket is used for developing all the other jacket styles, with the exception of some soft (often unlined) dressmaker jackets, cardigans or coatees, not requiring any real tailoring, for which the ordinary Bodice block can be used as it is, or with minor adjustments.

THE JACKET BLOCK – FIG. 1

After outlining the Bodice block to the Hip line (22 cm), leave a little paper all round, particularly beyond the CF for wrap and lapels. The block may be made 20 cm long below the waist if preferred.

BACK

(*a*) Raise NP 1 cm.
(*b*) Raise SP 1 cm.
(*c*) Draw shoulder seam making it 0·5 (1) cm longer (curving slightly up to NP is optional).
(*d*) Draw neckline from new NP down to CB neck point. CB is generally also raised – 0·5 cm.
(*e*) Add 0·5 to Back width (sometimes 1 cm).

(*f*) Lower UP 1 cm.
(*g*) Draw a new and bigger armhole.
(*h*) Move HP 0·5 cm in and 0·5 cm down: draw a new Hipline.
(*i*) Re-draw underarm seam, first following the bodice seam or even keeping just *outside*, then passing 0·5 cm inside the waist and down to the new HP.
(*j*) The 2 cm Sl. CB can be used when the actual style has a CB seam. It is shaped as usual.
(*k*) A *reduced* Sl. CB – 1–1·5 cm in – is often used for jackets with less CB shaping.
N.B. More addition to shoulder and back width when fashion demands it.

FRONT

(*a*) Move NP 1 cm *out* (widen neck) and then *raise it* 1 cm.
(*b*) Raise SP 0·5 cm and move it 0·5–1 cm out, i.e. lengthen shoulder.
(*c*) Reduce the Shoulder dart by 1·5 cm (on side nearest neck).
(*d*) Move lower point of Shoulder dart 0·5 cm towards CF and 2 cm up to shorten the Dart.
(*e*) Re-draw the shorter and smaller Dart, slightly *curving its outer side* towards the armhole.
(*f*) After pinning the new Dart draw the shoulder seam across it from the new NP to the new SP.
(*g*) Lower UP 1 cm to match the back.
(*h*) Add 0·5 cm to Chest line and re-draw the armhole.
(*i*) Move HP 0·5 cm in and 0·5 cm down, as in the back.
(*j*) Re-draw underarm seam, guided by outer edge of bodice block, keeping just outside the line at the top and just inside at the waist and lower, down to the new HP.
(*k*) Mark a point 0·5 cm *outside the CF waist* and rule a *new CF line* from the base of the neck through this point. This will add width to the hips, just where needed.
(*l*) Re-draw neckline keeping it very flat, almost in a straight line in the lower part, but hollowing it out well at the side, half-way up the curve. Two extra construction lines may help to give it the right shape: a perpendicular from NP intersected 6 cm lower by a straight line from the CF neck point.
(*m*) Add a 3 cm wrap parallel to the *new* CF (to be varied).
(*n*) Dip the lower edge of the block 1·5 cm on CF.
N.B. The wider neckline and reduction of Dart are not necessary if a classical Tailored collar is *not used*.

EXPLANATIONS OF THE VARIOUS ADJUSTMENTS OF THE BLOCK

Some Fitting points

BACK

(**a**), (**b**) and (**c**) adjustments give an **easier-fitting** and slightly longer **shoulder section** suitable for an outer garment which, more often than not, is lined. Extra

JACKET BLOCK
B 92

FIG. 1/x

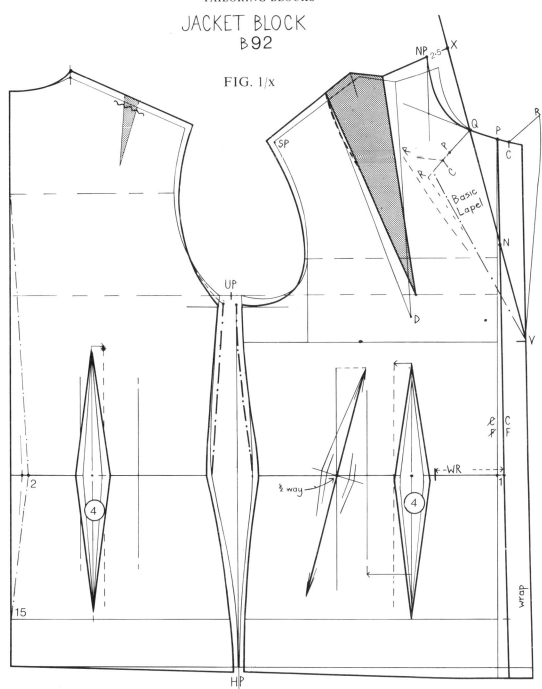

squaring, by raising SP further, can be done for fashion.

(d) – the NP in a jacket is usually 3 cm higher than CB neck.

(e) – **The Back** in the block is made only **slightly wider,** but in adaptations it is often further widened to suit style, type of jacket (e.g. sportswear) or fashion.

(b), **(e)** and **(f)** adjustments give the new points for the bigger armhole which will take a wider sleeve.

(h) reduces again to average size the hip width increased by the slanting out of the CF (see Front – **k**).

(i) shows that *easing* of fit on bust level in classical jackets is achieved by just keeping to *outer* side seam. A very slight 'bulging' of side seam at the top also provides extra ease for what is known as 'underarm drape'.

N.B. It will be noted that in the Jacket block no extra width is allowed on bust level, as in classical tailoring the ease provided by the outer seams of the Bodice block would be considered sufficient for light jackets. Since in modern tailoring an easier fit is preferred, a minimum of 0·5 cm may be added to the side seams (dot-dash lines), back and front, often increased to 1 cm and more in adaptations.

(j) refers to the Sl. CB *when used as a seam*. At a fitting it is sometimes possible to take it in a little more but, as with the more shaped side seams, there is always a danger of overfitting (on some figures and in some fabrics).

(k) is an additional detail—a *reduced* Sl. CB (1–1·5 cm) much used in classical tailoring and sometimes also in very short styles without a CB seam. In the latter case it may be continued below the waist, losing some hip width which is made good on the side seam: this gives a clinging fit on the hips at CB as required by some styles, but is not suitable for all figures.

FRONT

(a) – The widening of the neckline is equivalent to transferring part of the Shoulder dart into the neckline: hence the corresponding reduction of the main Dart. This *redistributes the width over the bust*, giving more ease over the CF part and so helping to keep the front edges together when jacket is unbuttoned. The extra neck width presents no danger since it is controlled by a correct back neckline.

(b) – Raising SP and NP gives an easier shoulder section. The *extra* added above NP is to allow for any possible tightening (pulling up) of the foreparts, by canvasing and pad-stitching. Often it is not required and can be taken out (at a fitting). It is usually unnecessary in the softer type of jacket.

(c) – Shoulder dart is reduced because of wider neckline.

(d) – These are just 'tailoring style' details.

(e) – Slight curving of outer side of the Shoulder dart, which is optional, causes a little 'fluting' in the armhole, giving ease just over the prominence of the shoulder bone (the armhole here may also be stretched).

(g) and **(h)** refer to the armhole which must be given a good shape after lowering UP to the level of the back.

(h) – The Chest has already been widened a little by slanting out CF and raising point of Dart. Additional ease is advisable to produce the little fold near the armhole which modern fit demands.

(j) – The side seam should allow full width on the bust level and must not be overshaped at the waist.

(k) – The 0·5 cm addition swings the CF forward and improves the 'wrap' of the jacket. The extra hip width of the front has already been reduced at the side. Some types of figure (with prominent bust) are better without this addition, as they need tightening rather than loosening of the front below the bust.

(l) – The neckline is reshaped mainly to suit the classical tailored collar. For various other collars it will be of a different shape, either following the ordinary Bodice block or more cut out, or even blocked in.

(m), **(p)** and **(q)** deal with the wrap, the width of which varies with style (SB, DB or Link), as does also the slant of the 'Crease line', which may start from a higher or lower **'Top Button level'**, and from the edge of a wider or narrower wrap (see FIG. 2). Every change in these details affects the Crease line which, in turn, influences the construction and set of the collar.

WAIST SHAPING

The basic principle of waist shaping is that the WR must be well distributed round the figure. This applies to jackets and coats as much as to dresses.

It is particularly important to remember that fabrics used in tailoring are usually heavier than average dress materials, that they will not 'give' as much in wear nor adjust themselves so easily to the figure without extra manipulation or correctly planned darts and seams.

The overshaping of the underarm seam is an ever-present danger. In classical tailoring the side seam does not take a big waist suppression and should be handled carefully to avoid such defects as bagginess under the arm, diagonal drags from the side waist, etc. It is a safe plan to keep to the outer shaped side seam and to tighten seam only if a fitting shows that this is possible (as it will be on some shapes of figure).

The possibilities of **the CB seam for waist shaping** are also limited, for the *middle* of the back is flat, or only slightly curved (as distinct from the shoulder blade part). Overshaping of this seam easily causes a baggy fit between the shoulder blades and 'drags' at the waist. The 4 cm suppression allowed on the Sl. CB (2 cm on half-pattern) can sometimes be increased a little at a fitting, on some figures and for some styles.

The front Waist dart, under the bust, has to be kept comparatively small for the average modern figure, to avoid tightness *below* the waist and over the hip bone, or a 'pinched-in' silhouette (unless the latter happens to be fashionable). Few figures can have more than 4–4·5 cm taken out in the front darts, usually less, at least in the *classical* styles. In fact, whenever the style provides other possibilities for waist suppression (e.g. extra seams) it is generally the front Waist dart that is reduced. It is also often placed nearer to the side seam and slanted (Fig. 2), a position which makes it less conspicuous, yet provides even better waist shaping for the jacket.

The **biggest waist reduction** is possible in the back, **under the shoulder blade,** where a panel seam, one or several darts and sometimes just easing (secured by a tape) can dispose of a considerable amount of waist fullness.

The best plan, therefore, is to use the side seams, the CB seam (if it is in the style) and the front darts to their *safe maximum*, and to take out the remaining fullness in the back, planning darts or seams accordingly.

On the Tailoring block mark the **usual position of the Waist darts.** First measure the waist from CB to side seam and continue from front side seam until $\frac{1}{2}$ waist + 6–7 cm is reached: beyond, as far as the new CF, is the WR. Measure it and divide it equally between back and front

Waist darts. With a bigger WR the back dart usually takes more since the front dart soon reaches its maximum.

It will be noted that the **12–14 cm ease** allowed for the waist in this block represents an **average allowance** for a fairly shaped jacket, but the ease may vary from 8 to 15 cm, though jacket waists are seldom tighter or looser.

THE WRAP OF A JACKET — FIG. 2

The width of a wrap varies from 2 cm to 9 (10) cm. Edge-to-edge jackets have no wrap but 1 cm beyond CF is often allowed as a precaution.

The three classical wrap styles are the Single-breasted (SB), the Double-breasted (DB) and the Link button front.

The SB wrap is usually 2–3 cm and up to 4·5 cm wide
The DB wrap 6–8 cm and up to 9–10 cm wide
The Link wrap 2 cm wide *at the waist* only.

In classical tailoring, jackets with low-rolling lapels may have SB wraps 4–4·5 cm wide and the buttons may not be on the CF but slightly to one side. The DB wrap can be as wide as 9–10 cm. The Link button jacket has some 'wrap' provision, near the waist level, for the single button usually placed 2 cm above the waist.

The shape of the wrap varies considerably according to style and **shape of lapels.** It may be the same all the way down, curved or cut away at the bottom, made narrower or, more often, wider at the top, to give the right shape to the lapels. The way to establish the correct shape is to draw the lapel as if folded back, *inside* the Crease line (as in the basic method for Revers) and then to transfer it to its correct position *outside* the Crease line.

THE CREASE LINE AND LAPELS — FIG. 2

The Crease line (or Break line) passes through a point which is 2·5 cm away from NP-point X (FIGS. 1 and 2). The line always starts *from the edge* of the wrap, but from *different levels* on it, according to the style and shape of lapels, and in each case it has a *different slant*. It can begin as low as the waist level or as high as the Chest line and from any point in-between. In each case it not only slants differently, but it also intersects the neckline at a slightly different point (point Q – FIG. 2).

The point where the Crease line cuts the CF line gives the *depth* of the 'neckline' in the front (N), as it appears when the jacket is *buttoned* (in practice this is affected by set of collar on the figure). Thus a Crease line starting from the Bust line level will not give a 'neckline' down to that level but much higher.

The other factor affecting the run of the Crease line is the *width* of the wrap: the wider it is, the more slanted

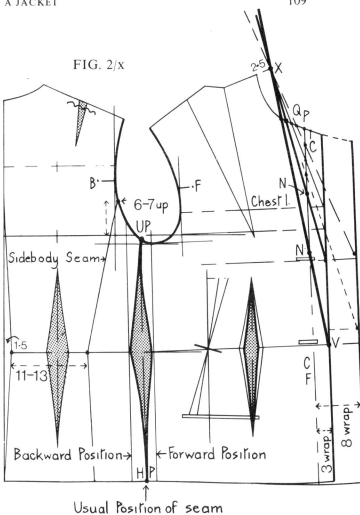

FIG. 2/x

Usual Position of seam

the Crease line (FIG. 2), and the higher it will cross the CF; it will also intersect the neckline (point Q) closer to CF. All this can be ascertained by trying out several lines *through point X*, but from the edge of different wraps.

From the above it should be clear that, whatever the fashion in lapels and in jacket 'necklines', high-rolling lapels usually go better with a narrower wrap, and vice versa. Where this is not so, care must be taken to co-ordinate all the points in such a way that the result is not an unwearable jacket with a clumsy, choking fit at the neck. It is not advisable to design a jacket style which, when buttoned up, has a 'neckline' depth *down CF* of less than 7·5 cm.

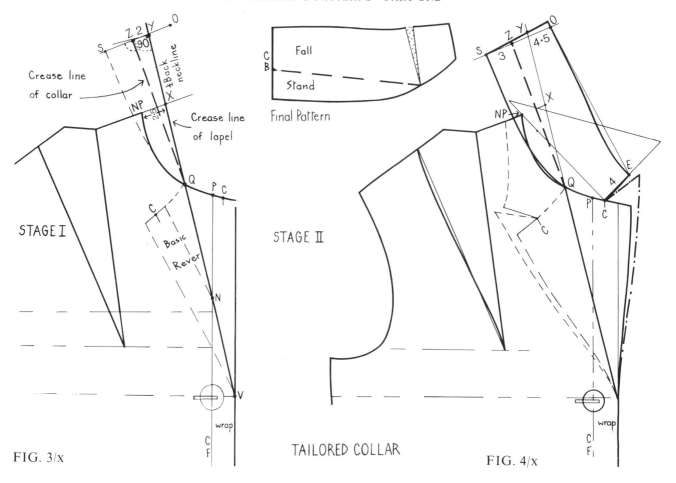

FIG. 3/x

STAGE I

STAGE II

TAILORED COLLAR

FIG. 4/x

THE TAILORED COLLAR — FIGS. 3 and 4

This is **the basic drafting method** for a classical tailored collar. The pattern is that of a standard shape which can serve as a general model for other styles.

On the extension of the **basic Crease line** measure from point X upwards ½-width of back neckline plus 0·5 cm, i.e. in this case 7 + 0·5 = 7·5 cm. Mark point Y. From Y, at right angles to the Crease line measure 2 cm and mark point Z. Connect Z with Q (at neckline intersection): this gives the **Crease line of the Collar,** the line on which the collar turns over and which separates the Stand from the Fall. Note that in the draft it is at an angle to the basic Crease line, an angle which can be varied *to change set of collar.*

Through point Z square a line to the collar Crease line Z–Q, extending it a little right and left: this is the provisional CB on which **the CB width of collar** (7·5 cm) is measured, to the left of Z — the Stand (3 cm to point S), and to the right — the Fall (4·5 cm for point O).

From S draw **the Sewing-on edge** of the collar, passing about 1 cm inside NP to make a good line, and into the front part of the neckline, through Q and P (pit of neck

on CF) to 1 cm beyond CF (point C), where the collar ends.

For the **end of the collar** place a set square with the 90° angle on point C and one side touching NP, and draw the collar end 4 cm up, along the other side to point E. This, of course, is only a standard shape given to this basic collar for general guidance. It may vary in other styles both in shape and in the way it joins the lapel.

Complete the **Outer edge of the collar** by connecting points O (on CB) and E and going 0·5 cm *beyond* O, from where the final CB line is drawn to S. Curve the final outer edge line as shown in FIG. 4.

It will be noted that the length of the Outer edge has already been slightly increased: 0·5 cm was added at point O and, at the beginning, the collar crease line Z–Q was placed at an angle to the basic (lapel) Crease line which also lengthens the Outer edge. Manipulation of the edge (by stretching under the iron) will further increase its length. It is nevertheless advisable for present day fit, which is usually looser, to add further length in the pattern by slashing from the edge to Q and opening it on the edge 0·5–1 cm, as shown in the *final pattern,* FIG. 4.

THE TAILORED ROLL COLLAR
(Shawl collar) – FIG. 5

This is an important adaptation of the standard collar with the Outer edge running straight into the lapel, as shown in FIG. 5. The undercollar has a join along line Q–C, but the top collar is cut *in one with the facings* and there is a seam in the CB. The dot-dash outline shows position on jacket when combined collar and lapel are turned back.

THE FLAT TAILORED COLLAR
(or French collar) – FIGS. 6, 7, 8

Style A – FIGS. 6 and 7 is a fashion collar much used in present-day tailored suits, particularly those with cut-away necklines. It has a much flatter fit.

It could, of course, be produced by drafting, placing point Z further away from point Y and slashing the Outer edge more (see Coat collar, FIG. 18/Chapter Eleven); but it is simpler to cut the pattern as shown in FIGS. 6 and 7, which are self-explanatory.

It may be used as a *Two-way collar*, buttoned up at the neck or worn open in Rever-style.

Style B – FIG. 8 – is similar in cut but less flat, and is suitable for various styles, including jackets without lapels, i.e. with the front edges just meeting.

ADJUSTING THE FIT OF A TAILORED COLLAR

Referring to the basic method of collar construction it will be remembered that the longer the Outer edge in relation to the inner or Sewing-on edge, the flatter a collar will set and the looser will be its fit, and vice versa.

In a tailored collar there is also the additional influence of the *roll* of the lapels and of the width of the wrap to be considered. Thus low-rolling lapels and narrow wraps (the two do not necessarily go together but, when combined, increase the effect) tend to *loosen* the 'neck-line', so that for a good *tight* set of lapels a higher and *closer-fitting collar* is required, while high-rolling lapels and wide wraps have the opposite effect and should therefore go with a flatter and looser collar.

This does not take into account any special fashion influence, such as fitting collars away from the neck, nor the actual *shape* of the neck, both of which may affect the tightness and set of a collar.

On glancing at the basic collar draft it is obvious that the method already adjusts it to different conditions through the change in the slant of the collar Crease line. It is useful, however, to know what exactly controls the looseness or tightness of a tailored collar and to understand where an adjustment can be made.

In the draft the Outer edge of the collar is shortened or, more often, lengthened by addition at CB (0·5 cm or more), by slashing or darting the edge, and by *adjusting*

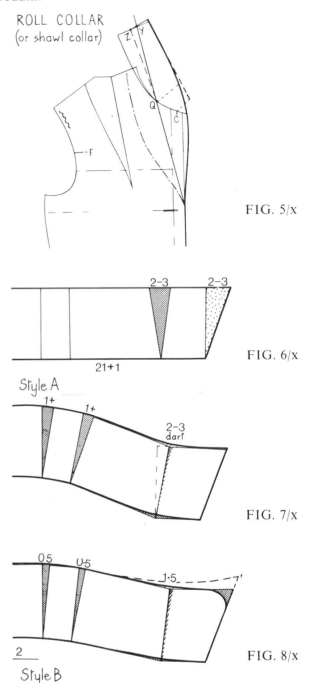

ROLL COLLAR
(or shawl collar)

FIG. 5/X

FIG. 6/X

Style A

FIG. 7/X

FIG. 8/X

Style B

the angle between the basic and the collar Crease lines Y–Q and Z–Q, i.e. by placing point Z closer or further away from Y. If, for instance, the distance between Y and Z is increased, the Outer edge becomes longer and the collar sets flatter and vice versa.

At an actual fitting, collar and lapel tightness is adjusted mainly by taking in or letting out the neckline seam which joins them, between C and Q. The end and the Outer edge of the collar must then be re-shaped, to regain their original outline.

CLASSICAL JACKET STYLES

The Jacket block is already a **simple jacket style** which can be varied in many ways: by using different wraps, lapels, collar styles, arrangement of buttons, and shape, size and position of pockets. It can be made longer (23–25 cm) or shorter (13–15 cm) below the waist. The design can also be varied by a different arrangement of the Waist Reduction: the darts can be divided into 2–3 smaller ones, stitched only to the waist giving a 'pouch' above, moved slightly *out* or, in the case of the front Waist dart, placed half-way towards the side seam and slanted. Some of these **detail variations** are shown on the block, FIG. 1, and in FIG. 2.

In addition to the simple basic jacket and the Straight jacket, there are two styles which embody the main **variations in cut** used in classical tailoring: the **Panel jacket** and the **Lounge jacket,** based on the cut of a man's suit. They should be studied in detail as most other styles are but variations of these well established patterns.

It will be noted that one of the chief features of a classical cut is the position of the underarm seam which is often moved back (3–5 cm) from its middle underarm position. This happens in such strictly tailored styles as the Chesterfield coat (or long jacket based on it), in the blazer and other similar styles. This makes the back narrower and the front wider, and usually requires an additional 'dart' or even seam placed further forward, under the arm. Sometimes the side seam is moved *forward*, usually to make room for an additional seam in the back, as happens in the Sidebody jacket. In all such cases the block is joined on the underarm, UP and HP touching, and the waist gap between is measured and treated as an extra 'dart'. The position of the new seam or seams is then planned.

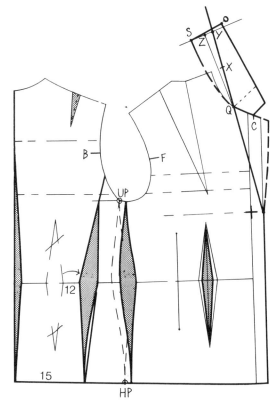

FIG. 9/x

THE LOUNGE JACKET or Sidebody jacket—FIGS. 9, 10, 11

This is a style in which the usual underarm seam is replaced by two seams: one slightly to the front, the other —well to the back (more than 5 cm). The first may be either just a long 'dart' from the armhole, or a complete seam, in which case *a separate underarm section*—known as **a sidebody**—is outlined and detached from back and front. Generally this style has also a CB seam.

After joining pattern at UP and HP, move the underarm seam of block 1 cm forward, as shown in FIG. 9. Shape the seam, as originally, or *reduce* the gap slightly.

Use reduced (1·5 cm) Sl. CB and shape back seam as usual. Then plan the sidebody seam position (see FIG. 2). From Sl. CB measure at the waist a distance equal to $\frac{2}{3}$ of Back width of jacket, i.e. 12 cm. At the hem measure, from ordinary CB, 3 cm more i.e. 15 cm. For the top point measure along the back armhole 7–8 cm up from

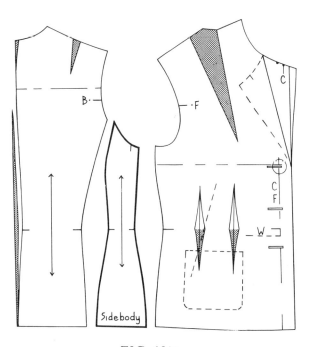

FIG. 10/x

the *usual* UP. This point can also be found by measuring 5 cm straight up from armhole level, i.e. from Bust line, or else by coming down the armhole 4–5 cm below point B. Connect the three points and curve the seam slightly, as shown in FIGS. 9 and 10.

The back Waist dart is moved into the sidebody seam. Complete the other side of the seam, curving it a little (this provides the slight 'drape' under the arm).

·After cutting away the sidebody (FIG. 10) complete the details of the front, which in this case has a 2·5 cm wrap without a point (widening 1 cm at the top), i.e. the simplest type of lapel. The Top button is placed on the True Bust line, as in the block. The patch pocket has its lower edge parallel to the hemline of the jacket.

The Back Waist Reduction here is mainly in the seams and since there is an extra one on the CB, suppressing 1+ cm, this amount can be taken either from the front Waist dart or from the forward underarm seam (to give the sidebody a less narrow waist). The front Waist dart is split into two and it is therefore not so important here to reduce it, as it is in some other styles. Though the WR is differently arranged, the *total* suppressed is still as in the block.

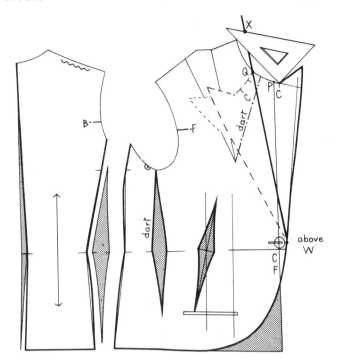

FIG. 11/x

THE LOUNGE JACKET WITH A LINK BUTTON FRONT – FIG. 11

This is another style of jacket based on the same cut but *without a separate sidebody*. It has an additional dart from the armhole, *replacing the forward seam*. This dart is usually a little smaller (3 cm), the excess going to the CB seam. The front Waist dart, moved out and slanted, is also reduced a little, 0·5+ cm going into the CB seam. The Dart ends in a jetted pocket, placed 13 cm below NW.

The front finish is that of a typical Link jacket with a 2 cm wrap at the waist, where the single button is placed 2 cm above NW. The wrap disappears completely in the cut-away and curved lower part, while at the top it widens considerably, with 4 cm added beyond point C for the lapel.

THE PANEL JACKET – FIG. 12
Classical style

The planning of the seams is similar to that used in dress patterns (see Panel bodice – Chapter One).

In dress patterns it is generally considered preferable to match the Panel seams on the shoulder. In tailored jackets they often do not come together, the idea being that since the two Panel seams are never seen together, it is more important to place each seam to the best advantage on the figure. The front seam is often kept straighter, as being more slimming, particularly for a large figure, while in the back the Panel widens out a little more towards the shoulders to balance the slight widening below the waist. The two seams are, therefore, planned independently, but a gap of less than 1 cm on the

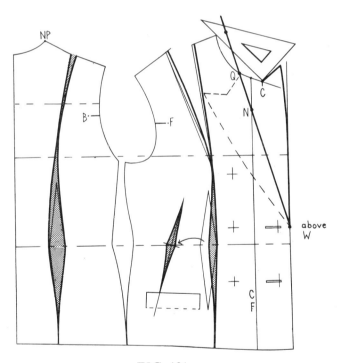

FIG. 12/x

shoulder should be avoided so as not to appear as a mistake.

As usual, the Panels are planned first, after which the waist suppression is worked out. The other side of each seam is then completed, outlining Side front and Side back.

For the Back Panel mark the following points:

On the shoulder a point in the middle, by measuring half shoulder length from NP.

At the waist—a point on the inner side of the Dart.

At the hem—1 cm further out from CB than at the waist.

For the Front Panel mark the following points:

On the shoulder keep a distance of at least 1 cm from the Back Panel.

At the waist—a point on the inner side of the Dart.

At the hem—1 cm more than at the waist from CF.

All these points, back and front, may, of course, *vary according to style and fashion*. Thus, when a straighter and looser fit is fashionable, the panels are made wider at the waist (points placed inside the Darts) and the same width is given at the hem in the front, with less widening towards the hips in the back. The panels can also be *matched on the shoulder*, if preferred.

After outlining the panels as shown in FIG. 12, plan the waist suppression in the two main seams. In the back the full back Waist dart of the block can usually be taken out in the seam. But in the front the Waist dart is generally *reduced* to avoid an over-shaped fit unsuitable for a classical tailored jacket. It is therefore necessary to have an *additional waist dart* which is placed half-way between the Panel seam and side seam, and slanted. The end of the dart often goes into a pocket—welt, or jetted—placed 10–13 cm (according to length of jacket) below the waist.

This classical style is often cut with a DB front, i.e. a 7–9 cm wrap with a double row of buttons, 10–12 cm apart. Note that here the lapel instead of widening towards the top, as in the Link jacket, FIG. 11, is on the contrary made narrower to avoid having too much width to fold back. The collar is taken a little further beyond the CF point (2 cm).

A very popular variant is a style with the panel running from the armhole instead of the shoulder (as shown in Chapter One). The line is usually curved, but may also be shaped at an angle, to appear, in fact, as if starting from a yoke.

The lower part of the front panels may also curve or turn sharply (at an angle) sideways, usually to form a hip pocket, before reaching the side seam.

STRAIGHT JACKETS — FIGS. 13, 14, 15

The cut of what is generally described as a 'Straight jacket' may be interpreted in different ways, and it is difficult to give a single basic pattern, as can be done for the more definitely shaped classical styles.

Generally speaking, straight jackets are loose and

have perfectly straight seams. But in some styles, and these often the more strictly 'tailored' ones, slight shaping of side seams is not only permissible but even necessary to reduce unwanted fullness under the arm. In most jackets of this particular type (the semi-sac or blazer type) the side seam is placed 3–5 cm to the back and slightly shaped. Many straight jackets are quite *long* (e.g. finger-tip length) and therefore may be considered as short coats.

The really short, loose straight jacket generally has a perfectly straight side seam which is in its usual position. It is wider than the Jacket block on the bust level, across the back, and usually also across the chest, but the hip width is much more a matter of style and fashion.

Width addition can first of all be made down CB—0·5–1 cm, increasing the width **right through.** At the top the extra width is either left in the neckline (eased or darted) or it is moved into the shoulder and added to the dart (FIG. 13). A *deeper shoulder blade dart* (or more ease, or both) is in any case important *for the good hang of a straight back*. Further width addition **on Bust line**—0·5–1 cm is generally made at UP—back and front—with the new side seam **running into the old,** unless extra hip width is also desirable. **The hip width,** however, is a more variable detail and may be increased or kept tighter, according to style. On an average 10–12 cm over the Hip measurement is quite usual when no particular 'figure hugging' or 'swing-away' effect at the hem is aimed at. Slight adjustment can be made at a fitting.

The correct hang of the back is a most distinctive feature of a well-cut straight jacket and it varies with style and fashion. The back may be required to hang quite straight, as much as possible in a vertical line; or to slope *in* a little, clinging to the hips or, on the contrary, to stand away and even swing *out* from the figure. The line is usually definitely indicated by the style and must be observed. But, style and fashion apart, the problem of correct hang may arise also in connection with **the shape of the figure** which may have a pronounced 'stoop' (round back) or, on the contrary, an over-erect 'sway-back' posture. Just to achieve *a normal straight hang* on such a figure it may be necessary to adjust the pattern to a more clinging or a more swinging out line on the hips. In this way many defects, such as diagonal folds (drags) from the shoulder blades and pulling up of hem at CB on the round-shouldered figure, or rucking at the waist and riding-up of the lower part of the jacket on the hips on an erect, hollow-waisted figure, can be avoided. These are the problems encountered when fitting a straight back and in connection with this there are two important adjustments which may help to improve the hang of a straight jacket.

The first is shown in FIGS. 13 and 14, and is generally applied to all patterns of 'boxy' jackets. It makes the back detach itself from the figure on the hip level and produces an easy and more elegant hang with small vertical folds at the armhole which are considered correct

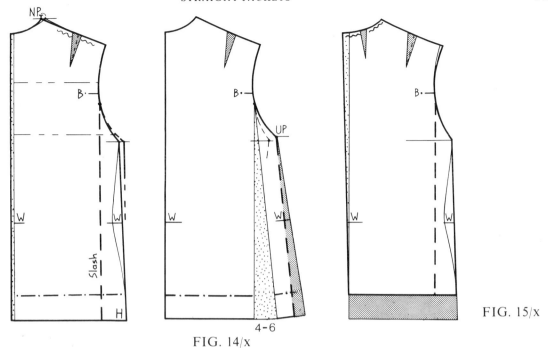

FIG. 13/x

FIG. 14/x

4-6

FIG. 15/x

for this particular type of back. It is much used for normal postures, to give the back a good line but is, of course, particularly important for the erect figure with hollow back and over-developed hips.

After slashing the back on a line parallel to CB up to a point on the armhole 3–4 cm below B, open slash at the hem 4–6 cm according to length of jacket. Note how the back armhole swings up in the lower part, 'setting' the small vertical fold. If the extra hip width is excessive for style, reduce it at side seam by $\frac{1}{3}$ of the amount gained (or more, if there is no drag from shoulder blade).

The other adjustment, FIG. 15, is an addition of width beyond the CB *at the top only*, with CB line *sloping in*, so that no width is gained on the hips. The extra neck width can be dealt with as in FIG. 13.

The effect of this adjustment is to give more ease across the shoulder blades and prevent hem pulling up at CB. The two adjustments can sometimes be used together on average figures.

In connection with all straight jackets in general, it must be noted that the hang is improved by **greater raising of NP** – 1·5–2 cm instead of 1 cm, with CB neckline also slightly raised. Some figures may need it in other styles as well, but it is particularly the fit of the straight jacket back which benefits from this adjustment.

There is little to say about **the Front** which usually has a Shoulder Dart or a **Neckline dart**. The latter is *suitable for most jacket styles*, and is much used in classical and modern tailoring. The Underarm dart, though used occasionally, is less satisfactory. Dividing the dart between two positions, e.g. neckline and underarm or hem, is often convenient but all these details usually follow the style.

THE TAILORED TWO-PIECE SLEEVE AND ARMHOLE – FIG. 16

The general method of cutting this sleeve has already been given in Chapter VI, so only some additional points will be mentioned here. These refer mainly to the more classical shape of this sleeve, in connection with the jackets dealt with in this chapter.

As already stated elsewhere, present fashion demands a looser, less shaped jacket sleeve, as given in Chapter Six. The classical shape is more curved, and generally less wide, particularly in the wrist part.

Extra shaping or curving is added to the Two-piece sleeve as shown in FIG. 16. From Elbow point E slash the top sleeve as far as the middle and, taking out a 0·5 cm dart on the opposite edge, inside the elbow, open the slash. This extra length is eased into the under-sleeve over the elbow. Reduce the inner edge of under-sleeve by a similar dart until the two edges of false Forearm seam match. Later pressing and slight stretching of this seam makes the *real* Forearm line tighter and smoother-fitting inside the arm.

The wrist width is reduced by 2 cm, taking in 1 cm on each back seam edge and running off to nothing at point E. This also increases the *curve* of the sleeve (FIG. 16).

With regard to the **width of the sleeve,** this depends largely on the armhole and to a certain extent on the crown depth required. In the classical jackets, given earlier in this chapter, the armhole is increased by 1 cm in the top part (above B and F) through the 0·5 cm addition above SP. The 1 cm lowering of UP increases the armhole another 1–2 cm, so that *when no extra under-arm width*

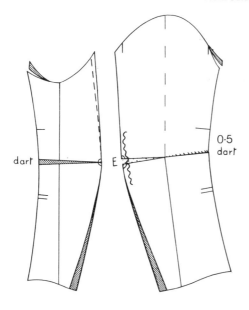

FIG. 16/x

is added on bust level the total increase is 2·5–3 cm. The sleeve must therefore gain on the crown edge and so the crown goes up 0·5 cm, is hollowed out 1+ cm and the remaining 1+ cm is obtained by widening the sleeve block. The classical tailored sleeve is therefore less wide and generally fits into a smaller armhole than a modern jacket sleeve.

If a jacket armhole is further increased by *width addition on bust level*, the sleeve head edge must be further lengthened by giving the sleeve *more width across*. However, since *the fashion fit* of a sleeve nowadays depends so much on a *deep crown* (i.e. more hollowing out and shorter underarm), it is obvious that too much sleeve width, even in a looser jacket, is not desirable either. A correct *balance between width of sleeve and depth of crown* is therefore most important.

THE PLANNING OF VARIOUS DETAILS IN JACKETS

To complete this survey of classical tailored jackets a few general remarks must be added about the planning of pockets, buttons, collars and lapels.

BUTTONS AND BUTTONHOLES

The most important button – **the Top button** – is marked on the level from which lapels begin to turn back and from where the Crease line (passing through X) is marked.

The **Waist button** is also quite important. More often than not it is placed above NW, though it may be below.

In Link jackets it is the only button (a linked double button) and is always 2 cm above NW to prevent lapels bulging. In many present day styles it is the middle button, or often the lowest button, while in classical tailoring, with low-rolling lapels, it was usually the Top button.

It is convenient to be guided by these two buttons and to plan the others in relation to them. Space between the buttons varies considerably with style and may be as small as 6 cm (sometimes less) or as big as 15 cm (average 9–10 cm).

In SB styles the distance of buttons (the shank) and of buttonholes (the eye), from their respective edges should *in theory* be the same, or almost (making allowance for the slight further projection of buttonhole to accommodate the shank). This applies particularly to styles with narrow (2–3 cm) wraps, since here the buttons are meant to be on the CF line. In practice, tailored buttonholes are usually made fairly close to the edge of the wrap, i.e. 1–2 cm in from the edge, while the buttons are often sewn further in (for better inside wrap) and are sometimes moved in or out to tighten or loosen the fit of the jacket. In styles where such displacement from the CF might be too noticeable (e.g. high buttoning jackets) this should of course be avoided.

In DB styles the distance of the two rows of buttons from the CF is largely determined by width of wrap which in styles with higher-rolling lapels, and buttons *above* as well as *below* the waist, is usually narrower, 6–8 cm, with buttons 10–11 cm apart; while in classical tailoring, with low lapels and buttons, it can be as wide as 9 cm and even 10 cm and buttons often 14–15 cm apart.

When **planning buttons and buttonholes on a DB jacket** the holes on the wrap-over side are usually marked 1–2 cm *in* from the edge and *their distance from CF* is then measured on the opposite side of the CF line for the sewing on of the second (inner) line of buttons (there are of course no buttonholes on this inner line). On the under-wrap a single buttonhole is usually made to go over an inside button to keep the under-wrap edge in position.

In fancy styles, in which any type of buttoning can be used, one must follow the design, guided as much as possible by the CF line and the Top and Waist buttons.

POCKETS

There is great variety in the shape, size and position of pockets, especially in modern tailoring when pockets are sometimes the main fashion feature. As in the case of wraps and lapels, many definite rules of classical tailoring have been relaxed or completely waived and the designer's ideas or the wearer's preference are now often the deciding factor.

The opening or mouth of a **Hip pocket** is usually 13–14 cm long, but may vary from 12 to 15 cm. Patch pockets are basically rectangles 13–14 × 13–15 cm deep on an an average, but they can also be any shape and size, and *outsize* pockets are often used.

Breast pockets are usually smaller, 9–10 cm long: But still smaller as well as bigger fancy pockets, particularly of the 'Patch' or 'inside stitched' variety, appear in many modern jackets.

The position of a pocket on a jacket also changes with fashion. In the past most hip pockets were placed a little above the 'Yoke' line i.e. 12–13 cm below the waist, leaving just enough room for a small pocket bag below. In modern styles pockets are generally placed higher, 6–8 cm below the waist, and sometimes just below the waist (e.g. flap pockets). Slanted pockets may begin almost at the waist.

The inner end of a hip pocket usually comes on or inside the Waist dart, on an average 9–11 cm from CF. In Panel jackets – a little further out, just outside the Panel. The outer end is generally at least 2·5 cm from the side seam.

Breast pockets are placed between Chest and Bust lines, the present tendency being to place them higher than before. The classical *slanted* welt pocket was usually *on* the Bust line and slanting (3–4 cm) upwards from it. But much depends of course on the size and shape of the pocket.

The inside of a pocket, the pocket bag, must be considered in the pattern, so that enough depth is left for it.

A Patch pocket is usually placed with its lower edge parallel to the sloping hem of the jacket.

All these are general observations rather than rules. Changes in the tailoring technique as well as fashion have affected considerably details even of classical jackets, details which in the past were much more rigid and definite.

COLLARS AND LAPELS

Different lapels have already been given in connection with the various styles. The Tailored collar can also vary in shape and so can the way in which it *joins* the lapels. It can be wider or narrower, set flatter or higher. The exact way in which the collar-end joins the lapel must be carefully studied and correctly reproduced, for this detail often represents a most characteristic fashion feature in tailoring.

Most of the **tailored collars** of traditional design end just beyond the CF or sometimes on the CF. But in some cases, particularly in more fancy styles, collars may be shorter (not reaching CF) or longer going well beyond CF, even to the end of the lapel, without forming a step or notch.

When tailored collar and lapel are joined so that their combined edge forms a *continuous curved* line, the foundation for a 'roll collar' (or Shawl collar) is obtained. The join between the under-collar and lapel (see FIG. 5)

is covered by the facing which has a seam in the CB. Many fancy variations can be planned on this basic collar.

The Rever-collar used in dressmaking is also used in jackets of the 'dressmaker type', as are many other collars, such as Eton-cut, round or pointed styles, the high Stand collar (Military collar), and a variety of Roll collars of different shapes and sizes. Some could be adapted to the 'collar drafting method' given in this chapter, but the majority can be cut best by following the basic method of collar construction. It is not so much the actual pattern, as the working and finish (interlining, pad-stitching, etc.) which distinguishes a jacket collar from a dress collar.

The neckline given in the Jacket block is mainly an adaptation *for the classical tailored collar*, as well as for some of its modern versions. With **fancy collars** the usual neckline of the bodice block should be retained and adjusted (blocked in or cut away) as required by style and fashion.

TAILORING PATTERNS
Part 2—Coats, Capes

Coat patterns can be cut from the Jacket block or from the ordinary Bodice block. The most convenient, however, is to have two simple basic coat patterns—one for the straight and one for the shaped coat styles.

From these two patterns a big variety of styles can be produced, often with only slight changes in details—wraps, lapels, collars, pockets and buttons. The introduction of secondary seams, such as panels, yokes, etc., however fancy, usually presents little difficulty once a

correct basic outline and proportions suitable for a coat fit have been obtained.

It is impossible in the space of one chapter to do more than deal with the most important coat silhouettes, and the two classical styles given here—the Straight and the Shaped coats—are certainly the most important basic patterns. They can therefore be used as **Coat blocks.**

THE STRAIGHT COAT—FIGS. 1 and 2

This is a loose coat with perfectly straight side seams.

The adaptation is more conveniently made from a **Bodice block,** because the additions and adjustments are more clearly seen than in relation to a Jacket block. If, however, for some reason, the latter is used (there are cases when this may be more convenient, as when adapting a Sidebody jacket to a Chesterfield coat which has the same cut), then the various additions must be reduced accordingly since the Jacket block already has extra ease.

The extra width addition in a loose straight coat is at least 8–10 cm on the bust and hip levels. In its final shape, the coat, as shown in FIG. 2, actually measures a little more, but there are styles for which this is excessive.

When outlining the Bodice block, back and front separately, 8–10 cm apart at the hips but correctly aligned on the same level, allow paper all round for the various additions, particularly for the length below the Hip line. The average CB coat length is 112–116 cm.

BACK—Stage 1

(a) Add 1 cm down CB.

(b) Raise NP 2 cm.

(c) Raise SP 1 cm.

(d) Move NP 0·5 cm to the left, only partly reducing the neckline; this leaves the shoulder 0·5 cm longer.

(e) Draw shoulder seam; lengthen it 0·5 or 1 cm, to obtain the 1 cm *extra shoulder length* and also to allow for a full 2 cm dart, which is important for straight coats.

(f) Draw neckline down to 0·5 cm above original level at CB.

(g) Lower UP 2 cm.

(h) Add 1 cm width at UP.

   N.B. If preferred, the *whole* bust width addition can be made *at the side seam*, instead of partly down CB.

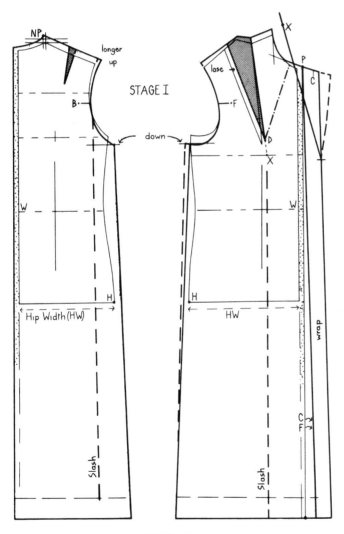

FIG. 1/XI

The extra *Back width* and *shoulder length* must then be added separately and armhole re-shaped accordingly. This does not affect the final result.

(*i*) Re-draw the armhole to the lower level.

(*j*) Continue CB down to full length.

(*k*) Draw the hem, making it equal to *Bodice block Hip width* plus 5–6 cm.

(*l*) Rule the straight side seam from new UP down to the hem width marked, passing outside point H.

FRONT–Stage 1

(*a*) Add 1 cm down CF. As well as adding width on bust and chest it also widens the neckline (as in jacket).

(*b*) Raise NP 1·5 cm.

(*c*) Raise SP 1 cm.

(*d*) Reduce Shoulder dart 1 cm: this lengthens shoulder 1 cm.

(*e*) Raise Dart point (D) and move it 0·5 cm in.

(*f*) Draw the shoulder seam over the closed Dart.

(*g*) Re-draw the neckline, *raising it* a little (1 cm) on the CF (additional construction line intersecting 6 cm from NP may be used).

(*h*) Lower UP 2 cm to match the back.

(*i*) Addition of 1 cm width at UP is optional but needed in some styles.

(*j*) Re-draw armhole as shown in diagram.

(*k*) Draw a *sloping* CF line through a point 0·5+ cm outside CF at the waist. This adds about 2 cm to hem.

(*l*) Complete hem making it 5 cm more than *Bodice* Hip width.

(*m*) Rule side seam from new UP down to hem width.

(*n*) Add a wrap, minimum 4 cm wide for a SB front.

At this stage (**Stage 1**) the pattern can already be used as a block for some styles (narrower coats). To improve its 'wrap' and its 'hang' in the back, however, the following adjustments are usually made:

BACK–Stage 2

After cutting out pattern, slash from hem to a point on the armhole, 3–4 cm below B, and open the slash 6 cm at the hem. This improves the hang of the back (as in 'boxy' jackets). If hem width is excessive, *some* of the width gained can again be lost at the side (2–3 cm).

FRONT–Stage 2

After cutting out pattern, slash below the Shoulder dart from hem up to point D (or X) and close enough of the Shoulder dart (usually 1–2 cm) to open the slash at the hem 5–6 cm (less for some styles). Transfer the remainder of the Shoulder dart into the neckline, cutting to point D from a point 4–5 cm inside the CF. This is the best position for the Dart in this type of coat, though it can also be used on the shoulder or sometimes in a Panel seam.

Transferring part of the Dart into the hem improves the 'wrap' and corrects the tendency of the coat to open out in the front. If the hem width is thought to be excessive for the style, a little (2–3 cm) may be lost at the side. But care must be taken to see that when the coat is worn, the side seam does not slope towards the front but hangs either quite straight or with a slight swing to the back. Since shape and posture of figure may have some influence on the hang of the seam, it is not advisable to reduce hem width too much before seeing the coat on the figure.

STRAIGHT COAT ADAPTATIONS

The final size of a coat pattern depends very much on the *type* of coat it is, on the fabric and, of course, on the style. If this is a real *overcoat*, to be worn over a suit or other heavy clothing, it must naturally be looser and have a larger armhole. Generally this applies to coats made in heavy fabrics. On the other hand, the same pattern can serve for closer-fitting or *straighter* coats in

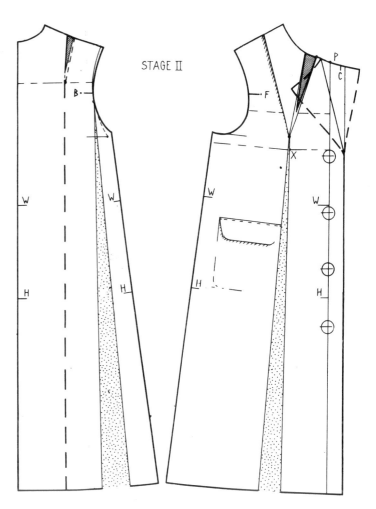

FIG. 2/XI

lighter fabrics, with less bulky sleeves and smaller arm-holes (e.g. a summer coat). It is useful to know where and how to reduce or increase the block pattern.

The Back, as already stated, can be reduced a little in hem width at the side seam (sometimes just to make it swing correctly). But for a very straight silhouette, clinging to the hips or even with a definitely **sloping-in line in the CB,** one can actually slope the CB of the pattern, losing 1–2 cm at the hem. In more extreme styles this effect is sometimes exaggerated and achieved not only by losing some hem width, but also by adding more width (folds, gathers, etc.) to the top, in the neckline or on the shoulder.

At a fitting, this adjustment of '*pulling-in*' the hem at the back is achieved by undoing the side seam and moving the back *up on the front* (back UP 1–1·5 cm *above* front UP), and only then losing hem width at the side and adjusting the length. This is largely a style and fashion adjustment, but some *inward sloping* of back may some-times be useful for round-shouldered figures.

In most other cases the straight back is more elegant when it has an easy hang, slightly detached from the hips, and with some fullness draping in *vertical* folds under the arm (i.e. the 'boxy' effect).

For a fuller **back swinging out at the hem,** width can be added also through a slash made from the hem *up to the shoulderblade dart.* The latter can be slightly lengthened to meet the slash on the Back line, and it can be either partly or wholly closed to give, according to style, 10–15 cm more width at the hem.

For a very full **'swagger' style back** width can also be added at the CB, e.g. 15 cm and up to 20 cm, off to nothing at the top. This, as well as the other width additions, gives the hem 30–40 cm more, well distributed over three points.

Front adaptations are on the whole simpler and less varied than those in the back. The hem width added by the slash below the Bust dart may be reduced in some cases (i.e. slash opened out less than 6 cm), either to achieve a very straight effect or to prevent the fronts swinging forward too much. In some styles the slash may simply be unnecessary, as when the coat has a Panel seam through which extra width for a better wrap can be added. It is therefore also useful to have a front pattern without a hem slash (as Stage 1), for use as a block in some cases.

A small reduction in hem width (2–3 cm) can also be made at the side, taking care that no 'drag' develops from the bust, and that it does not make the side seam swing forward noticeably.

Sometimes a slash is made from the hem up to the arm-hole, exactly as in the back, to achieve a small vertical 'fold' under the armhole, in which case the slash under the Bust dart would not be used. All these are, however, details of line and style rather than general points of cut and fit.

Fancy style lines, such as panels, narrow sections, yokes, etc., are introduced into the simple Straight coat in the usual way (using either 1st or 2nd stage); and so are various types of pleats often seen in straight coats. Wraps of different width, rolling higher or lower, and widening at the top into various shapes of lapel, also different shapes and sizes of pockets and button arrange-ments—all these provide much variety in design without changing the basic cut of a straight coat.

THE SHAPED COAT—FIGS. 3 and 4

This type of coat is often referred to nowadays as a 'Redingote'. It represents a line or silhouette which *follows the shape of the figure,* but without fitting it closely, widening out slightly towards the hem.

In style adaptations, it can, of course, be easily trans-formed into a real close fitting coat, with a flaring hem-line, the effect being achieved mainly by the addition of extra seams, e.g. Panel seams.

The basic Shaped coat is adapted from the Bodice block in a similar way to the Straight coat, the main difference being in the shaping of the side seams. Less width is added round the bust (5–6 cm extra only), to be increased when necessary.

BACK—Stage 1

(*a*) Add 1 cm down CB.
(*b*) Raise NP 1·5 cm (2 cm for some figures). For very light coats this may sometimes be reduced to jacket proportion.
(*c*) Raise SP 1 cm.
(*d*) Draw neckline, reducing it (moving in NP) 0·5 cm only.
(*e*) Draw the shoulder seam, lengthening it another 0·5 cm.
(*f*) Lower UP 2 cm.
(*g*) Continue CB to full length. Complete the hem as usual making it 6 cm wider than the Hip width of the Bodice black: this can always be reduced *for style,* if necessary.
(*h*) Draw the side seam from new UP, passing a little out-side the Bodice block, towards a point just inside the waist, and from there, curving into the Bodice seam, to join a straight line ruled up from the hem.

FRONT—Stage 1

(*a*) Add 1 cm down CF.
(*b*) Raise NP 1·5 cm and SP 1 cm. As in the back this may be reduced to Jacket proportions for very light coats.
(*c*) Reduce Shoulder dart 1 cm, thus *lengthening shoulder* 1 cm.
(*d*) Make the Dart shorter and slope its point inwards.
(*e*) Complete neckline, *raising it* slightly at CF.
(*f*) Lower UP to match the back and re-draw the armhole.
(*g*) Draw the sloping CF, as usual.
(*h*) Complete the hem, making it 5 cm wider than Hip width.

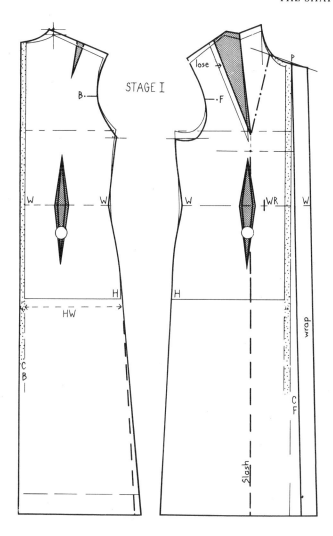

FIG. 3/xi

Stage 2 — FIG. 4

After completing the basic outline of the front, make a slash from the hem and, partly closing the Shoulder dart, transfer 3–4 cm into the hem, to improve the wrap. The remainder of the Dart then usually goes into the neckline (as in the Straight coat), to be more or less hidden by the lapel, though there are of course styles where the Dart is used on the shoulder or in a Panel seam.

There are shaped coat styles where this adjustment is unnecessary because there are additional seams, e.g. Panel seams, which can provide extra width for a good 'wrap'. As in the case of the Straight coat block, it may therefore be convenient to have two fronts — stage 1 and stage 2 — to be used according to style requirements.

WAIST SHAPING

The waist shaping of this block is most conveniently marked by two simple Waist darts, exactly as on the Jacket block. Measure the total waist, as usual, from

(i) Draw the side seam as in the back, slightly *in* at the waist, but keeping the *full width* at the top.

(j) Add 4 cm beyond CF for SB wrap or more, according to style.

N.B. It will be noted that alternative jacket proportions are mentioned at some points. This is because coats nowadays are made in such a variety of fabrics — from heavy woollens to light cottons and silks — that in some cases, e.g. when they are worn over sleeveless or thin dresses, they are, as far as fit goes, little more than jackets extended to full length. This, of course, applies also to Straight coats, though, by tradition, they are generally looser fitting, even in light fabrics. The latter may now include every type of silk and even lace, chiffon, etc. Although such coats can hardly be considered as *tailored* garments, they are nevertheless cut from patterns which structurally are very similar to those used in tailoring, and it is therefore difficult not to mention them in this connection.

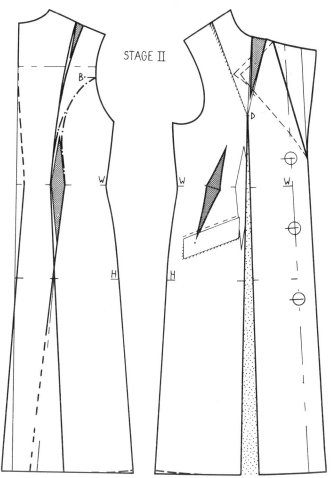

FIG. 4/xi

CB, until the WR point is found: beyond it is the WR.

In a coat the waist is usually about 15–16 cm looser than the Waist measurement, though in some styles it may be tight (e.g. in real Princess styles), especially in light fabrics, and always when fashionable. The block should have a semi-shaped rather than a close fit. So that in this case (Waist 70 cm) *the final waist* should be 35 + 8 cm, i.e. 43 cm on the half pattern.

The actual position of the Waist dart, when used as a single dart, will depend on the style, but it is quite usual to move the front Waist dart towards the side, as is done in jackets. This is a good position both for the closer-shaped waist, but particularly for the more moderate shaping of so many classical coat styles. It reduces surplus waist width without unduly emphasizing the hollow below the bust, i.e. without overshaping.

SHAPED COAT ADAPTATIONS

There is quite a variety of style lines in shaped coats. The most usual is the addition of a CB seam which takes over part of the waist shaping. In such a case by slightly increasing the waist shaping *at the sides*, it is often possible to eliminate the back Waist dart completely. The slanted front Waist dart is quite a feature of this style, and usually goes into a pocket.

The best known style adaptation is the **Panel coat** or **Princess coat** (the latter made closer fitting and fuller in the hem). The planning of the seams follows the classical method already described in the Panel jacket (Chapter Ten). Panel seams may run from the shoulder or from the armhole (FIG. 4). A popular classical coat style (a typical Redingote) has a Panel in the back, more often from the armhole, and a plain front, with a slanted Waist dart.

Another classical adaptation is a style similar to the Lounge jacket—the Chesterfield coat. It has either a complete Sidebody, sloping out naturally below the hipline or, sometimes, only a downward running dart (as in jackets). The planning of the Sidebody seam is very much the same as in jackets, but the amount of sloping-out below is decided according to final hem width required, which is usually that of the basic coat or slightly more.

As well as these classical styles, there are many fancy variations, sometimes with partial or whole seams round the waist and a flaring 'skirt part', sometimes with many more downward sections (10- or 12-gore styles), sometimes with addition of pleats or side-flaring. For all these the usual basic methods are followed.

COAT SLEEVES—FIGS. 5, 6, 7

Three types of sleeve are used for coats: the Straight sleeve, the Semi-shaped sleeve and the Two-piece sleeve.

The Straight sleeve is exactly like the block except for the increase in size shown in FIG. 5, and the subsequent reduction at the wrist.

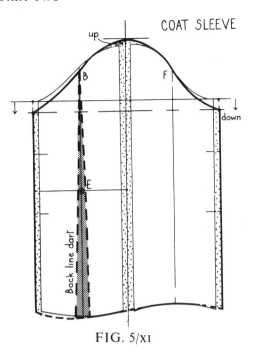

FIG. 5/XI

For a big coat, with an armhole 8–9 cm bigger than on the Bodice block, **the Straight sleeve block is widened across** by 5 cm, adding 2·5 cm through the middle and the other 2·5 cm divided equally between the two edges. This equal division makes it unnecessary to move points B and F and is more convenient for a bigger addition than for a jacket sleeve. (**N.B.** For coats with smaller armholes use less width across).

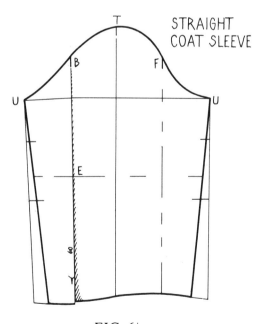

FIG. 6/XI

The crown is made higher by raising it 1·5 cm above point T and hollowing it out 2 cm below point U, on both edges (with a higher *original* crown, 1 cm lowering may be sufficient). Re-draw the sleeve head passing below points B and F. The total increase of the crown edge should be 9 cm, suitable for an armhole increased by 8 cm.

Measure carefully the size of the sleeve head and compare it with the coat armhole: a slight excess of sleeve head length (over and above the usual 2 cm extra of a *dress sleeve*) can be overlooked as it is not difficult to dispose of it in a *big* armhole, and also because the coat armhole itself may increase a little through stretching.

For the **correct final size** the sleeve must be reduced at the wrist and elbow. Allow 13–15 cm more than the wrist measurement, i.e. on an average 30–32 cm at the wrist. Excessive sloping of seam is not advisable and to avoid this the 'Back line dart' from point B, taking out 3 cm at

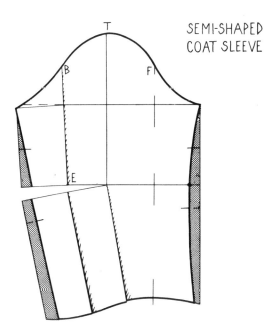

FIG. 7/xi

the wrist, should first be used (as is done for Semi-shaped and Tight sleeves). After that the seam can be sloped 2–3 cm, equally back and front, reducing wrist to 30–32 cm. Draw the final seams straight down from U (FIG. 6) and check to see that elbow width is at least 5 cm more than Elbow measurement.

The Two-piece sleeve follows the usual method given in Chapter Six, *after expanding the Straight sleeve block* to a correct *coat size*, as described above.

The Semi-shaped sleeve – FIG. 7, is also produced from the Straight sleeve by first taking out 3 cm at the wrist in a 'Back line dart' from point B – the usual *preliminary stage* in all shaped sleeve patterns.

After that, slash on the elbow level from the back edge as far as the middle, and at the wrist take out a 'dart' up the Middle line *to meet the slash*, making this 'dart' big enough to open slash 3–4 cm. The sleeve is now shaped and the wrist *partly* reduced.

For **the final width of the sleeve** allow 5–6 cm more than elbow width on the elbow level, taking out the rest equally on both edges. At the wrist, take out 1 + cm inside the front edge, and enough inside the back edge (e.g. 2–3 cm) to reduce it to the required size. This wrist can be a little tighter than in the simple Straight sleeve.

THE KIMONO COAT – FIGS. 8, 9, 10, 11, 12

A distinctive feature of Kimono coats, at least in present day styles, is the very sloping line of the sleeve. Some styles have an ordinary gusset, similar to the gussets described in Chapter Three. Many styles have high fitting or invisible gussets. But there are also some styles which have no gussets, or in which the gusset is so small that its effect is quite insignificant. These are usually the more voluminous coats, so wide in the 'armhole' part and sleeve, and so little clinging to the figure, that the effect is almost that of a cape. The arms move freely inside, as under a cape, and gussets can be omitted. In fact, some kimono styles merge into capes or cape-like coats.

The basic kimono coat given here has all the features of a simple *straight* coat, almost tubular in shape, but, in adaptations, it can of course be expanded and widened at the hem in various ways, according to style.

Outline the Kimono block *after slanting the sleeve 3 cm more*, as explained in Chapter Three. This basic block therefore now has a 10–11 cm slant. Generally, when very sloping kimono sleeves are in fashion, an *additional Kimono block* should be available to save time over this preliminary operation.

BACK – FIGS. 8 and 10

Placing the block on to a large sheet of paper, slash from SP to U and open the slash 3 cm (at SP). Secure the block in this position. Continue CB to length required.

Straighten the underarm seam, i.e. make it parallel to CB (it may be sloped later if necessary), and draw it down. Straighten also the sleeve underarm by making it parallel to the Top line.

Add 2 cm width to the side seam, measuring first at the waist and lower. Draw new side seam.

Add 2 cm width to the sleeve underarm in the same way. Draw the new sleeve underarm *to cross* the new side seam line: the point of crossing is **the new Underarm point U** which is lower than point U of the block. The more width is added to both underarm lines, the lower point U comes down. The sleeve can now have its width in the lower part (wrist) reduced to the required width: ½ wrist plus 2 cm (i.e. 17 cm for a 30 cm wrist width).

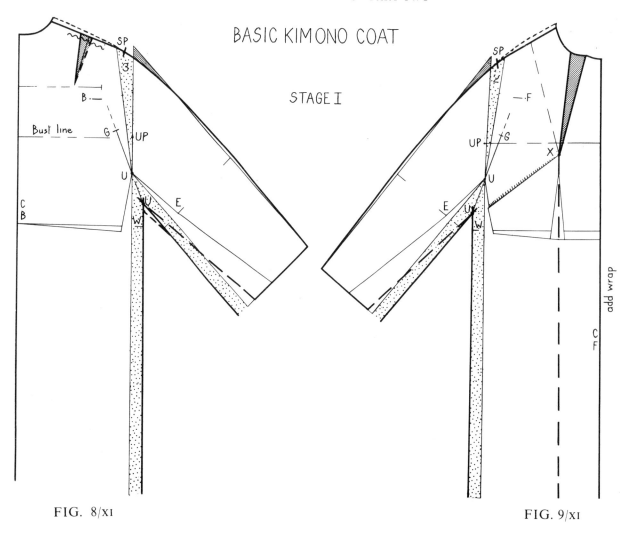

BASIC KIMONO COAT

STAGE I

FIG. 8/XI   FIG. 9/XI

Finally raise NP 1·5 cm and draw a new shoulder line to SP.

N.B. It is advisable not to add height above the actual SP (but see special note on Kimono styles, page 126).

FRONT—FIGS. 9 and 11

As in the back, slash from SP down to U but open the slash 2 cm only: the extra *back shoulder length* is added to the back shoulder blade dart or eased into the front.

Transfer the underarm Bust dart of the block into the neckline. Straighten the underarm lines, exactly as in the back and then add the extra 2 cm width to both. Reduce the wrist to ½ final width minus 2 cm.

Raise NP 1 cm and run the new shoulder line to SP.

Outline the whole pattern—back and front—to the required length (in this diagram it is a ¾ or ⅞ length = 96–100 cm down CB). The shoulder-sleeve line should be gently curved over the SP *without exaggerating the angle*: slight tightening over SP is preferable as, with a deep armhole and wide sleeve, it helps to improve the 'hang' of the coat from the shoulders.

It must be noted that in these patterns *with underarm additions*, the length between W and U, on back and front, changes and *becomes unequal*: this must be adjusted by moving point U up or down on back or front, *until the two lengths W–U match*. This may affect slightly width of back or front sleeve at the top.

To this simple, straight outline various additions can now be made for style and fit.

Some styles require more width down CB which can be added either straight down, or often more at the top and sloping in towards the hem. Sometimes CB width is added at the hem only, without increasing width at the top.

The Gusset is planned in the usual way and can be

shorter or longer down the underarm, back and front (FIGS. 10 and 11). It is seldom cut high up the Gusset line, usually 5–6 cm only, since in a coat which is so loose under the arm it is less important to regain much of the lost underarm length.

For an invisible gusset it is essential to have a style with an underarm section (see FIG. 12).

In the front add the sloping CF line, as usual. Then add a basic wrap, parallel to it (4–5 cm).

Complete the neckline and Neckline dart (slightly shortening it) and plan the gusset (if used) to match back.

The front may be slashed from the hem and connected as usual with the Dart, to add 3–5 cm to hem for better wrap.

COAT STYLE WITH UNDERARM PANEL
– FIGS. 10, 11 and 12

This is a very popular adaptation because it provides the possibility of having a high underarm or invisible gusset. The *Bust line* of the original *Bodice block* should be indicated for reference, as well as the original UP.

From point G, on the original Gusset line, measure 3 cm inwards, i.e. towards CB and CF and place this point on the UP level or just above it (point X). Connect this point with point U: this gives a *more inward slanting Gusset line* (FIGS. 10, 11).

Plan **the Underarm panel seam** by taking it from point X and drawing the line down the back and front, parallel to CB and CF (dot-dash line). The width of each section – back and front – will be between 8 and 9 cm.

The sleeve need not necessarily have a separate underarm section but, if it has one, the line will be taken from a point at the wrist, 4 cm from the underarm and going up to point X (as shown in FIG. 11 – front).

Cut away the underarm sections of back and front and *join them*, balancing them correctly at waist level, as shown in the detail of FIG. 12.

Measure on the back, from point U, the distance to UP level (dotted line, FIG. 10). Take 3 cm from this length (approx. 13–14 cm) because a coat armhole is always lower and so in any case below the original UP level. Then allow this length (10–11 cm) up the middle line

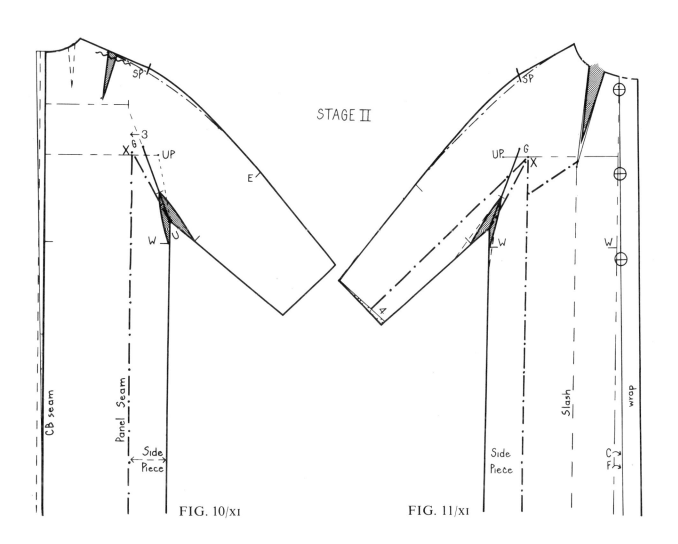

STAGE II

FIG. 10/XI   FIG. 11/XI

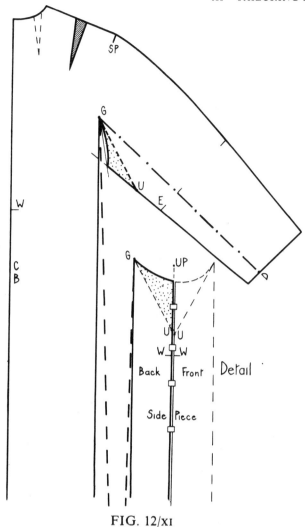

FIG. 12/XI

of the joined underarm panel (FIG. 12—detail), *to build it up to the level of an ordinary coat armhole.*

The underarm section thus represents the lower part of an ordinary armhole, while the top part of the sleeve remains a kimono sleeve.

The underarm of the sleeve part, if not cut away, can be built up 8–9 cm, in fact as far as the coat panel seam will allow, for there must be a gap of at least 2·5 cm for the turnings. *The advantage of cutting away this part is obvious:* it enables the sleeve underarm to be built up *higher,* i.e. to the normal underarm length of a coat sleeve, and provides all the necessary turnings. In this way the *total* underarm—sleeve and coat—can be as long as with a set-in-sleeve.

After cutting away the underarm section it is possible to add extra width to the hem by sloping out the panel seam a little. This is particularly important in the back where the usual 'armhole slash' is not practicable in a kimono. The underarm panel section can also be widened a little towards the hem.

SPECIAL NOTE ON KIMONO STYLES

In style adaptations it is important to distinguish between two types of kimono coat: the coat which—whether straight or with a Princess line—is shaped closer to the figure, has a neat underarm and **well outlined shoulders;** and the type of cape-like kimono which **hangs from the shoulders** without moulding them, has a deep armhole and a wide, loose underarm, often reducing itself towards the hem.

In the first case the shoulders are usually *squared,* either to suit the figure, or to follow fashion (shoulder pads). The underarm can be quite neat, as in an ordinary coat, and the UP is kept as high as various gussets will allow (see coat with side panels—FIG. 12).

In the second case the fit of the coat depends so much on the hang from the shoulder points, that it is essential not to loosen it at SP (*no addition above SP* and often further *tightening* at fitting). The 'armhole' must be kept deep and *loose,* and any tightening of sleeve at SP must be compensated under the arm and by further lowering of SP.

CAPES—FIGS. 13, 14, 15, 16

Capes for outdoor wear are best designed on a coat foundation and the Straight coat block is the most suitable for this purpose (used either in its 1st or 2nd stage).

There is a big variety of cape styles, but the most distinctive feature of a cape is not so much its style as its *outline* which varies from a very full cape, falling in folds round the figure, to a close-fitting silhouette, almost moulding the figure round the arms and shoulders and with a hem no wider than that of an ordinary Straight coat.

The basic problem in cape cutting, therefore, is to know how to achieve the correct 'line' or silhouette before introducing into the pattern the style lines or other details of the design—seams, pockets, buttons, collar, yoke, etc.

The most convenient is to make first the pattern of a **Half-circle cape,** a simple and definite pattern with a hem width of about 4 m on a full length of 100–110 cm down the CB. This can then be used as a **basic pattern** for cutting other cape styles, both those with a fuller as well as those with a tighter hemline.

THE BASIC HALF-CIRCLE CAPE—FIG. 13

On a Straight coat block close both the Bust (i.e. Neckline) dart and the shoulderblade dart and, slashing below, transfer them both into the hem. The block is now 'dartless'.

On a large sheet of paper place the coat back and front with SP's touching and with CF and CB at right angles to each other, i.e. place pattern inside a right angle, as shown in FIG. 13. Outline the coat, marking through the shoulder and the neckline, the position of the *closed darts* and the *width of the slashes* at the hem. Remove the pattern.

The gap between the NP points is the **shoulder dart of the cape**. In this case it measures about 11–12 cm. Halve it and mark *NP in the middle of the gap.*

Continue line NP–SP straight down to the hem: this is the side seam. Measure on it the CB length plus 5·6 cm for **the side length of the cape.** Passing through this last point and following hem of coat block, complete the hem. Measure it: it is about 200 cm so that the whole cape has about 4 m round the hem. This completes the **basic pattern of a cape**.

CAPE WITH REDUCED HEM WIDTH
FIGS. 13, 14, 15, 16

After cutting out the basic cape, cut away the shoulder dart.

The first reduction of hem width can be made **at the side,** but *it is limited.*

At the top measure the distance between the two UP points marked here as A and B: it is 18 cm. This is one of two controlling levels in the pattern where a check is made to prevent the cape getting too tight over the arm (the other is higher and is referred to later). The length A–B

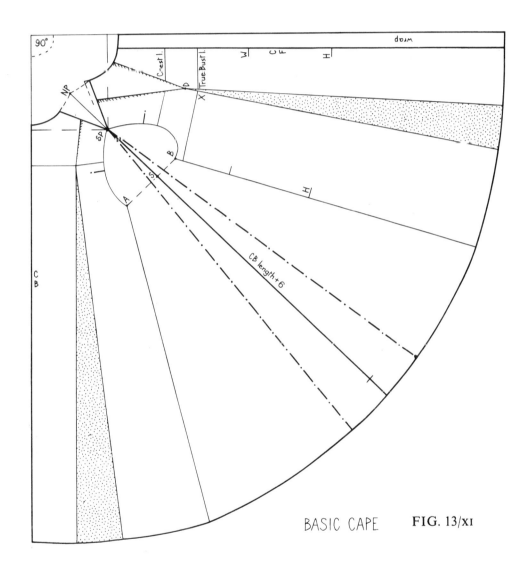

BASIC CAPE   FIG. 13/XI

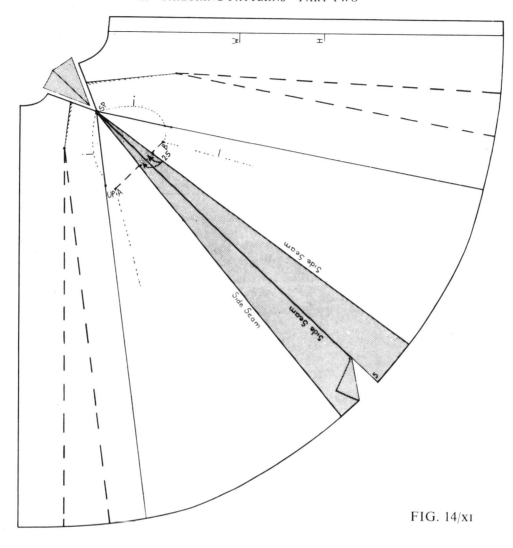

FIG. 14/XI

can be reduced until it is equal to half the width of the back between CB and UP (i.e. point A), but should not be allowed to get smaller. Since CB to UP on the coat block measures 24–25 cm (the slash addition here should be ignored) 12–13 cm must be allowed between A and B and the rest, i.e. 18 minus 13 = 5 cm, can be taken out. To do this, mark on level A–B 2·5 cm each side of the seam, and from SP draw two lines *through these points*: this will give the amount which can be lost *at the hem*, i.e. about 23–26 cm. No further reduction should be made down the side from SP, since this may make the cape too tight *above the elbows*, though some tightening here may be possible at the final stage or at a fitting.

From SP rule two straight lines—one down the back armhole and one down the front armhole—either following the armholes or passing just outside (3 cm or over). Continue these lines straight down to the hem (FIG. 14). Then from SP cut along these lines 20–23 cm down and fold out below enough width at the hem (about 10 cm) to *open each slash* 2–3 cm at SP: this lengthens and 'squares' the shoulder and at the same time loses width at the hem (FIG. 15).

Hem width is further reduced by putting both the Neckline and shoulder blade darts (now in the hem) back into their original position at the top, and folding out the corresponding hem width. This will reduce the hem

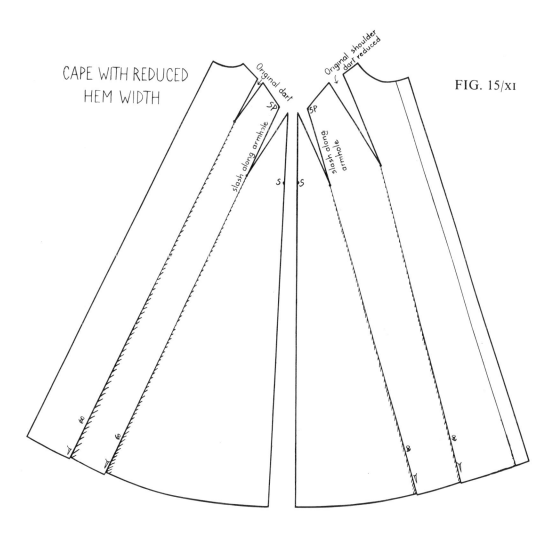

CAPE WITH REDUCED HEM WIDTH

FIG. 15/XI

width to less than $1\frac{1}{2}$ m on the half-pattern. **N.B.** If the Coat block used has no extra hem width (as in Stage 1 block), then only $\frac{2}{3}$ of the front Dart fullness should be put back into the neckline, leaving some of it in the hem for a better 'wrap', as in a coat.

CLOSE FITTING CAPE—FIG. 16

A still closer-fitting cape with a tighter hem can be produced by simply reducing the hem at the side seam, losing on each part, but in such a way as not to reduce the width at point S (the A–B level), or only a little, enough to make a good line.

The outline of such a tight cape is shown inside the Standard cape in FIG. 16. The width lost makes the hem now more or less like that of a basic coat or only slightly over.

For a final **check of the width at the top** in all closer-fitting capes, use a measurement taken on the figure on a level 12 cm down the arm and on or just below the Chest and Back lines, *with arms slightly raised*: this is usually 110–115 cm all round (on average figure). Apply it to pattern on this level (broken line, FIG. 16). It is equal approximately to $\frac{1}{2}$ Back + $\frac{1}{2}$ Chest + $\frac{1}{2}$ sleeve width.

COLLARS AND NECKLINES IN COATS AND JACKETS—FIG. 17

The shape of the neckline is not only connected with the type and style of the lapel and with the exact way it joins the collar, but also with *the way the coat is to be worn*, i.e. with the lapel always folded back (as in most classical jackets and some coats) or always buttoned up at the neck, or either way. A coat neckline, for instance, is often a 'two-way' neckline requiring a two-way collar.

The classical tailored jacket collar is a particularly tight fitting one, with a high roll at the back and sides, clinging well to the neck. It is a collar drafted specially for a very loose 'neckline'. It cannot be worn buttoned up at the neck: it is too tight for that.

This *tight* collar can be used on coats which are of the same type, i.e. worn with lapels always folded back, in fact coats which are a longer version of the classical jacket (e.g. the Chesterfield coat). The collar would be drafted as for a jacket but a little wider (stand—3–4 cm and fall—5–6 cm), and of course to fit into the bigger coat neckline.

More often, however, the coat neckline and therefore the coat collar are of the less 'set' type, so that the coat can be worn buttoned up as well as open, with a casually folded back rever. This may apply also to many jacket styles not conforming to the real classical cut, e.g. sports jackets and various modern fashion styles.

Three different coat lapels and neckline styles are shown in FIG. 17. The lowest line simply follows the neckline of the block (which is slightly raised in the CF because of the deepening of neckline by the addition at NP). It is the one which would be used with the traditional Tailored collar. The middle line is a very usual coat neckline, slightly higher on CF, to bring it up well to the neck, and worn either buttoned up high or in casual rever style. It generally goes with a looser type of collar, a 'two-way' Storm collar or Round collar, buttoned at the neck. Finally, the highest (dot-dash) line represents a more fancy but very usual coat neckline with a particularly *high rever*. It is generally unsuitable for buttoning at the neck. It must be noted that this type of neckline forms an angle at point Q and a flat-fitting Storm collar, for instance, must be tightened a little *at*

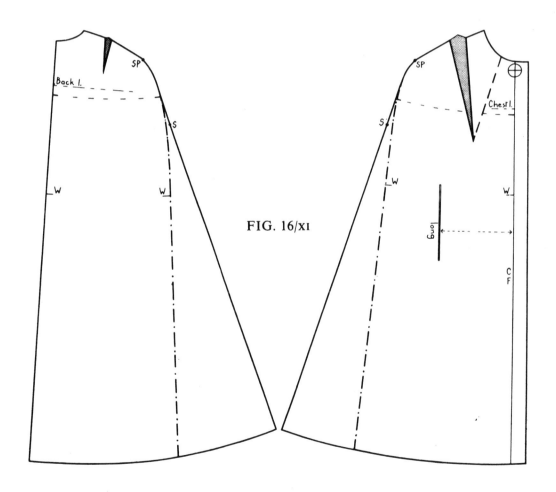

FIG. 16/XI

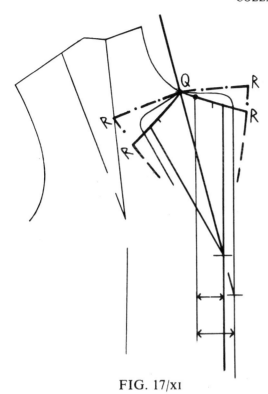

FIG. 17/xi

which is seldom more than 4 cm, often only 3 cm, and a fall which can be anything from 5 cm upwards (usually 8–10 cm or more), the difference can be quite big. Distance Y–Z will increase accordingly to provide a longer Outer edge, which is generally further lengthened (usually by half of Y–Z quantity) either *by slashing and expanding* Outer edge, by adding beyond CB or by manipulation (i.e. stretching); often by a combination of all three methods. In some cases, where manipulation is difficult because of the fabric texture (e.g. in rainwear), the *stand is cut separately* and joined by a seam to the fall which, once detached from the stand, can be widened on the Outer edge of pattern as much as necessary.

Method 1 – the classical draft of a Storm collar, 12 cm wide. FIGS. 18, 19, 20.

This follows the method given for the jacket collar in Chapter Ten (FIGS. 3/x and 4/x). On the extension of the Crease line, above point X, measure back neckline plus 1 cm and mark point Y. Pivoting from point Q (neckline intersection) sweep a circular line through Y and

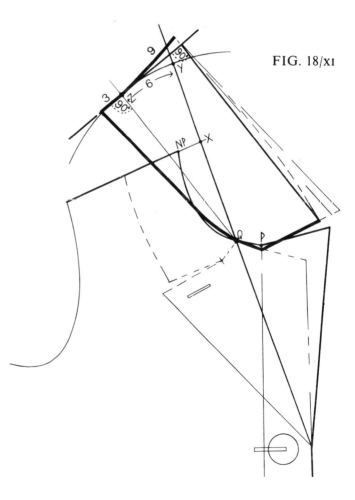

FIG. 18/xi

this point by darting its Outer edge, to prevent any fluting and to increase its front roll.

The coat collar, therefore, is generally a looser, flatter-rolling type of collar which in many cases can be worn either way and which of course can be of any width suitable for the design, while in the tight, clinging jacket collar the width limit is soon reached. Thus most coat collars are fairly wide, slightly curving bands, and the so-called **Storm collar** can be considered as **a basic pattern** for most of them. It is essentially a two-way collar but it can be made tighter to improve the set of the open lapel or looser (flatter) to ease it for the higher buttoning, all this according to the style.

THE STORM COLLAR – FIGS. 18, 19, 20, 21

Two methods of making the pattern are given here: one is based on the traditional collar drafting, resulting in a slightly tighter fit; the other is a very simple collar draft, giving a somewhat looser fit. The latter can, however, be easily adjusted to a higher roll, when necessary.

In the classical draft of the Jacket collar (Chapter Ten, FIGS. 3 and 4) the distance between points Y and Z is really based on the difference between stand and fall (increased by 0·5 cm). Since the classical jacket collar varies little in width, the Y–Z distance is more or less fixed at 2 cm, e.g. 4·5 cm fall minus 3 cm stand gives 1·5 plus 0·5, i.e. 2 cm. But in big coat collars with a stand measure on it 6 cm to find point Z (3 cm stand and 9 cm fall give a 6 cm difference). Connect Z and Q—the collar Crease line. At right angles to Z–Q from Z measure to the left 3 cm for the stand, and to the right 9 cm for the fall.

Complete the collar as usual, drawing the Sewing-on edge straight into the neckline, even slightly crossing it and finishing at point P (CF) or slightly below (for a flatter fit). Draw the collar end to go with the style of lapel (with a gap of 0·5–1 cm between them). Finally complete the Outer edge, first at right angles to CB, then according to style and width of lapel. Add 1·5 cm length *beyond* CB.

After cutting out the collar (FIG. 19) the Outer edge is usually further lengthened by two slashes in the back (4 cm apart), adding at least 2 cm more, in addition to the 1·5 cm at CB. Any further lengthening is according to style (FIG. 20).

A Coat collar witn a separate stand, i.e. **a seam** between the stand and the fall, can be cut from this pattern by detaching the stand (shaded in FIG. 19) and then lengthening the Outer edge of the fall, by slashing and opening it as much as necessary, without affecting the

length and fit of the stand. Stand and fall are then joined by a seam.

Method 2—The simple Storm collar draft—FIG. 21
The Storm collar can also be drafted as shown in FIG. 21. The diagram is self-explanatory. The method, though simple is quite satisfactory and has been much used for a big variety of coat patterns.

The collar works out less tight than the one produced by the classical method (Method 1). It is flatter-rolling, particularly in the front part where it must be tightened a little by darting (1–2 cm) from the Outer edge, as indicated in the diagram.

It will be easily understood that this collar could also be produced by the standard method of cutting collars. See, for example, the flatter-fitting jacket collars in Chapter Ten (FIGS. 6/x, 7/x and 8/x), the second style of which (B—8/x) is very similar to it in shape. However, the simple draft (Method 2) has always been found a most convenient method for obtaining an accurate and easily adaptable pattern for what can be considered as the basic type of collar in coats.

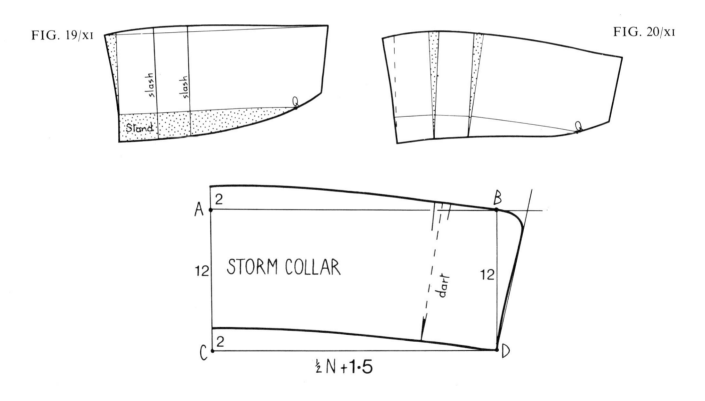

FIG. 19/XI

FIG. 20/XI

FIG. 21/XI

SPORTSWEAR PATTERNS
Trousers, shorts, divided skirts

All the main block patterns – bodice, skirt and sleeve – are used for sportswear. The pattern of trousers is an important addition to these blocks.

Although trousers or slacks are now worn both for work and leisure – in fact for almost any occasion requiring either a practical or high fashion garment – they are, nevertheless, an important *basic pattern* from which garments used more specifically for sport are produced (e.g. shorts). This is therefore an important pattern in this chapter, in which only a selection of sportswear styles and adaptations are given.

BASIC PATTERN OF TROUSERS
FIGS. 1, 2, 3, 4, 5

Measurements

Hips – 98 cm ($\frac{1}{2}$ Hips = 49)   Hips = 94 cm ($\frac{1}{2}$ Hips = 47)
Waist – 70 cm ($\frac{1}{2}$ Waist = 35)   Waist – 68 cm ($\frac{1}{2}$ Waist = 34)
Side length = 96–102 cm   Side length = 96–102 cm
Bodyrise = 28–29 cm   Bodyrise = 27–28 cm

The Bodyrise is a measurement taken from the waist down the side with the figure in a sitting position. The person measured should be sitting upright, preferably with legs crossed, and on as flat a surface as possible (a table is often quite suitable), so that the maximum height of the part of the body between the waist and the legs is registered (average 27–28–29 cm). This is an individual measurement not always necessarily related to the total height of the figure. A person of any height can, for instance, be more or less long-legged.

The pattern of the trousers is **adapted from a skirt block.*** As, however, the Standard skirt is 'shaped' to stand away slightly from the figure, this may give the trousers pattern too much length down the CB line, and it is therefore advisable *to straighten it* first in order to reduce this CB length. If *easy* fitting, one can also *reduce it in width* by losing at least 0·5 cm down CF/CB (see Tight fitting Trousers and Fig. 6).

PREPARATORY STAGE

The method for straightening the Standard skirt is basically the same as for obtaining any straighter skirt pattern, i.e. by darting it from the hem up (see D.P.D.–Ch. XI, Fig. 4).

Outline a Standard skirt to Knee line level only. Draw a straight line at right angles to CF exactly on Hip level

* When a skirt block is not available, a simple draft, given in Chapter XIV (p. 171), can be used instead (FIG. 19/XIV).

(or do this by folding pattern, as shown in Fig. 1). Though the two lines – the curved and the straight (or creased) coincide at or near the CF, there is a definite gap between them on the CB. In the trousers pattern this represents the 'seat angle'. In a Standard skirt this angle is usually too big for the small or average figure which is fairly flat in the back, and so needs reducing to obtain *less slope* and *less length* on the CB of the trousers.

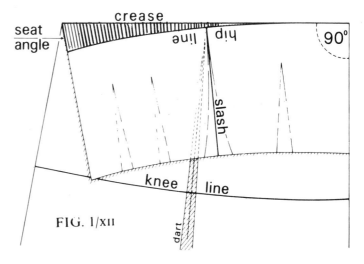

FIG. 1/XII

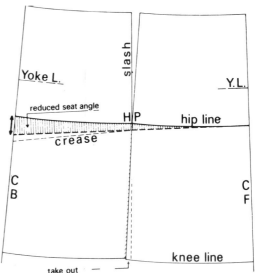

FIG. 2/XII

Cut from the waist down the centre side seam of the skirt to just below the Hip level, and from the lower edge (Knee line level) take out a 'dart' 1·5–2 cm wide, up to the end of the slash which will open at the waist. This *straightens* the skirt and on the CB *reduces the angle* between the two lines, approximately from 5 to 4 or even 3 cm. **N.B.** Since now the former *creased* line breaks halfway, to re-establish beyond the break the straight line from CF a *new straight Hip line has to be drawn higher* (Fig. 2). The size of the 'dart' from the hem may have to be varied slightly, according to size of pattern, to achieve the same (4 or 3 cm – as desired) angle on the CB (3 cm for smaller and flatter figures).

METHOD OF ADAPTATION TO TROUSERS

Place the *straightened* skirt on a large sheet of paper 10–12 cm, according to Hip size, from the right hand edge of the paper and parallel to it, and outline it down to 12–15 cm below the Hip line (Fig. 3). After outlining, *trace through* the curved Hip line, and indicate the beginning of the Yoke lines on CF and CB edges. On removing the skirt pattern, mark on the Hip level the middle point HP exactly half-way between CF and CB; then, between the waist and Hip level (half-way), draw an additional curved line parallel to the other curved lines: **the High Yoke line,** on which a corresponding measurement, taken on the figure, can be checked when the pattern is completed.

Measure from point O (waist) down the CF line **the depth of the crutch** for which the Bodyrise measurement is used – in this case 28 cm for Hips 98 (27 cm for Hips 94). Mark point X – the crutch point.

At X square a line to CF, taking it a few centimetres to the right, beyond the CF. On this line measure from $X - \frac{1}{10}$ of Hips minus 5 cm. This will give, for H 98, 9·8 minus 5 = 4·8, i.e. 5 cm (for H 94 = 4·5 cm, and with 4 cm as a *minimum* for all sizes). Mark point F – **the front Fork point.**

Placing a metre stick on this short line, extend it back through the 'skirt' beyond the CB. This is the **Basic line** of the trousers pattern, which must be *absolutely at right angles* to CF.

Along the Basic line measure to the left from point F $\frac{3}{4}$ Hip measurement* minus 5 cm (or minus 4 cm for easier fit or in large sizes), and mark the back Fork point B. For 98 Hips this will be $\frac{3}{4}$ of 98 = 73 minus 5 = 68 cm (for 94 Hips = 70 – 5 = 65 cm). This proportion is not constant and it is varied to suit different figures and style requirements, using in some cases minus 6 (tight), but in others only minus 2 or 3 (looser fit). This is an average for a *fairly close fitting* block pattern of trousers.

Placing the set square with one side to the Basic line, so that the other passes exactly through the midway point HP on the Hip line above, draw **the Side seam** upwards to the waist (point S), and then continue the line *down* to the full length of the trousers (Fig. 3).

* See Table p. 104.

Measure the side length (96–102 cm, or as required) from point S down, and on this level rule a horizontal line *parallel to the Basic line*, for the lower edge of the pattern – **the Bottom line** (BL), drawing it also right across. Here the lower edge of the trousers will be worked out.

Measure the distance between the Basic line and the Bottom line, *halve it*, and 5 cm higher draw **the Knee line** (KL), again right across and parallel to Basic line.

This completes the various construction lines of the pattern, the details of which can now be drawn in.

Draw the **front Fork line** (CF seam) curving into the CF under the Yoke level. In the back **drop point B** 1·5 cm below the Basic line, and starting from here draw the **back Fork line** (CB seam), at first almost horizontal, then curving into the CB of skirt, as shown in Fig. 4.

For the Crease lines (or balance lines) which are at right angles to the Basic line, *divide in half* the Basic line *between point F and the Side seam*, and from this point, marked 'm', drop a perpendicular on to the Bottom line for the **front Crease line**. Measure exactly *the same distance* beyond the side seam to find point 'n', from which the **back Crease line** is drawn parallel to the other line. The remaining part of the Basic line, beyond point 'n', is usually a little wider.

Crease lines are used for getting a correct balance when planning the leg seams, placing the pattern correctly on

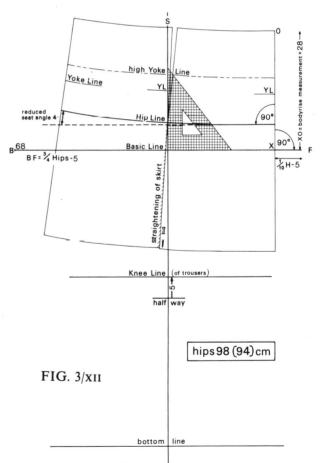

FIG. 3/XII

hips 98 (94) cm

material (SG along the Crease lines) and pressing the creases of the trousers (folding).

On Knee line level measure the Knee width, adding to the basic knee measurement, as required by the style. The most usual width for the block is 6–8 cm more than tight knee, i.e. 44–46 cm in smaller and medium sizes. A quarter of this, i.e. 11–11·5 cm, is measured *both ways* from the two Crease lines.

The Bottom width is entirely a matter of style and fashion, and can be anything from a very close fit (e.g. in trews or 'drainpipes' 2–3 cm more than ankle measurement), to the more usual 44–46 cm for straight slacks and up to 60 cm and more for the 'bell-bottom' styles.

Through all these points, marked at Knee and Bottom level, draw the **Inner and Outer leg seams,** from F and *lowered* B points, curving them (1–1·5 cm) above the knee as shown in Fig. 4. The inner back leg seam is slightly stretched at the top between B and K *to match* the front between F and K.

At the waist reduce the width to Waist measurement plus 2 cm. In this example of a 70 cm Waist it will be 72 cm, i.e. 36 cm on the half-pattern (for Waist 68 − 35 cm).

The **total Waist Reduction** (WR) is generally distributed more or less **equally between back, front and side** waist, thus keeping all the darts rather small and short, and running them off to nothing on the Yoke level or a little above. This depends on the shape of the hips.

Some width is taken out on the CB (1–1·5 cm) and − shape of figure permitting − on CF (1 cm).

Darts: in the back draw (at least on the block) two 2 cm darts, their guide lines parallel to CB, the first 8–9 cm from CB, the second usually 8 cm farther (but not too near to side seam). In the front use a 2 cm dart or a 3 cm pleat (more suitable for some figures or styles), in line with the front Crease line, and a second 2 cm dart half-way between the first and the side. Often the outer darts (particularly the front) must be made shorter to fit over the curves (e.g. high hip bone) of the figure. If preferred, one can have only *one dart*—back and front—and these single darts would be bigger. One can also replace the basic dart arrangement by yokes, front only or both back and front; or use an elastic in the back.

The remaining width is reduced in the side seam. The **Side dart** in the seam is generally planned in such a way that, after taking out all the darts (including CB and, if used, CF reduction), the back and front waists each measure approximately a quarter of the total waist width required (in this case 18 cm), unless observation of shape of figure at the fitting shows that a different distribution would be an advantage and would give a better run to the side seam at the top. This means that the Side dart will usually not be equidistant from the side seam, but generally more *curved towards the front.* The two lines meet near or below the Yoke level.

The **Outer leg seam** can now be completed from the top, running smoothly into the leg seam below.

The waistline is usually lowered 1 cm on the CF, provided this is suitable for the figure.

On completing the pattern, check the **total crutch length** (FIG. 5), measuring the CF and CB seams from waist down to points B and F and, if possible, compare this with a 'checking' measurement taken on the figure between the legs (not too tightly): if the difference is more than 3–4 cm, either way, it may be advisable to adjust the pattern by lengthening or shortening the CB seam (seat angle), or taking a deeper or less deep crutch level from the waist.

Finally check the **width on the High yoke line** and compare with a measurement taken on the figure, 10–12 cm below the waist. In some cases it may be too tight and darts will then have to be shortened or even let out.

Sometimes the waist is lowered 5–6 cm for a **Hipster style** effect. On some figures, catching tightly on the hip bone, this may prevent 'slipping' down from the waist.

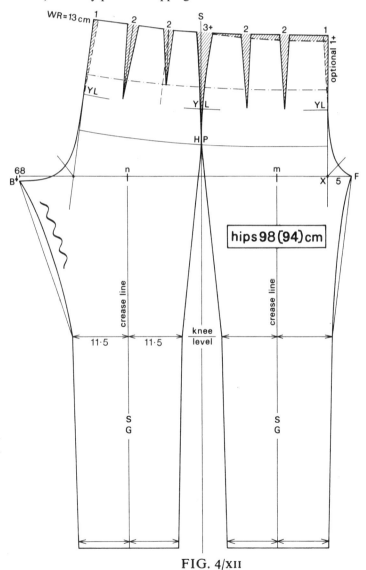

FIG. 4/XII

total crutch length

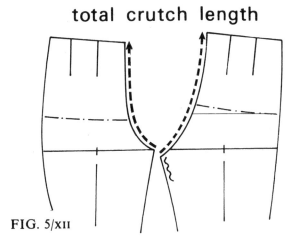

FIG. 5/XII

SOME IMPORTANT POINTS OF FIT OF THE BASIC PATTERN

The basic pattern of trousers, as given above, will not necessarily fit every *shape* of figure or be suitable for all *styles*. It is therefore important to understand its construction, in order to be able to control and, if possible, to adjust it correctly.

Special note must be made of the following features of the draft: (a) the *difference* in length between CB and CF seams; (b) the seat angle and how to adjust it; (c) the depth of crutch (Bodyrise) and its adjustment; (d) the Basic line B–F and its change in length; (e) the tightness on and *above* the Hip level.

All these points may have to be considered both in *style* adaptations and fitting, as they vary according to *shape* of figure, conditions of wear (movement), style and fashion.

For example, whatever the total crutch length, it may have to be *divided differently* between back and front, giving proportionately more length to back seam for figures with more prominent seat, or in tight fitting styles, and dividing more evenly for the flat figure, or in looser styles. Changing seat angle is one way of dealing with this problem.

The same applies to depth of crutch, corrected from the waist, or by a tuck across pattern at hip level: the closer the fit, the shorter it will usually be; while for styles hanging loosely between the legs, and wider trouser styles generally, crutch depth may have to be increased in order to keep CB and CF crutch length more evenly divided (e.g. culotte).

The Basic line B–F changes in length, often according to requirements: in sportswear, e.g. in skiing trousers, more B–F length may be needed to provide for a good stride. In general, a longer B–F means greater ease in movement.

Finally, it is also advisable to consider at an early stage the *tightness of fit in the upper part*, above the Basic line, in preference to fitting adjustments later (see Tight Fitting trousers, Fig. 6 and details).

TIGHT FITTING TROUSERS—FIG. 6

For a closer fit of trousers, particularly on and above the hips, the **skirt block should be made tighter** by losing, i.e. cutting away or folding back (see detail) equally down CF and CB of skirt block sufficient to make the width on the Hip line equal to $\frac{1}{2}$ Hips $+ 1$ cm. The middle HP must remain in its central position.

The adaptation follows the general method of the basic trouser pattern, but the Basic line B–F can be made $\frac{3}{4}$ H minus 6 cm (occasionally minus 7 cm), and the CF and CB seams are well hollowed out (preferably after fitting). The tighter proportions will be used mainly in small and medium sizes, on flatter figures, or when using stretch fabrics. In large sizes, everything depends on *shape* of figure.

The tighter fitting top can be used for **a variety of styles,** both tight and easy fitting, below the Basic line, i.e. the leg part for straight slacks or trousers, for instance, may be continued in the usual way, as described for the basic pattern.

If, however, a close fit is required for the leg part as well—as for trews, 'drainpipes' or whatever they may be known as—then some **additional measurements** must be taken **for a tight leg fit.**

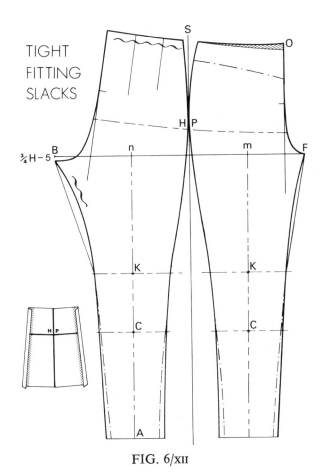

FIG. 6/XII

Knee measurement – tightly, but with knee flexed.

Calf measurement, 12–15 cm lower, over widest part.

Ankle measurement – just above instep, over the bone.

Reduction of leg width may be considerable and should be measured outwards from the middle, i.e. the Crease lines, equally in both directions. (N.B. Crease lines in some cases are brought a little closer together.)

The Knee width is made equal to measurement + 3 cm, e.g. 39 + 3 = 42 cm: ¼ of this (10·5) is measured outwards from point K marked on the Crease line. The Calf width is the tight measurement + 3 cm, divided into four, e.g. 33 + 3 = 36 cm, giving 9 cm to be measured in the same way. Finally the ankle width is the measurement increased by 3–5–7 cm, according to style (some tight slacks widen towards the hem). A very tight ankle requires a placket, or the use of stretch fabric.

SHORTS – FIG. 7

This is the simplest adaptation, since tailored shorts, as distinct from skirt-shorts (given lower), are merely the top of the trousers pattern. However, except when the fit is to be tight and clinging to the back of the leg (usually the lower edge of shorts is *loose*), it is advisable to reduce the seat angle by 1–2 cm, to correct a possible 'baggy' fit in the back (FIG. 7).

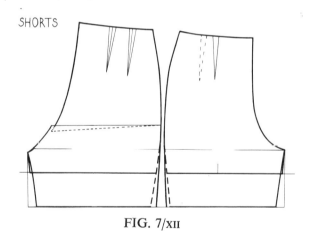

SHORTS

FIG. 7/XII

They may be **quite short,** just 5–8 cm below the Basic line. These are a popular style for sportswear, with a plain hem or with a 'turn-up' or cuff, and they are usually fairly loose at the lower edge.

The **longer variety,** known as Bermuda shorts, may be 15–20 cm below the Basic line and, according to the style, either quite loose (reduce seat angle), or close fitting in the lower part. For actual details of finish, i.e. waist, placket, etc., style and fashion are followed.

SKIRT-SHORTS – FIGS. 8 and 9

This is a different type of shorts which can be worn either separately or be part of a dress (e.g. a tennis dress).

The pattern follows the method given in Chapter Nine for the 'skirt-knicker' block. It is a very short skirt with a crutch part added to it, and cut either on the Standard skirt block (as in this example), or on the Quarter-circle pattern, as in Plate 41, Chapter Fourteen.

After outlining the skirt block to a length of 40–45 cm, mark down the CF and CB the depth of the crutch using **Bodyrise measurement plus** 3 (4) cm. This should be a fairly loose crutch fit as it is not advisable to tighten it too much because it may pull in the shorts between the legs and prevent them hanging away from the figure, like a skirt.

On this crutch level (both on CF and CB) draw lines at *right angles* to CF and CB, and measure from X in the front $\frac{1}{10}$ H minus 2 cm and in the back $\frac{1}{10}$ H plus 2 cm. The back is thus 4 cm wider than the front.

Draw the front and back seams as shown in Fig. 8. The waist may be raised slightly (1 cm) in the back: this is not essential, but is generally done when joining shorts to a bodice for a complete dress (it may of course be a fitting adjustment).

The skirt-shorts are seldom used plain and generally have pleats. The most usual is to have an inverted CF and CB pleat. In some styles there are also additional pleats, e.g. through the middle of the front (FIG. 9) and sometimes also at the sides. First these crutch parts are cut away, and then the pattern is cut where necessary to introduce the pleats. After adding the pleats, the crutch parts are joined again, taking care to place them on the correct level: this is ensured as usual, by folding out all the pleats, before joining the various pieces into a complete pattern. There is generally a seam at the side, as well as on the CB and CF.

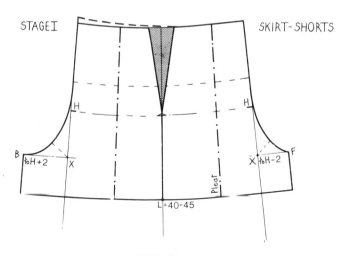

STAGE I · SKIRT-SHORTS

FIG. 8/XII

To improve *the hang in the back*, i.e. to make it stand away more from the figure, it is very usual to slash the pattern from the hem up to 5 cm above Hip level, and to open it 3–4 cm at the hem, while reducing (darting out) some of the waist width at the top, *above* the slash (FIG. 9).

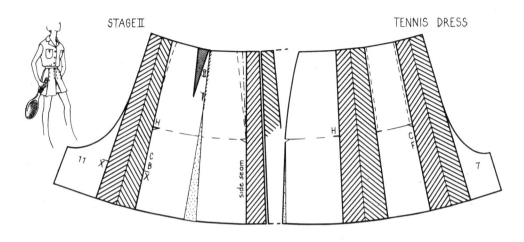

FIG. 9/XII

DIVIDED SKIRT (Culotte) – FIGS. 10 and 11

This pattern is similar to the skirt-shorts (FIGS. 8 and 9) and is really a longer version of it. It is, in fact, a *full-length* skirt with a crutch part, with CF, CB and side seams, and usually with inverted pleats on CB and CF.

The width of the skirt (the Standard skirt block) is slightly increased in such a way that 3 cm are added down CF and CB *at the hem only* and nothing at the waist, so that the CF and CB slope out more, adding width on the hips, but mainly at the hem: Point X is moved further out.

The crutch part is thus added to a new CF and CB, on a *lower* level, i.e. 4 (5) cm *below Bodyrise* measurement, as the skirt must not be allowed to pull in between the legs.

For the crutch part, add from the *new* point X (4 cm below Bodyrise) $\frac{1}{10}$ H for the front and $\frac{1}{10}$ H + 5 or 6 cm for the back, i.e. for H 98 = 10 cm for F, and 15–16 cm for B. This addition is bigger than for shorts to enable a *longer* skirt to hang away more from the figure and to retain its 'skirt silhouette'. If, however, considered excessive, e.g. in a *shorter* skirt, then it can be reduced as for shorts. Complete the crutch parts down to the full length, either making them the same width right through or slightly wider at the hem (broken line).

After cutting away the crutch part (Fig. 11), pleats are added, as usual, before the crutch parts are rejoined to CF and CB, exactly as in the pattern of shorts, and always after first folding out the pleats to ensure that all parts come together correctly.

SOME GENERAL REMARKS ON SPORTSWEAR

All blocks, in one form or another, are used for sports garments, skirts, slacks and knicker patterns being probably the more important ones. A few general observations and suggestions on the use of other blocks – Bodice, Sleeve, etc. – may be helpful.

Blouses, bodices and jackets, with some exceptions mentioned lower, must generally have plenty of ease for freedom of movement. To be of real benefit, however, this ease must be secured in a correct position on the figure, i.e. over the chest and *particularly the back*, where it is most needed, for nothing constricts movement of arms so much as an insufficiently loose back. This extra width or fullness must not be allowed to hang off the shoulders (as a dropping armhole) or to stand away too much from the figure under the arms: underarm addition increases width but does not necessarily provide the comfortable *all-over ease* required for a sports garment. Width addition must therefore be planned in such a way that it comes where it is most needed.

The popularity in sportswear designing of **yokes,** with fullness eased into them, and of **pleats** (e.g. CB inverted pleat in blouse or jacket), is due mainly to the fact that they are a means of providing and *keeping* fullness exactly where required, and not just under the arm (though some addition is made here in most cases). Yokes and pleats give ease in the right place without interfering with the movement of the arms, as too much shoulder length and unnecessary underarm width often do.

The close fitting bodice may also be quite suitable and is even traditional for some sports, such as skating and particularly swimming. The close fit in these cases is not restricting so long as the legs and arms can move freely. This freedom of movement is ensured either by a complete absence of sleeves, or by a long underarm and a sleeve fitted *high on the shoulder* (as is also usual for ballet dresses). Finally, not only tight bodices but even brassiere patterns are sometimes used for some sports garments (see Plate 38 over the page).

The sleeve often presents a special problem. A deep crown restricts movement and for sportswear, or for any other *comfortable* wear, when it is important to be able to move arms freely, sleeves should have a long underarm and consequently a shallower crown. For method of *flattening* the crown (e.g. in shirts) see Plate 38 and FIG. 12 in Chapter Thirteen.

Sometimes sleeves have a special gusset extension on the underarm seam to compensate for lowering of armhole or simply to provide more length for high arm swinging (e.g. in golf jackets).

The Kimono, in spite of its appearance of easy fit, is not always the best cut for sportswear because of its movement-restricting fit under the arm. Only short-sleeved kimono patterns with a small sleeve *slant*, are suitable for sportwear. The 'sleeve' part of the kimono must be very short, preferably 'cap sleeve' type, and even then a gusset often has to be used for complete freedom of arm movement (gussets, however, do not always stand up well to hard wear).

The same does not necessarily apply to the **Raglan sleeve** which, provided it is cut reasonably high under the arm, can be quite comfortable.

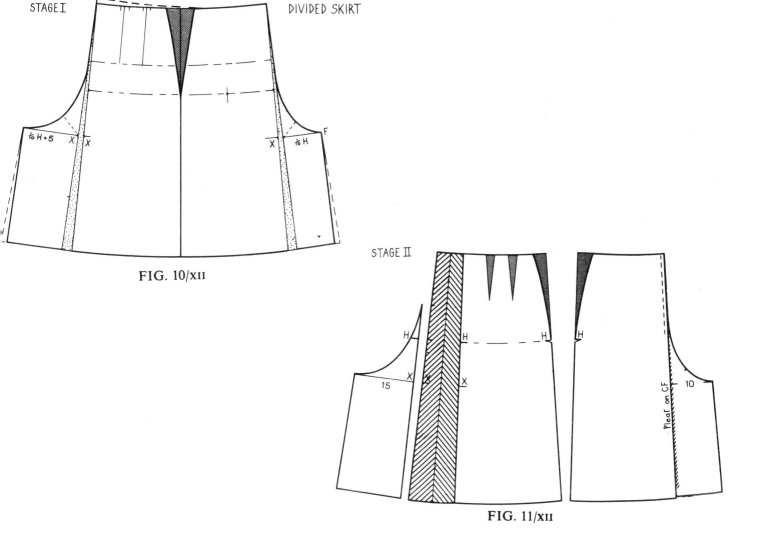

FIG. 10/xii

FIG. 11/xii

PLATE 38—A BIKINI SWIM SUIT AND PLAY SHIRT

Contributed by Edna Green, F.C.I.

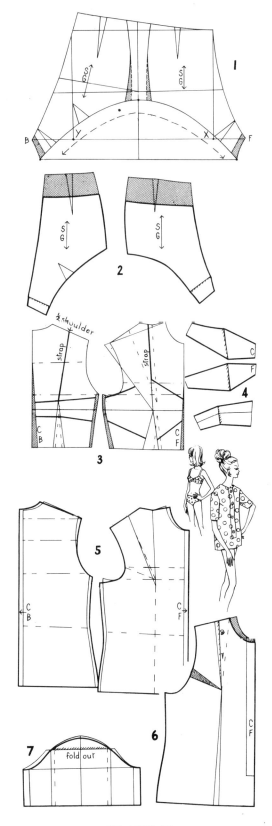

THE SWIM SUIT

The swim suit consists of short close fitting trunks and a 'bra'.
Trunks—FIGS. 1 and 2.
Use either the trunks given on page 99 (Fig. 12) or follow FIGS. 1 and 2 on this page which are self-explanatory. This adaptation here is of a *Standard knicker block* and consists mainly of size reduction, losing *width* through the middle, length down the side to 25 cm, shortening crutch by 3 cm at B and a F, and tightening the *lower* edge by darting *to fit tightly* round the thigh (average about 60 cm). Shorten also from the waist down by 8–12 cm for 'hipster' style fit.

Bikini Top or Bra—FIGS. 3 and 4

Build pattern as for any type of Bra, planning it equally **above and below the True Bust line.**

For **the Back** use inner side seam and Sl. CB. To tighten the fit take 1·5 cm off the side seam and double the Waist dart before folding it out. Plan pattern 3 cm above and 3 cm below at CB and near the Waist dart, and 4 cm above and below at side seam.

For **the Front** use also inner side seam and Sl. CF and take 1·5 cm off at the side. **Double both Darts** and plan pattern 4 cm above and below on CF, and on side seam, and 10 cm on the level of the darts.

After cutting out the outline of the Bra, cut along the Basic line and fold out both darts to their full depth, which gives a *horizontal seam*. The top and lower edges can be curved instead of being left pointed.

THE PLAY SHIRT—FIGS. 5, 6, 7

With 7–8 cm extra width it is very loose and also *flat fitting* (no bust shaping). The bust *dart must therefore be lost.*

Back: Add 1·5 cm down CB, moving the extra neck width into the shoulder. Add another 1 cm length at the armhole, thus making shoulder 2·5 cm longer. Add 0·5 cm on side seam and lower armhole 1 cm. Cut out neckline 2 cm (for style).

Front: Add 1 cm down CF and 0·5 cm at side seam, as in the back. Lower armhole 1 cm to match back. Cut out neckline 2 cm.

Shorten Bust dart to Bust line level. Make a slash to this point from the armhole (on Chest level), fold out enough of the dart to open slash 2 cm. Keep 1·5 cm of the Bust dart *to lengthen shoulder* and transfer the rest into the hemline.

As a result of all this the armhole increases by 4 cm, so that the sleeve must be widened 2 cm each side of the seam, with B and F moved 1 cm out. To allow for longer shoulder *flatten the crown* by a 1+ cm tuck taken right across, and set the sleeve quite flat into the armhole (no ease).

PLATE 38

CHILDREN'S PATTERNS
The blocks

Patterns for children are cut very much as patterns for adults and the *basic methods* of style and pattern adaptation are the same. Adding fullness for gathers, pleats, tucks or smocking, outlining yokes or panels, flaring skirts and flounces or obtaining a correct set of a collar — all this is done by following the general principles and methods of pattern designing.

Children's styles are certainly simpler and less varied, and many of the difficulties met with in pattern cutting for adults never arise. Thus one seldom has to deal with difficult textures of material, with problems of grain, with elaborate effects of draping or dart shaping. Fabrics used for children are mostly strong and hard-wearing. The fit of the clothes is easy, so that dart shaping is of little importance. Details of design are not complicated. Styles are more standardized and functional and do not follow closely every change of fashion. Even when the influence of fashion does show over a certain period, the change is gradual and little noticeable under ordinary working conditions. All this makes pattern designing for children very much simpler.

Nevertheless, there are some **special problems in the production of children's clothing** which affect considerably the planning and cutting of the patterns and these problems must be examined and understood as they are of great importance for good practical results.

The biggest problem is the constant **change in size and shape** of a growing child's figure, and the necessity of providing for this. It affects the whole approach to children's pattern cutting by making *size* and *proportions* so much more important than style interpretation. There is also the difficulty of fitting children or sometimes even of getting reliable measurements. Finally, there exist a number of **practial limitations** imposed by requirements of comfort, hard wear and frequent laundering: these limitations can seldom be ignored. Pattern cutting for children is very much influenced by all these considerations.

The main problem — that of changing size and fit — can be dealt with by making **averages sizes and proportions** the foundation of all pattern cutting for children. It is of great help in this work to understand and always to bear in mind how an average child grows and develops, and a Table of Average sizes for *various age groups* is indispensable (see Table at the end of the chapter).

But since a block for one particular age, e.g. a five-year-old, cannot show the *changes* which occur as a child grows, it is advisable to produce **a range of blocks** to represent a growing child through several stages, between two and thirteen years. It gives a better picture of the problems one has to deal with. Four bodice blocks are therefore given here, and the sizes in between can be obtained by simple grading.

Where individual measurements are easily available, they should be used mainly to correct the relevant proportions of the nearest average block (e.g. longer waist, wider back, etc.). Of course the whole pattern can be drafted to individual measurements, if preferred. But with children, far more than with adults, it is often quicker and easier to adapt an average block.

The four standard sizes drafted are:

Size 1 for an average child of 3 (small size).
Size 2 for an average child of 6 (small-medium size).
Size 3 for an average child of 9 (medium size).
Size 4 for an average child of 12 (big size).

N.B. An 'Infant size' — age 18 months — can also be drafted or obtained by *grading down* from the small size.

Size 1, for an average three-year-old, would also fit a *big* child of two or a *small* child of four. To fit an *average* child of four or two the pattern must be *graded up or down*. The same applies to the other sizes, so that the whole range from two to thirteen can be covered by the four standard blocks.

The following general observations may be helpful:

(*a*) It is not easy to measure children and it is better to get a few good measurements rather than many inaccurate ones, working out further pattern details by average proportions: e.g. skirt equal to $1\frac{1}{4}$ or $1\frac{1}{2}$ bodice length, armhole equal to $\frac{1}{2}$ Breast measurement, etc.

(*b*) Since children grow all the time, an easy fit is essential and, with a few exceptions children's garments must not be cut to fit tightly.

(*c*) An easy fit, however, must not be made an excuse for ill-shaped garments. The clothes must have a good *cut* and line, not dependent on shaping them to the figure, e.g. the waist must be in the right place, the hem of correct fullness, the armhole must not slip down the arm, etc.

(*d*) Comfort in wear is important and nothing in the *design* must hamper or restrict a child's movements.

(*e*) As they grow, children change in shape as well as in size. Allowance must be made for these changes also.

MEASUREMENTS

The following measurements are **essential** and should be taken in every case:

> Length to Waist (LW down CB).
> Breast or Bust measurement (B).

Other **useful measurements** which help to reduce fitting are:

> Back width.
> Waist (also Hips in bigger sizes).
> Total length of garment (dress, skirt, etc.).
> Sleeve length.

Additional measurements may be taken as required by style.

The essential measurements can, of course, be taken from a Table of Average Proportions for Children, or even worked out theoretically from the age, as for instance the **Length to Waist** (CB) can be taken as being equal to $\frac{1}{4}$ height of a child, and the height can be found as follows: a child of 3 is taken as being 95 cm tall, i.e. just under 100 cm. For every year up 5 cm is added, and for every year down 5 cm taken off. Thus a child of 2 is 90 cm tall, a child of 6 – 110 cm. etc.

> **N.B.** Children are actually taller now and these proportions are quite artificial. But they still work quite well for finding the LW, often better than if the correct actual height of the child is used, for a $\frac{1}{4}$ of real height may give too long a waist.

Nevertheless, although the above proportions are fairly reliable, it is *always advisable to check the basic measurements individually*: variations in size among children of the same age group are considerable. Although many clothes for children are actually bought *by age*, this is not always very reliable. Even when dealing with a big group (e.g. a class), the two basic measurements should always be checked: it may make all the difference between a reasonable fit and one which turns out to be completely wrong.

All the other measurements, however, can be worked out reasonably well from the two basic ones if it is not possible or convenient to take them individually.

Because of this reliance on **proportions derived from two basic measurements,** or even just from the age, the technique of establishing correct proportions plays a very important part in pattern designing for children.

PROPORTIONS FOR FIGURE AND PATTERN

The following figure proportions can be derived **from Length to Waist (LW):**

> Back width = LW, or slightly more.
> Chest width = LW.
> Shoulder length = $\frac{1}{3}$ of LW (or $\frac{1}{3}$ of Back/Chest).
> Length from Waist to Hips = $\frac{1}{2}$ LW.
> Length from Waist to Knee = $1\frac{1}{2}$ times LW.
> Length from Waist to ankle = $2\frac{1}{2}$ times LW.
> Length of Arm = $1\frac{1}{2}$ times LW, but more in bigger sizes.

from Breast measurement:

> Armhole = $\frac{1}{2}$ B (just over or just under).
> Neckline = $\frac{1}{5}$ B – 2, – 3, – 4, – 6 cm.
> Top Arm = $\frac{1}{3}$ of B (slightly over).
> Waist = B – 3, B – 5, B – 8 or 10, B – 12 or 15.
> Hips = B + 3, B + 5, B + 8, or 10 (always an easy measurement).

It will be noted that the above proportions are affected by a child's age and by the way a child's figure develops. Thus in big sizes extra allowance is always made for a more *rapid* increase in length of arms (legs), while a small child's arms are comparatively short and grow more slowly. The *difference* between Breast, Waist and Hip measurements increases considerably in the top age group (and continues to do so beyond it), while for a small child these measurements are more or less the same (actually so for a baby). The shoulder of a small child is square, the back straight, the chest and front well filled out and *curved*, for which allowance is made in the pattern. As the child grows, the shoulders become more sloping, the front flatter; the back becomes less straight and may even develop a curve (round shoulders).

PROPORTIONS FOR GARMENTS

The Length of a:

Dress = twice LW in smallest sizes increasing to $2\frac{1}{2}$ times LW (knee length) in big sizes. Nowadays, however, the length is usually shorter.

Skirt = LW for small sizes, increasing to $1\frac{1}{2}$ times LW in big sizes. Now usually shorter.

Nightdress = $3\frac{1}{2}$ times LW (big sizes slightly over).

Pyjama trousers = $2\frac{1}{2}$ times LW (or over).

Knickers-side length = LW or less *according to style.*

The Width of a:

Bodice (as block) = 10 cm more than B measurement. On small children this may even be a little loose.

Sports or School blouse = 12–15 cm more than B measurement.

Pyjama coat, Overall = 12–15 cm more than B measurement.

Coat, Dressing gown = 15 and up to 20 cm more than B measurement.

Skirt = minimum 8–10 cm more than hips, often looser, being mainly gathered or pleated.

Hem width = $1\frac{3}{4}$ B measurement minimum or twice B measurement and often much more. In some cases (e.g. coats) it may be slightly less.

Sleeve width = Top Arm + 5 cm or more.

Wrist width = just over half of above proportion.

It must be noted that every extra garment worn by a child adds considerably to its 'size' (more so than in the case of adults), and therefore a good allowance must be made in *outer* garments, such as coats or overalls, to accommodate the extra bulk of garments worn underneath.

BODICE BLOCK SIZE 1 and 2—FIGS. 1 and 2

SIZE 1—average child of 3 (big 2-year old or small 4-year old).

> LW = 24 cm   Breast = 56 cm

SIZE 2—average child of 6 (big 5-year old or small 7-year old).

> LW = 28 cm   Breast = 64 cm

N.B. The instructions which apply to both sizes are actually given for Size 1 with proportions for Size 2 *in brackets*.

Take a rectangle of paper equal to:

$$\tfrac{1}{2}\,\mathbf{B} + \mathbf{6\,cm} \times \mathbf{LW} + \mathbf{5\,cm}$$

or simply a *square* equal to $\tfrac{1}{2}$ B + 6 cm (i.e. 34 cm): unnecessary length can be cut away later. Rule a line parallel to the right-hand edge and 1 cm inside it: this is the CF which is sloped out later by using the extra 1 cm beyond.

BACK

Down the left-hand edge, the CB, measure 1·2 (1·5) cm from the top and mark point O (nape of neck).

From O measure down CB the LW = 24 (28) cm and draw the **Waist Line** right across the paper.

Halve distance O–LW, mark a point 2 cm *lower* (in Size 2, 2·5 lower) and draw **the Breast Line** right across.

Halve O to Breast Line for position of **Back Line**. Take it right across: on the front it will be the **Chest Line**.

N.B. The exact position of the Back line does not affect the draft: it may be placed a little higher or lower to avoid awkward fractions. Accurate paper folding, however, should make it possible to avoid any difficult calculations.

Halve O to Back Line and 1 cm above this draw the **Shoulder Line** which also goes right through to the front.

All these construction lines must be squared to CB or obtained by careful paper folding at right angles to CB.

From point O square a short line—the **Neck line**—and measure on it the **back neck width** equal to $\tfrac{1}{8}$ Breast meas. + 2 cm, taking **half** of this for the half-pattern, i.e 4·5 (5) cm. Take this point up to the top edge and mark NP. Draw **back neckline** from NP down to O.

On the Back Line measure $\tfrac{1}{4}$ Back width. This may, of course, be an *individual* measurement. By the 'proportion method' it is equal to $\tfrac{1}{2}$ LW = 12 (14) cm, but is usually increased a little (0·5–1 cm) in small sizes. Draw a vertical construction line through this point to cross the lines above and below.

On the Shoulder Line measure from CB 0·5 cm more. Mark SP and draw **the shoulder** between NP and SP, as usual.

Find middle of paper (halve the Breast Line), excluding the 1 cm beyond CF, and from here take 0·5 cm back for UP. Drop perpendicular from UP, slant underarm seam 1+ cm from it.

Guided by the vertical line draw **the Armhole**.

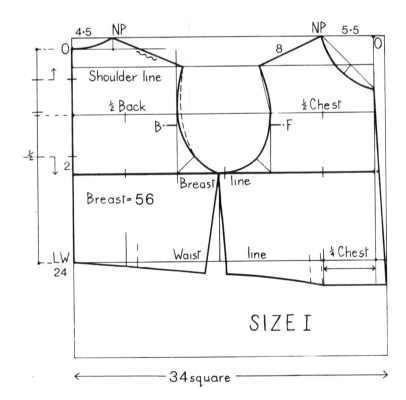

FIG. 1/XIII

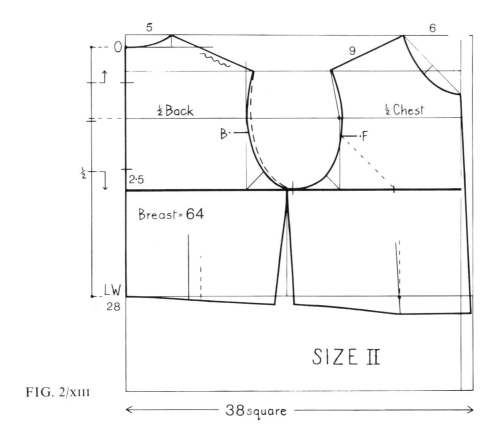

FIG. 2/XIII

← —————— 38 square —————— →

FRONT

Along the top edge, from the right, measure the **Front neck width** making it 1 cm more than in the back, i.e. 5·5 (6) cm.

Down CF measure neck depth equal to neck width. Draw the neckline with the help of the usual construction line.

Draw the shoulder from NP on to the Shoulder Line, making it equal to $\frac{1}{3}$ of LW, i.e. 8 (9) cm or $\frac{1}{3}$ of Chest.

On the Chest Line mark $\frac{1}{2}$ Chest width $= \frac{1}{2}$ LW, i.e. 12 (14) cm, and from here drop a perpendicular on to the Breast Line to guide the drawing of the armhole.

Draw underarm seam, slanting it 0·5 cm from perpendicular.

Dip the final waistline 2·5 cm on CF (2 cm in Size 2), going up to 1 cm below the basic Waist Line on the side. Then *slope out* the CF from the neckline to a point 1 cm out at the waist, and re-draw **the final CF line** as shown in the diagram. This provides more ease across the front and allows for the natural posture of a small child.

If the waist needs reducing (this would depend on the style), small darts (1–2 cm) can be used in the usual position at $\frac{1}{4}$ Back and $\frac{1}{4}$ Chest or a little further out. If the dress has no waist opening, the waist must remain loose enough to allow the child to get in easily, i.e. 10–12 cm over the Waist measurement, which is usually the width of the block, as drafted, without the darts.

N.B. The method of drafting for the two smaller sizes is the same. If, however, the Breast Line in Size 2 is placed only 2 cm below half-point, as in Size 1, the armhole may work out a little too small. It should be 2·5–3 cm below half-distance.

BODICE BLOCK SIZE 3 and 4—FIGS. 3 and 4

The general method of drafting is the same, but there are some differences in detail which must be mentioned.

The **width of the paper** is equal to $\frac{1}{2}$ Breast ($\frac{1}{2}$ Bust) $+$ 5 cm and there is no extra 1 cm for the sloping out of the CF. This is quite straight, as in a block for adults.

Point O (top of CB) should be 1·5 cm below the top edge. If preferred, this proportion can also be used in the smaller sizes (e.g. Size 2) instead of 1·2 cm.

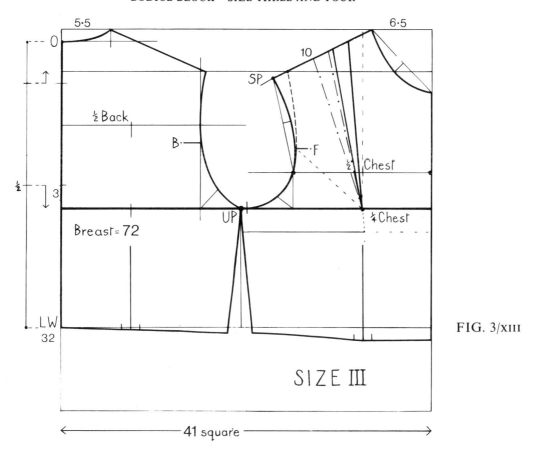

FIG. 3/XIII

The **Breast Line** (or **Bust Line** in Size 4) is placed 3 cm below the half-point between O and LW.

The **Shoulder Line** in the biggest size (Size 4) is 2 cm above half-point (or 3 cm below O, as for adults).

The **Chest Line** is not on the same level as the Back Line. It is 4 cm above the Breast (Bust) line.

The **underarm seam slants** 1·5 cm in from the perpendicular, back and front, and in Size 4 may slant in 2 cm.

A Shoulder dart is introduced by the usual method of slanting it 2 cm on the shoulder from a guide line which is parallel to CF. In Size 3 it is only 2 cm deep. In style designing it may sometimes be placed further out, in the middle of the shoulder, as for instance in most Panel styles (e.g. in coats, particularly for younger children).

In Size 3 the Dart is generally used in its *underarm position.* Sometimes it is transferred into the waist, this being *equivalent to sloping out the CF* in the smaller sizes. Sometimes it may be *omitted altogether* and the armhole is then moved in (shoulder shortened). This depends on style (e.g. some loose blouses can be dartless), as well as on the *shape* and *posture* of the child, and also on whether the child is below or above *average* size. Thus

a child of 7 may be as big in size as a child of 9 and require the Size 3 pattern, but still have the *shape* and posture of a younger child. On the other hand a small child of 10–11 may be no bigger than Size 3, but would probably have a different shape and posture from the big child of 7. Thus the same average pattern may require variation in detail, especially as regards use of dart and its position.

In Size 4 the Dart is 3 or 4 cm (according to the shape of the figure) and in style adaptations it may also be moved further out on the shoulder, i.e. slanted more (with point in the same position, at ¼ Chest width). In some cases, the depth of the Dart may be even more than 4 cm as at this stage a girl's figure sometimes develops very quickly. In the underarm position the Dart is placed 4 cm below the armhole.

The final waistline dips only 1·5 cm, as in the block for an adult figure.

Over the ages of 12–13 the usual Standard block is used according to Bust measurement, and no special proportions have to be considered, except that the LW may still be shorter than in the corresponding adult size.

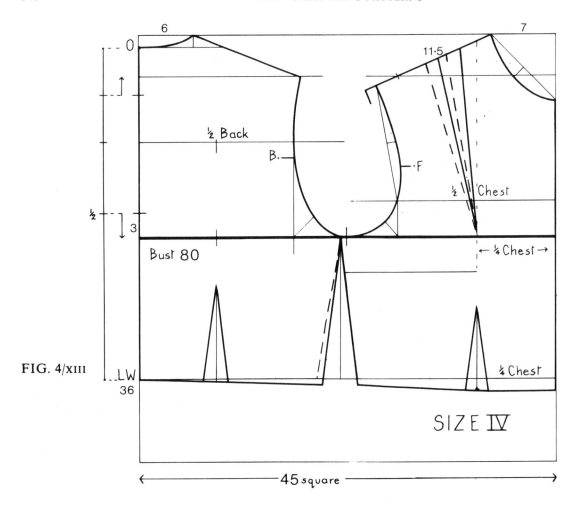

FIG. 4/XIII

SIZE IV

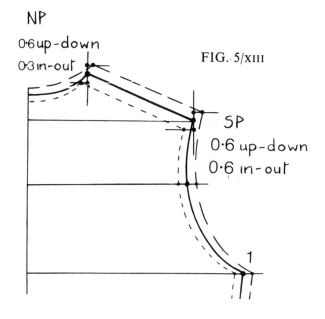

NP

0·6 up-down
0·3 in-out

FIG. 5/XIII

SP
0·6 up-down
0·6 in-out

GRADING FOR THE INTERMEDIATE SIZES—FIG. 5

Sizes which come **between the four average blocks** can be obtained by simple grading, i.e. by increasing or decreasing all the important measurements and proportions. The Back and Chest width, the Shoulder length and the height above/below the top are increased or decreased 0·5–0·6 cm (just *over* ½ cm); the length at the waist is increased by 2 cm or decreased by 1 cm (for safety); the neck-line by 0·3 cm and the underarm width at front and back UP by 1 cm.

This is only a very simple way of changing to one size above or below the sizes given in each of the four groups. For Trade grading, where one deals with a whole range of sizes, involving careful measuring, a more systematic approach must be followed. But even with this simple grading, accuracy in measuring is essential. **Short vertical and horizontal lines,** on which all the measuring is done, are drawn *at right angles* to the CB (CF) and to the Back or Chest lines (see Fig. 5).

THE SLEEVE BLOCK — FIGS. 6, 7, 8, 9

MEASUREMENTS

Length of arm = $1\frac{1}{2}$ times LW in Size 1, then 2–3–4 cm more.

Top Arm measurement = just over one-third Breast measurement.

Width of sleeve = Top Arm + 5 cm (the block minimum).

Wrist = $\frac{1}{2}$ Width of sleeve. Add to this 3–4 cm for ease (more for coats).

	Length	Top Arm	Sleeve width	Wrist width
SIZE 1	34	20	25	13 + 3–4 cm
SIZE 2	42	22	27	14 + 3–4 cm
SIZE 3	50	25	30	15 + 3–4 cm
SIZE 4	58–60	28	33	16 + 3–4 cm

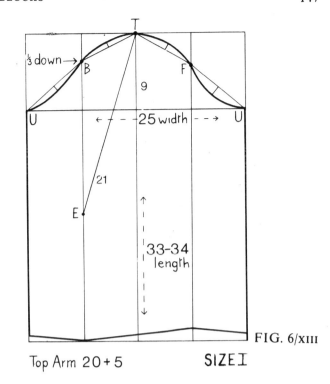

The draft of the sleeve follows the standard method for the Straight sleeve block.

Paper — a rectangle = Length by Width of sleeve.

Mark Depth of Crown (DC) making it equal to $\frac{1}{3}$ of Width of sleeve or just over, e.g. 9 cm for 25 cm width of sleeve, 10 for 27 width, etc. (FIGS. 6, 7, 8, 9).

Measuring from the top edge, on the left place point B $\frac{1}{3}$ of Crown Depth down (or a little over). Point F is marked on the Forearm extension 1 cm lower than B. The Elbow point may be found by measuring from T to E, the Top Arm measurement plus 2 cm (in smallest sizes + 1 cm).

Complete the sleeve connecting U, B, T, F, U, first by straight lines, then curving 1 cm above and below in the back, but more in the front (see FIGS. 6, 7, 8, 9).

N.B. For a deeper sleeve crown, when required, draw DC line 1 cm lower and bring points B and F 0·5 cm down. But a deeper crown and shorter underarm restrict movement and are generally acceptable for children only in tailored garments.

GRADING OF SLEEVES

This is done by making *half* of the addition or reduction through the middle and the other half, divided equally, down the sides of the pattern. The crown is slightly (0·5 cm) raised or lowered. If the whole width addition is made down the sides, the Inset points must move down by half of the addition (FIG. 8).

OTHER BASIC SLEEVE PATTERNS

The sleeve is used mainly in its simplest shape, long or short. In long sleeves, the wrist width, according to style, is either gathered into a cuff or *reduced*. The reduction, which affects also the elbow width, is made along the seam, and for a closer fit also by darting at the wrist.

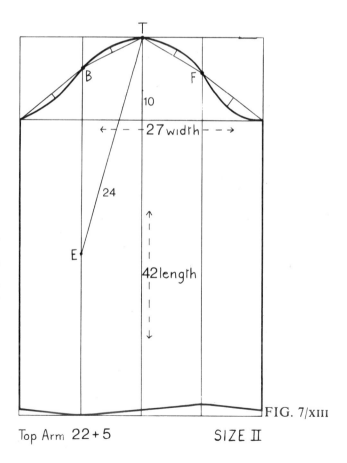

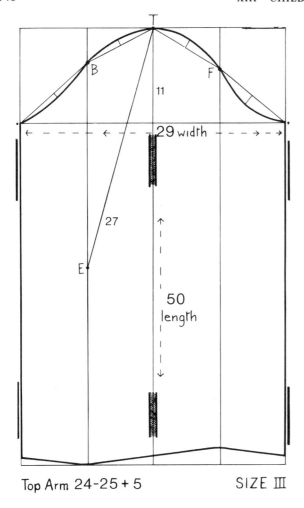

Top Arm 24-25 + 5   SIZE III

FIG. 8/XIII

though more often than not *extra width* is added through the middle or just at the wrist. Lose length equal to the cuff depth on the Forearm, less on the Back line.

Puff sleeve

This is a very popular style, particularly in small sizes. Make the pattern 4–5 cm long on the underarm, cut into 6 sections right through or, according to style, through the lower edge only, and spread the sections to add extra width, allowing half as much again on the lower edge, e.g. 12–14 cm. At the top, when it is also gathered, allow less—8–9 cm. To make the final pattern come together correctly, fold out additions as pleats in the usual way.

Two-piece sleeve

This follows the usual method. Example in Chapter Fourteen, where an example of a **Raglan sleeve** is also given.

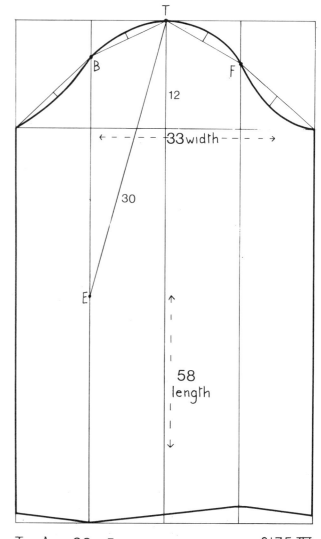

Top Arm 28 + 5   SIZE IV

FIG. 9/XIII

Closer-fitting sleeve — FIG. 10

For a 'reduced width sleeve' measure on Elbow level 1–2 cm inside the seam (on both edges) and through these points rule straight lines from U down to the wrist. Width is lost both at elbow and wrist.

Semi-shaped sleeve — FIG. 11

The Semi-shaped sleeve is used in jackets and coats or as a closer-fitting sleeve in dresses.

Slash pattern on Elbow level from the back edge, as far as the Middle line. Take out a dart on the Middle line or simply cut on it and overlap the edges, enough to make the elbow gap open 2 or 3 cm in big sizes. Excess length is eased into the front edge of seam. If this is done on a reduced-width sleeve (broken line, FIG. 11), the *width lost by overlapping*, e.g. 2 cm, should be added to the wrist beyond the front edge, running line into original line at elbow level (dot-dash line). Wrist can be tightened more (in big sizes).

Bishop sleeve

This is simply the block gathered into a cuff at the wrist,

SLEEVE CROWN ADJUSTMENTS

For some garments, mainly jackets and coats, the crown of the sleeve is made deeper and higher. For other garments, mainly sportswear and nightwear, the crown is flattened, i.e. made shorter with a corresponding increase in the underarm length.

Raising the crown

Add 0·5–1 cm above point T and re-draw the upper part of the crown, running into original line below points B and F. This increases the length of the sleeve head, i.e. top edge. See example in Chapter Fourteen, FIG. 4.

When the armhole is lowered (e.g in tailored garments) the sleeve crown is also hollowed out, i.e. *deepened*, coming down below points U 1 cm, seldom more. This shortens, of course, the underarm seam.

Lowering the crown – FIG. 12

A flatter crown is used for some children's garments to provide for more freedom of movement (easier raising of arms) by giving the sleeve a longer underarm. It is used mainly for sportswear, pyjama coats, and some blouses.

Make a tuck across the crown, taking out 1–2 cm (sometimes more) and *lengthen sleeve* at the wrist by the same amount. As this also reduces the sleeve head (top edge), making it too small for the armhole, the sleeve is widened to regain size. For a 2 cm tuck (1 cm on the double) 0·5 cm more added on each side of seam is usually sufficient to replace the loss. But if the armhole itself is to be increased, then the sleeve width addition must be bigger. *Check the armhole and sleeve head length* carefully (holding tape measure on edge) – they must match. These sleeves are usually set in quite flat, with no fullness.

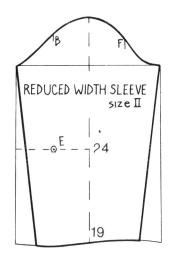

FIG. 10/XIII

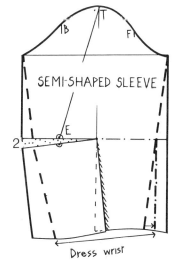

FIG. 11/XIII

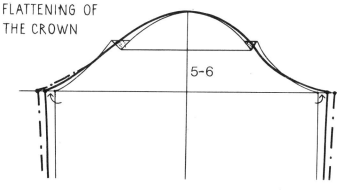

FIG. 12/XIII

THE KIMONO OR MAGYAR BLOCK
—FIG. 13

The draft follows the method already given for the Simplified Kimono in Chapter Two. In the smallest sizes the method is even simpler and so it is repeated here — with a few changes — for Sizes 1 and 2 only (proportions for Size 2 are given in brackets).

Using a square of paper equal to ½ Breast + 6 cm, rule a line 1 cm inside the right-hand edge and fold the paper in half *on to this line* to mark the centre of the pattern.

From the top edge measure 1·5 cm down CB: mark O. From O measure down CB the LW = 24 (28) cm and rule the waist right across. Halve O–LW and take this point 3 cm down for the Breast line, ruled right across.

Along the top edge measure 5 (5·5) cm, i.e. 0·5 more than the neck width of the ordinary bodice block. Mark NP and draw the back neckline down to point O.

From NP *along the top edge*, measure length of shoulder 8 (9) cm and take this point 2 (2·5) cm down for SP. Rule 'shoulder-sleeve' line from NP through SP, as far as the centre line.

Repeat everything for the front, but bring SP 2·5 (3) cm down to slope the front shoulder more (which places the shoulder seam slightly more to the front on the figure).

Use the bodice block CF neckline depth, i.e. 5·5 (6) cm.

Complete pattern as usual, dipping the waist and sloping the CF line, as in the ordinary bodice block.

After cutting and separating pattern down the centre line, paste paper to the cut edges for the extension of the sleeve which is made by simply continuing the 'shoulder-sleeve' line to the required length beyond SP.

Because of the unequal sloping of the 'shoulder-sleeve' lines (which should be *avoided in baby sizes*) a little adjusting may be necessary on the lower edge and the underarm seam of the sleeve, to make the front match the back.

KIMONO FOR SIZES 3 and 4

The drafting of the kimono for the bigger sizes can follow the method given in Chapter Two (Simplified kimono), placing the Breast line 4 cm below the half-point for both sizes, but the back SP 3 cm (3) and 4 cm (4) below the top edge.

Instead of sloping the front 'shoulder-sleeve' line more, it is advisable in the bigger sizes to raise the whole back 1–1·5 cm, as explained in Chapter Two.

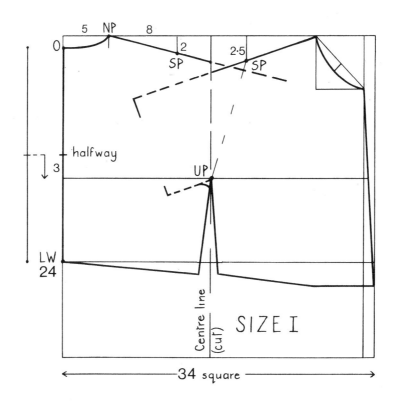

FIG. 13/XIII

SKIRT BLOCKS—FIG. 14

Children's skirts are very simple and consist mainly of straight lengths of fabric, gathered or pleated. There are also styles based on circle patterns: the Quarter-circle and to a lesser degree the Half-circle. Since straight full skirts require no block pattern, the circle patterns, particularly the Quarter-circle, may be considered as the main blocks, at least for the bigger girls.

The Quarter-circle block

This pattern can be used for a variety of styles—plain, gored, pleated and also gathered. It can be made straighter (tightened hem), or widened at the waist to introduce fullness (gathers), and generally used in many different ways (see Plates 40, 41, 42).

In the case of the bigger girls, for whom it is mainly used, it is advisable to draft the Quarter-circle skirt always to a 72 cm waist (which is generally the best, all-purpose size, even for smaller children). In this way there is sufficient width *below the waist* where this pattern tends to work out too tight when drafted to the actual waist measurement. The **extra Hip width** may be anything from 8 to 10 cm and upwards, but must never be less. The unnecessary **waist width** is reduced by small 'darts' in the side seam (3–4 cm deep) and in some cases by easing. To make sure the Hip width is not too tight, it should be measured and indicated on the block on two (three) different levels, suitable for *different heights and ages* of girls. In this way *the same block will serve different* sizes, the length being adjusted as required.

The Half-circle block

This pattern is used mainly for **flared skirts.** It is usually cut in two or in four gores. Like the Quarter-circle it can be reduced at the hem and widened at the waist to introduce fullness for gathers or darts. It can also be reduced at the hem (i.e. straightened) by 'darting' pattern up to the waist, but in such cases the *Hip width* must be controlled, while in the fuller styles it can be ignored. Used on the bias, it is a popular but not always a very becoming skirt for big girls.

THE KNICKER BLOCK

The children's block is drafted in the shape of 'Directoire knickers' but can be adapted to any style of knickers, panties, shorts or trousers.

The block is obtained by a method of direct drafting, based on a rectangle (FIG. 15).

It is usually sufficient to draft two blocks to cover quite a big range of sizes: a small one (corresponding approximately to Size 2), for children 5–6 years old, boys and girls; and a medium-to-big size, suitable for girls of 10–12 years, Hips 80 or 85 cm. The sizes above, below and between can be obtained by grading.

The two proportions which control the pattern are the same as for the adult size of knicker block:

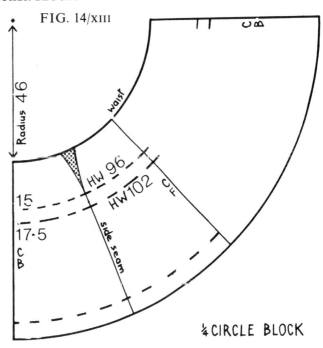

FIG. 14/XIII

¼ CIRCLE BLOCK

The **basic width** of knickers = ¾ Hips minus 3 cm (each leg).

The **crutch depth** (or rise) = ⅜ Hips minus 1·5 cm (or *half* the basic width).

MEASUREMENTS

The Hip measurement is the **basic measurement** from which all the necessary proportions are worked out. It is taken fairly loosely on the figure or obtained from the Breast measurement by adding to the latter 5–8 (10) cm, according to age.

The Waist measurement is useful at the finishing stage.

The side length is also used, mainly in adaptations. It is of little importance for the basic draft for which any length can be used without affecting the fit.

THE DRAFT—small size—FIG. 15

Hip measurement = 68 cm (5–6–7)

On a large sheet of paper (more than ¾ Hips wide) draw a rectangle = ½ Hips × ⅜ Hips minus 1·5 cm, placing it slightly over to the right. The rectangle O–X–Y–Z is equal to 34 × 24 cm.

The lower line, known as the Basic line, is extended right and left. To the right, from X, measure 1/10 H minus 1·5 cm for point F. To the left from Y measure 1/10 H plus 1·5 cm for point B. The *total length* of the Basic line from B to F is equal to ¾ Hips (51 cm) minus 3 cm = 48 cm. OX is half of it.

The leg part of the knicker block, below the Basic line is usually made equal to 1/10 Hips measured *down* a

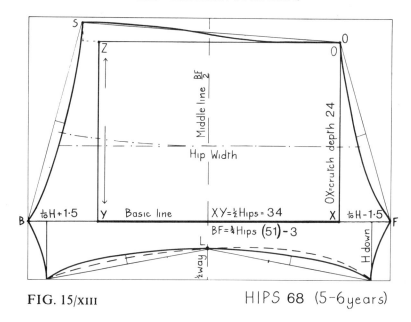

FIG. 15/XIII   HIPS 68 (5–6 years)

perpendicular which starts from a point 2·5 cm inside F and B. Connect the lower points with F and B by slightly curved lines which are the **inner leg seams**. Since they must match when sewn together, complete one leg seam first, then trace it through, after folding whole pattern *lengthwise* so that point B comes exactly over point F: the resulting crease, *bisecting* the Basic line, is the Middle line of the pattern on which **the side length** is measured.

In the block the length is marked half-way between Basic line and lowest level, and in this size it works out approximately 28 cm. But it will vary in adaptations. Complete lower edge as shown in FIG. 15: it goes up towards the middle (point L) and is curved above straight construction lines. If actually used for Directoire knickers (not as a block), the final curve is hollowed out more in the front (broken line).

Above the rectangle, in the back, add 2–3 cm and bring out this point (S) 2–3 cm beyond Z, to increase the waist if it is to be finished with an elastic (the most usual). It must go easily over the hips. Complete front and back seams, curving them 2 cm from a straight line. Draw final waist, curving it as shown in FIG. 15.

The difference in height between the back seam (S–B) and the front seam (O–F) usually increases for bigger sizes and may also do so for certain styles. It can be very small, or non-existent in babies sizes, as a baby's posture, makes front and back alike.

Basic proportions

It will have been noted, when drafting, that the various proportions used are all fractions of the Hip measurement. It is convenient to work out these proportions before beginning the draft and to write them down for easy reference.

For Hips 68 cm, for example

$\left.\begin{array}{l} \tfrac{1}{2}\,H = 34\ cm \\ + \\ \tfrac{1}{4}\,H = 17\ cm \end{array}\right\} = \tfrac{3}{4}\,H = 51$ minus 3 = 48 cm for Basic line BF.

Half of this = 24 cm (i.e. $\tfrac{3}{8}$ H minus 1·5 cm) used for depth of crutch O–X.

$\tfrac{1}{10}$ H is 6·8 = 7 cm.

If the crutch depth (24 cm) is found to be too deep by direct fitting or measuring of a smaller child, it can be reduced by 1–2 cm, making a horizontal tuck across the pattern at Hip level (or pulling up garment from the waist). The block is meant to have an **easy fit** in the crutch part and in the general width, which can always be reduced in adaptations.

It is useful to indicate on the block **the Hip level** which can be marked a little more (1·5 cm) than half-way down the rectangle. On this level is measured and *controlled* the actual **Hip width** of the pattern. A vertical tuck along the Middle line will reduce Hip width, if necessary.

THE DRAFT—medium size—FIG. 16

Hip measurement = 82 cm (age 10–11–12 years).

The method of drafting is the same. The proportions, *worked out in advance*, are:

$\left.\begin{array}{l} \tfrac{1}{2}\,Hips = 41\ cm \\ + \\ \tfrac{1}{4}\,Hips = 20\ cm \end{array}\right\} = \tfrac{3}{4}\,H = 61$ minus 3 = 58 cm for B–F.

Half of this = 29 cm used for O–X.

$\tfrac{1}{10}$ of H = 8 cm.

To establish the positions of points F and B, the smallest fraction, i.e. $\tfrac{1}{10}$ of Hips, is reduced (for F) and increased (for B) by 2 cm and not by 1·5 cm, as in the small size. This gives a bigger difference between the front and the back Forks. As will be seen in the adaptations the difference may have to be further increased for some styles.

The top of the back seam S–B is 3 cm (sometimes 4 cm) above the Front level (this will show clearly when the knicker pattern is folded lengthwise through the middle). The inner leg seams are taken 3 cm in from B and F (points C), and in some styles may go in even more to reduce width at lower edge (see alternative line).

Three different positions are shown for the back seam: the outer seam is for a loose waist finish, i.e. when the waist has an elastic and must go easily over the hips. The middle line, ending above point Z, is for a waist finish with a placket and darts or perhaps with just a half elastic (in the back only). The inner line is a guide line for a closer-fitting back seam, the kind of back seam that might be used in shorts and slacks. The line passes through point Z or just inside it, and there is more loss of both waist width and hip width. The line must therefore pass through a point (W) which controls the hip width, so that it does not become too tight. Remembering that the rectangle gives just half of the *actual* Hip measurement, everything beyond it must be controlled, as allowance for ease may vary according to the style (more ease for ordinary knickers, less for slacks, shorts, etc.). Examples given in Chapter Fourteen illustrate this point.

GRADING KNICKER PATTERNS—FIG. 16

To obtain other sizes, for every 4 cm more or less of Hip measurement, the knicker block must be increased or decreased by:

3 cm in basic width (from B to F).

1·5 cm in Crutch depth (unless shorter depth required).

The basic width is added or taken off as follows: half is added or taken off through the middle (see FIG. 16) and the remaining half is divided equally between back and front Forks, moving *in* or *out* at B and F. It is simpler, of course, to reduce a size than to increase it, since reducing means making a *tuck* through the middle (and across the pattern for crutch reduction), while increasing means slashing and inserting more width. The crutch depth, however, can always be adjusted *at the top* by simply raising the waistline for bigger sizes and lowering it for the smaller. When fitting knickers, they can be pulled up and cut away at the top, to reduce crutch depth, provided there is enough length in the leg part.

Adjust the front and back seams to the new points at B and F, and at the top.

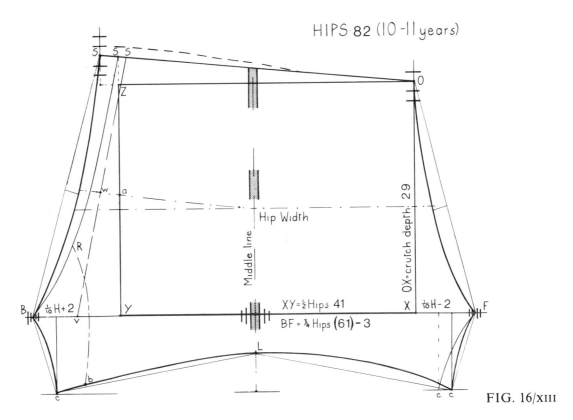

FIG. 16/XIII

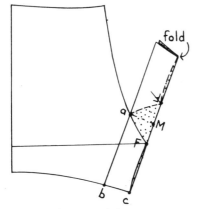

FIG. 17/XIII

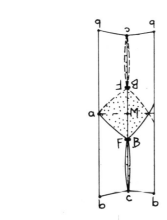

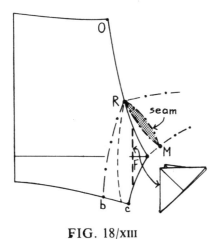

FIG. 18/XIII

GUSSETS AND REINFORCING PIECES

These play quite an important part in the cut and fit of children's knickers, and should be planned on the pattern.

Although the main object of reinforcing pieces is to add to the wear of the knickers by strengthening the part between the legs, in children's knickers they are often used also to increase the 'inner span' — the length between the legs (i.e. between points c), and so to provide for greater freedom of movement. In such cases they become real 'gussets', and the knickers naturally stand up better to hard wear.

Not all shapes of so-called 'gussets' are equally good: some economize material without adding to the comfort and good wear of the garment (the simple square gusset is often of this type).

Straight strip gusset — FIG. 17

This is an excellent gusset when hard wear as well as a good inner span, allowing for plenty of movement (running, jumping, etc.), are important. It is particularly suitable for school wear and therefore much used in small and medium sizes of children's knickers.

On the pattern outline a small section, F–a–b–c, 5 cm wide. A similar section, also 5 cm wide, is outlined in the back. Cut away the two sections. Make a duplicate of each and then arrange the *four* pieces as shown in FIG. 17, placing them to a straight line c–M–c, with B and F touching. Cut out the whole as *a continuous strip*, 10 cm wide. Join it to the main part of the knickers along the line a–b.

The straight strip gusset is of course doubled, i.e. faced with a piece of the same shape. The shaded part in the diagram shows the amount of *length gained* in the inner span.

Other shapes of gusset or reinforcing pieces—FIG. 18

A different shape, more suitable for the bigger sizes, is shown in FIG. 18 and is also outlined in the back in FIG. 16, line R–b.

This may be just **a lining piece** which simply reinforces the part between the legs and which is outlined to shape, R–b–c–F, but without anything being cut away from the pattern itself. Point R is placed 10–12 cm up the knicker seam, usually higher in the back than in the front, and on the lower edge the facing piece may be wider (point b) or narrower (point c), as preferred.

It may also be used as **a separate gusset,** by extending the shape slightly beyond F and B to form an extension (F–M), in which case it is cut *double*, i.e. faced; the whole double piece is then joined to the knickers along the line R–b or R–c.

The broken line (in FIG. 18) indicates the position of a simple square gusset, often used but not always recommended, particularly for children.

CHILDREN'S AVERAGE MEASUREMENTS AND PROPORTIONS

AGE	Group I 2–3–4	Group II 5–6–7	Group III 8–9–10	Group IV 11–12–13
BREAST (Bust)	56	64	72	80
LW-Length to waist	23/24	27/28	31/32	36/37+
Back and Chest	24	28	30	33–34
Hips	60	68–70	80	88–90
LENGTH	44–48	56–60	68–72	80–84
ARM-Length	34	42	50	58–60
T Arm (TA)	20	22	25	28
Wrist	13	14	15	16 17

In view of possible further calculations, it is an advantage to keep the measurements to *whole* and *even* numbers.

N.B.—When only one measurement is given for the whole age Group, the one above and below is arrived at by simple grading (see Fig. 5)

PATTERN DESIGNING FOR CHILDREN

As already stated in the preceding chapter, all the basic rules and methods of pattern designing apply to children's patterns. Since, however, the actual styles are so simple, few problems of *style interpretation* arise. Yokes, panels, simple pleats and flares and very simple dart manipulation is all one generally has to deal with when cutting for children. **Design variation** relies considerably on decorative work – hand and machine – and smocking, tucking, piping, binding, braiding, ruching and every kind of embroidery are much used on baby wear, and on summer and party dresses for young children. The foundation to which all this trimming and fine needlework is applied remains, however, the simple bodice or blouse, the one-piece dress, the gathered, pleated or slightly flared skirt, the plain or 'puff' sleeve and the Peter Pan (Eton) or straight band collar.

The technique of pattern designing for children therefore hardly ever involves any problems beyond those of good proportions and suitable size allowance, as will be seen from the examples that follow.

BODICE BLOCK ADAPTATIONS

When developing from a Bodice block a pattern for a dress bodice, blouse, one-piece dress or coat, the main points to be considered are:

(a) **good proportions,** as applied, for instance to the position of the waistline, or the depth of a yoke;

(b) **technical details of finish,** such as openings;

(c) **width and length allowance** suitable for the type of garment, the style and the age of the child, and the best method of achieving this within the limits of a particular design

All these details play an important part in pattern designing for children.

POSITION OF WAISTLINE – Plate 39

A correct waistline level is important, particularly in patterns for younger children (Sizes 1 and 2). It is usual to raise the waist a little for styles consisting of a bodice and gathered skirt – the classical dress of the little girl (FIG. 1 and sketch, Plate 39).

As a small child tends to be long in the body, i.e. short-legged, raising the waistline 3–4 cm above the normal level in Sizes 1 and 2 gives a more elegant silhouette, making the skirt a little longer in proportion to the bodice. Thus, for a 3-year-old (LW = 24 cm) the skirt will be more than half of the total 46 cm length (e.g. bodice 20 cm to a skirt 26 cm). After the age of 5–6 the waist may come down and in Size 3 (or even before) it is usually in its natural position. In every case the dipping of the front is maintained to improve the hang of the skirt.

All this does not apply, of course, to real 'low-waisted' dresses, when in fashion. Here the waistline is **lowered for style and usually placed several centimetres below the natural level, leaving only a very short skirt.** The same applies to a 'high-waisted' effect. In all these cases one must naturally be guided by correct style and fashion interpretation, and the effect must be quite definite so as not to appear as a wrong proportion.

YOKES – Plate 39

For babies' and toddlers' dresses yokes are generally about a quarter of the CF bodice length or slightly over. Back and front yokes must be on the same level, e.g. 2–3 cm below the Back and Chest lines.

The top of the gathered 'skirt' under a yoke is straight and includes the lower part of the armhole. Width for the gathers is added down CF and CB of pattern (not at the side).

If desired, yokes may be 'dipped' a little, though generally less than the bodice block waist (this is seldom done for babies' dresses). Further slight adjustment may be made at the hem level. However, in the case of very small children one does not always object to a dress going up in the front and the adjustment is optional.

OPENINGS IN CHILDREN'S DRESSES

The neckline opening is an important detail in the planning of a child's pattern: it must be long enough for the head to go through easily, remembering that a child's head is almost as big as an adult's. Twice the length of the opening plus neckline to equal 56–58 cm is a useful *minimum* to refer to.

Since necklines in small children's dresses usually fit close to the neck, to obtain the required total length equal to the above proportion generally means having a fairly long opening (more often down CB). In yoke styles, for instance, an opening always continues into the skirt part, usually as a 8–9 cm long slit below the yoke.

A waist opening is necessary for dresses with a fairly close fit at the waist (e.g. Waist + 5–8 cm). In these cases the neckline opening may be continued down to the waist (buttons down CB) and then, as a slit, into the skirt below the waist.

Two separate openings can also be used in dresses with darts at the waist (e.g. side and back or front opening at the top). In bigger sizes, when the neckline is sufficiently cut out, an ordinary side placket may be sufficient.

When the dress is not close fitting an opening can be omitted, provided the waist is loose enough to go easily over the shoulders. It must be at least 10–12 cm bigger than the Waist measurement (as in the block). Many such dresses without plackets are pulled in at the waist by belts, sashes and half-belts tied in the back, the latter being a particularly successful device for achieving a neat waist fit without the complication of a placket.

WIDTH ADDITION TO BODICE BLOCK
— Plate 39

Width is added to the block in the usual way. When the addition is small, e.g. just *to ease the fit* of the garment, a 0·5 cm added on each side seam edge (FIG. 2, Plate 39) gives 2 cm extra width to the pattern (suitable for a very simple blouse). An addition of 0·5 cm down CF and CB, as well as at the armhole, widens the pattern by 4–5 cm which is considered a necessary minimum for school or sports blouses, pyjama coats, etc. The shoulder is lengthened a little when NP is moved forward (to reduce neckline), but this is quite acceptable for this type of garment (FIG. 2, Plate 39).

With bigger additions for style, i.e. for gathers, smocking, pleating or tucking the width is usually added down CF/CB or, if more convenient, by slashing the pattern to introduce it where required.

SLEEVE AND ARMHOLE

The simple 2 cm width addition to the Bodice block makes the armhole 1 cm bigger. The sleeve must be increased accordingly by *widening* it by the same amount.

The armhole may be further increased by lowering it, but it must always be remembered that this shortens the underarm seam. Although quite acceptable for some garments, such as loose dresses or coats hanging from the shoulder, in other cases, e.g. in dresses fitted at the waist, undue shortening of underarm may give an uncomfortable fit (a pull from the waist) when the arm is raised.

The corresponding hollowing-out of the sleeve head (lowering of point U) is reserved mainly for coats and other tailored garments where shortening of sleeve underarm is acceptable. In many other garments, (e.g. sportswear) the sleeve underarm is on the contrary lengthened to allow for greater ease of movement (see flattening of crown in Chapter Thirteen, FIG. 12).

COLLARS – Plate 39

The classical collar for a small child's dress or blouse is the **round Peter Pan collar,** which, however, except in the smallest baby sizes, is seldom cut quite flat. It is usually cut as **an Eton collar** with the shoulders of the block overlapping 1–2 or 3 cm. The overlapping is less for blouses and dresses, and generally for small sizes, and more for jackets or coats, and for bigger sizes.

The popular round **collar cut in two halves** (dot-dash lines, FIG. 3, Plate 39), opening on CF and on CB, to go with the CB opening of a dress, is an Eton collar further *straightened* by darting the edge of the pattern to prevent it setting too flat, since a second (CB) opening would give it this tendency. Such tightening of the Outer edge may be used for various other round collars, e.g. in coats.

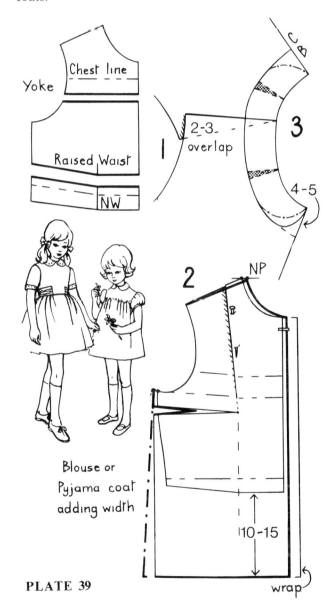

PLATE 39

The **Straight band** collar is also much used, mainly for open rever necklines, either in its simplest (rectangle) shape or with a small stand, i.e. 1 cm dip below the straight edge.

The **Two-way collar**, another version of the straight band with two slashes in the back opened 0·5–1 cm and a small dart in the front part, is particularly useful **in tailored garments**. It can be worn open or buttoned up.

The choice of a suitable pattern, therefore, is a matter of whether a looser or tighter edge is required to give the collar a flatter fit or a higher roll. One must always allow for the fact that small children have short necks (babies hardly any neck height), so that close fitting and high collars are unsuitable for them.

LENGTH ADDITION TO BODICE BLOCK

The waist-length Bodice block can be continued below the waist quite simply by ruling a straight side seam either parallel to CB/CF, as for instance in blouses, or by sloping it out a little from the perpendicular for pyjama coats, one-piece dresses and other longer garments (FIG. 2, Plate 39).

It is, however, useful to have also a hip-length Bodice block which is more convenient for some adaptations. A variety of longer garments, including jackets and coats, with either straight or shaped seams, can be cut from it.

HIP-LENGTH BODICE BLOCK—FIGS. 1 and 2

Continue the CB line straight down for half as much again as the LW. For a 28 cm LW this gives another 14 cm down, for 24 cm LW–12 cm and for 32 cm LW–16 cm down to **the Hip level**. On this level rule a straight line at right angles to CB, taking it right across to CF. If the pattern is *not enclosed in a rectangle* (as it is when drafted), it must first be aligned by placing Breast lines or basic Waist lines on the same level. The straight Hip line is ruled ignoring the dip below the waist, which can be added later below the hem. The CF line of the two smaller sizes continues to slope out below the waist (FIG. 1).

Along the Hip line measure from CB $\frac{1}{4}$ Hips + 1·5 cm and from the sloping CF $-\frac{1}{4}$ Hips + 4 cm, and complete the lower part of side seams (which overlap if the pattern is enclosed in a rectangle, as in FIG. 1). The addition gives 5 cm extra to the hip width on the half-pattern. For Sizes 3 and 4, allow $\frac{1}{4}$ Hips + 2 cm for the back and $\frac{1}{4}$ Hips + 3 cm for the front (FIG. 2). The 10 cm addition round the hips can, when necessary, be reduced to 8 cm by losing on every seam edge, for instance in jackets for bigger girls.

FULL-LENGTH PATTERN—FIGS. 1 and 2

Using a hip-length block, continue CB and CF to the required length (e.g. 60 cm down CB). On this level draw the hemline, at first parallel to the Hip line of the block,

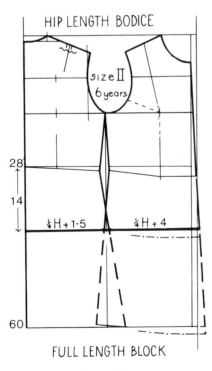

FIG. 1/xiv

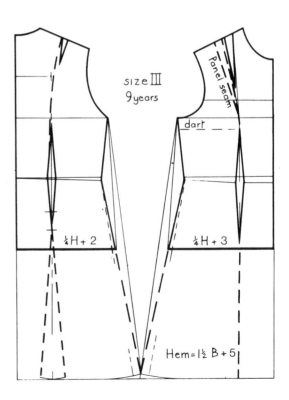

FIG. 2/xiv

and then curving it slightly upwards. Below the Hip level continue the side seams straight down, which gives a *basic hem width* usually equal to about 1½ times the Breast measurement. This represents a *minimum* hem width suitable only for a few styles (e.g. short straight tunics). More often it is increased by at least 5–8 cm on the half-pattern to bring it nearer to a width equal to about 1¾ Breast measurement. The extra width is added according to the type of garment and style, e.g. in panels when these are part of the design, through armhole slashes, through general width addition in coat adaptations, or simply by further sloping of side seams.

N.B. If at any time it is found inconvenient or unnecessary to have a sloping out CF line, it can be 'straightened' by pinning out a small Waist dart (in its correct position), making the dart equal to the sloping-out of the CF, 1 cm. This dart is then transferred into the shoulder, e.g. in a Princess style, or into the underarm or into the armhole where it can simply be 'lost' (dotted line, FIG. 1). Some children have a straighter posture than others and individual observation will show whether the CF sloping-out is necessary and at what stage it can be omitted. The sloping-out of the CF line must always be considered as the equivalent of a 'Shoulder dart' used in its waist (or hem) position and it can therefore be dealt with accordingly.

TAILORING PATTERNS FOR CHILDREN
GENERAL REMARKS

For Jackets use the hip-length block with shaped or straight seam, according to style. The method of adaptation, though simpler, is very much as for adult patterns, with shoulder raised 0·5 cm and Back and Chest widened 1 cm on the half-pattern. A total width addition of at least 5 cm is made on the Breast line, often more (e.g. in school blazers). In the blazer-type jacket the very slightly shaped side seam is generally moved 3–4 cm back from its usual position. Increase of armhole must be followed by a corresponding increase in the sleeve, as explained in Chapters Ten and Eleven.

Coats are also more conveniently cut from the hip-length block, though some simple coat patterns can be developed straight from the short Bodice block by making all the necessary additions on Chest and Back levels (usually 1 cm) and on the Breast line (5–10 cm extra).

COAT FOR SMALL CHILD – FIG. 3
Size 1 – Age 3–4 years

The coat is a classical style popular for both girls and boys. The pattern adaptation can therefore be considered as a basic one for small sizes. The style has a plain front and an easy, loose-fitting back, pulled in slightly by a half-belt. For greater ease in the hem (which is not very full) the coat has a vent in the CB seam. It can be worn open or buttoned up at the neck, and it can have a SB

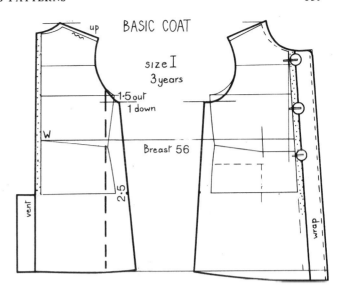

FIG. 3/XIV

or DB wrap. A Peter Pan (Eton-cut) collar or a straighter Two-way collar is suitable. The adaptation consists in adding length, width, raising shoulder and lowering armhole.

The length of a coat is usually 3–5 cm more than the dress length, e.g. 48 or more often 50 for a 46 cm length.

For extra width add 1 cm down CB and CF and move in the neckline *less* (to widen neck slightly). The Back and Chest are thus widened and the shoulder lengthened. Raise shoulder 0·5 cm and redraw neckline. Add another 1·5 cm at the side seam so that the *total extra width* added on the Breast line is 10 cm.

Lower armhole 1 cm. The *total increase in armhole* is now 1 cm on the shoulder (through 1 cm raising of shoulders), 2 cm in width across, and about 2 cm through the lowering of armhole, i.e. a total increase of about 5–6 cm. The sleeve must be increased accordingly (see lower).

Mark 2·5 cm beyond the hip width of the block – back and front – and through these points rule straight underarm seams from the new UP. This will give a hem width which, owing to the width additions at the top, is more

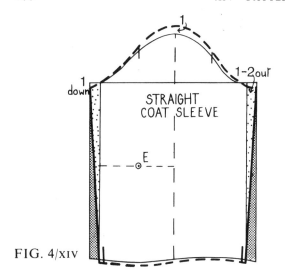

FIG. 4/xiv

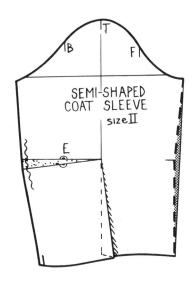

FIG. 5/xiv

than the minimum hem, being equal to about 1¾ Breast measurement.

A little more width can be added in the back by slashing from the hem up to the armhole (broken line) and opening 4–5 cm at the hem. The width is pulled in at the waist by a belt across the back.

Add the vent extension to CB seam, 4 cm wide, going up to Hip line. In the front add 3–4 cm for a SB or 6–7 cm for a DB wrap and plan buttons. Make a pattern of pocket (10 × 10 cm), belt (4 cm) and a round, 6 cm wide 'Eton' collar.

SLEEVES FOR COATS AND JACKETS
—FIGS. 4, 5, 6, 7

The coat sleeve can be either a simple Straight sleeve, as the block, a Semi-shaped sleeve or a Two-piece sleeve. For jackets the two last sleeves are mainly used.

The Straight sleeve—FIG. 4—is adapted to a coat or jacket sleeve as follows: Add 1 cm height above the crown, 1 or 2 cm width down each seam edge (1 cm for lighter coats and jackets), and lower point U, i.e. hollow out the sleeve head. Then **reduce the elbow and wrist width** by sloping the seam to the original width of the block (for a very loose wrist) or 1 cm further in. A coat wrist is about 8–12 cm more than the Wrist measurement in smaller sizes and 13–15 cm more in big sizes. Thus in Size 1 the coat wrist would on an average be 20 cm, while in Size 4 it would be between 28 and 30 cm. For jackets the wrist would naturally be smaller. The straight sleeve is, however, seldom used for jacket patterns.

The Semi-shaped sleeve when used **for a coat or jacket** would have the same additions at the top and would

first be reduced at the wrist (by sloping seam) to the width of the sleeve block.

The slash is made as usual on Elbow level as far as the Middle line and opened 1·5 cm (2–3 cm in big sizes) by taking out a dart at the wrist. This generally gives the right wrist width for a coat but it may have to be further reduced for a jacket. The back edge, now longer, is eased into the front edge which can be slightly curved (FIG. 5).

The Two-piece sleeve—FIGS. 6 and 7—follows the standard method given in Chapter Six, but with some slight changes. The false Forearm is placed 2 cm inside the

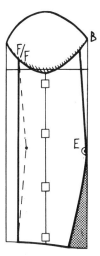

FIG. 6/xiv

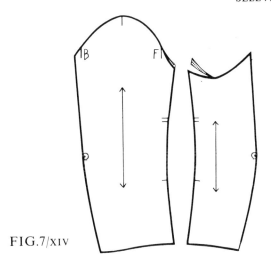

FIG.7/XIV

Forearm for small sizes, though it can be 2·5 cm in for big sizes. Point B is moved only 1 cm down towards underarm (2 cm in big sizes). For the shaping of the wrist in small sizes a 'dart' is measured from the Back line: 3 cm wide for coats and 4 cm wide for jackets. In the big sizes the standard method (see Chapter Six) can be used, i.e. the finished wrist width can be measured from the Forearm.

Before the adaptation the Straight sleeve would of course be increased to a jacket or coat size, as usual.

Coat and jacket sleeves for children are usually made a little longer, though raising the crown already increases their length.

A COAT WITH RAGLAN SLEEVE
—FIGS. 8, 9, 10, 11

Size 2 — Age 5-6 years

The basic coat adaptation of the hip-length block is done first (FIG. 8). Add the length down CB (5 cm more than dress length). Raise shoulder 0·5 cm. Add 1 cm down CF and CB, moving the neckline in less. Add 1 + cm at the armhole. Draw the coat side seams through points 3 cm beyond the hip width of the block. Measure hem width obtained to find how much will have to be added to it *for the style* which has a fairly full hem (equal, for instance, to twice Breast measurement).

Drop the armhole level for the Raglan sleeve 1 cm more than for an ordinary sleeve, i.e. 2–2·5 cm.

Add a wrap in the front, 3–4 cm wide for SB and 6 cm wide for a DB front finish.

The Raglan adaptation requires a slight change in the shoulder section: add 0·5 cm above NP in the back and take this amount off the front, i.e. lower the front NP

0·5 cm. Redraw the shoulder lines. In children's patterns it is not generally necessary to 'centre' the whole shoulder as it is usually already more to the front than in adult patterns and the moving of NP 0·5 cm forward should be sufficient.

Move the *side seam of the block forward*, adding 1 cm to the back and taking 1 cm off the front. The new seam runs into the old line at the hem.

Outline **the Raglan shoulder part,** making it 2·5 cm wide at the neck, both back and front. Draw the raglan lines as usual, slightly curved, down to the point 2·5 cm below the normal armhole: the 'centring' of the side seam has made the back raglan line longer and the front — shorter. To avoid complications, the back shoulderblade dart can be ignored and the extra length cut away at SP.

After cutting away the raglan parts, divide each into several sections *below* B and F (see details above FIG. 9) and cut *from the armhole edge* to within 0·2 cm of the other edge. The only adjustment to the sleeves is a 0·5–1 cm raising of crown.

Place the raglan parts as usual 1 cm above the sleeve (above its Middle line, not a forward line) and keep them 1 cm apart, with points B and F coming as near to B and F of the sleeve as possible and both UP's touching the DC line of the sleeve which is *extended in both directions.* The fact that the parts below UP overlap a little into the sleeve is of no importance. A dart opens out as usual on the shoulder: it is tilted slightly forward.

It will be noted that when the slashed Raglan parts are spread out, as shown in FIG. 10, considerable *width is added to the sleeve.* This is usually more than the width which would normally be added to an average coat sleeve. The extensions beyond the sleeve width need not be absolutely alike, but should not be bigger towards

FIG. 8/xiv

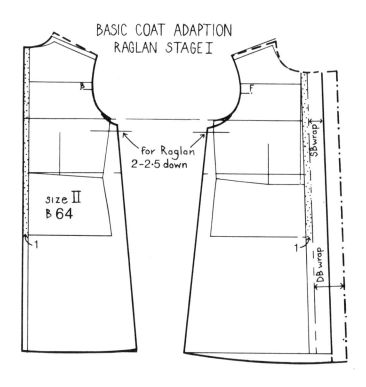

BASIC COAT ADAPTION
RAGLAN STAGE I

for Raglan
2-2·5 down

SB wrap

DB wrap

size II
B 64

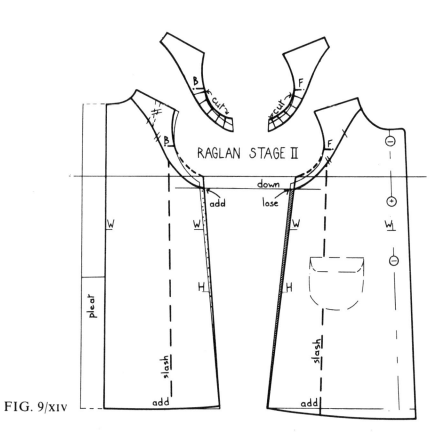

RAGLAN STAGE II

cut

down
lose

add

pleat

slash

add   slash

add   add

W   W   W   W

H   H

FIG. 9/xiv

the front. The 'centring' of the underarm seam of the coat usually ensures that they are more or less alike.

On the final pattern (FIG. 11) draw balance marks. The SG line goes down the middle of the sleeve. Reduce the wrist width to 23–24 cm (for Size 2 – Top Arm 20 cm).

The hem width in this style should be about twice the Breast measurement, i.e. about 120 cm. For extra hem width slash pattern, both back and front, along the lines indicated in FIG. 9 (broken lines), and cut from the hem up to points 3–4 cm below B and F. Open out at the hem to add 5 cm in the back and 4 cm in the front. If this does not give sufficient width (test by measuring hem) more can be added by sloping the side seams out further.

The armhole slash may be used for almost any type of straight-hanging coat. The front slash is used mainly in raglan styles, but the alternative slash would be the one from the hem to Shoulder dart (in big sizes which have no sloping-out CF line). This would improve the 'wrap' of the coat as well as add width to the hem. Both slashes help of course to avoid excessive sloping out of side seams which often spoils the hang of a loose straight garment, whether coat or dress.

Complete the pattern according to the details of the style. **The collar** is either a **round Eton collar** with 2–3 cm overlap of shoulder and one or two additional darts (according to age and size), or a **Two-way collar** (very similar in shape to a Storm collar) produced from a straight band in the usual way. The latter would be more suitable for a SB or narrow DB wrap which could be worn either buttoned at the neck or open with 'lapels' turned back.

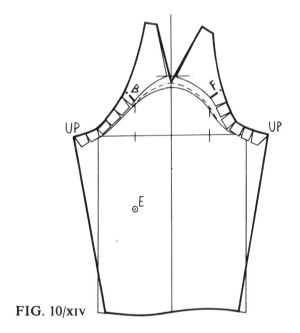

FIG. 10/XIV

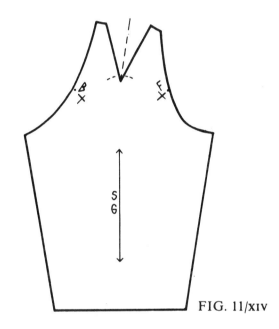

FIG. 11/XIV

In the following Plates are shown various styles which are all, in one way or another, based on the Quarter-circle pattern—a most useful and versatile block in pattern designing for children.

PLATE 40—SKIRTS

This shows a variety of skirts cut on the Quarter-circle which, as already stated, is the main skirt block for bigger girls (sizes III and IV).

The two principal styles are the 6-gore **Panel skirt**—FIGS. 1 and 2 (left sketch)—and a **Panel skirt with pleats**—FIG. 3 (right sketch). For the simple Panel skirt the usual method is followed and the diagrams are self-explanatory. The addition of knife pleats, pressed or unpressed, in the front (FIG. 3), though not necessarily always in the back, makes a very attractive and becoming style, suitable for many purposes—school wear, sports wear, etc.

A **straighter skirt pattern** can be produced quite easily from the Quarter-circle by darting the hem and opening the waist down to the Hip line, as shown in FIG. 4. Thus the hem may be reduced from 160 to 140 cm which is often a better width **for a pleated skirt,** i.e. for a style pleated all round or one with several pleats, back, front and sides.

A **straightened Quarter-circle** is also very suitable for many full styles, such as gathered skirts or skirts with folds (unpressed pleats). Its main advantage over the perfectly straight gathered skirt is that it can have *more hem width* with less bulk round the waist.

In adaptations the Quarter-circle can sometimes be straightened by adding more width at the waist (which, for instance, may be doubled) than the hem (FIG. 5, also Plate 42).

PLATE 41—SHORTS

This is a popular style of loose **skirt-shorts,** given here in its most usual version, i.e. with CB and CF inverted pleats (side pleats are optional, but are often also used). The shorts can be worn separately, with a blouse, or be *part of a sports dress.* The pattern construction is similar to the one given in Chapter XII (sportswear) but here the method is even simpler.

After outlining the Quarter-circle pattern to the required length (taken shorter for sportswear), measure the Hip width (HW) of the pattern along the Hip line which must of course be marked on the right level for the size (size III—15 cm down, size IV—18 cm down). Divide the HW, i.e. the Hip line, into 4 equal sections by folding the pattern twice lengthwise and obtaining 3 crease lines.

Make a note of the value of ¼ HW (e.g. 13 cm for size IV).

Measure the necessary crutch depth (e.g. 29 cm) down CF and CB, and mark points X. On this level draw short lines at right angles to CF and CB. Measure from X: in the front ¼ HW minus 4 cm (9 cm) for point F, and in the back the full ¼ HW (13 cm) for point B.

Complete the pattern as shown in FIG. 1. Cut away the crutch pieces and replace them *after adding the pleats.* The two knife pleats meet in the centre forming an *inverted CF pleat* and concealing the crutch part.

If side pleats are used, the side 'dart' will either come underneath the pleat (usually a knife pleat facing back), or the pleat can be added to a *straight* side seam by following the front *edge* of the dart at the top. This adds some width to the hem which can then be reduced (pinned out) in the middle of the front and transferred into a small waist dart (FIG. 2).

No reduction, however, is made in the back where it is advisable, to have more hem width so as to retain its full swing-out.

PLATE 42—DRESSES

In this Plate are shown two styles for bigger girls which are both based on the Panel skirt and can therefore be most conveniently cut from a Quarter-circle pattern.

Style A—a dress suitable for various occasions, is here shown as a party frock, with a fairly close-fitting bodice, very short sleeves (or sleeveless) and a Bertha-type circular yoke (FIG. 1), which could also be, of course, a real Bertha collar set on to a plain bodice.

The skirt has a small hip yoke, except on the front panel, and into this the fullness of the skirt is gathered in the back, on the sides and side fronts; the latter are folded over on to the plain front panel in two soft, unpressed pleats or folds, producing the effect of an overskirt.

Outline a shallow (8–10 cm) hip yoke all round (except on the front panel) and cut the skirt as for a panel style. The skirt is then doubled as shown in FIG. 3. The back, of course, is also doubled in the same way. Out of the front width outline the pleat which must be drawn a little wider at the bottom than at the top (e.g. 4 to 6 cm). Add a similar pleat extension to the front panel.

Style B is a summer dress with the skirt panels cut in one with a sloping hip yoke. The back is the same so that the yoke goes up into a point at the sides (pleats may be omitted). Only the side pieces of the skirt—front and back—are gathered. In this case the panel pleats are folded over on to the sides.

The bodice is quite plain, with short sleeves and a round collar.

¼ CIRCLE BLOCK PANEL SKIRT

72 waist

CF Fold

hip width
h w

hip line

side seam

C B

panel

back side gore

front side gore

panel

1

2

side gore

side seam

panel

CF Fold

3

side seam

pleat

pleat

CF Fold

STRAIGHTER SKIRT BLOCK

4

cut

hip line

take out 1-2

reduced hem

5

waist doubled

side

CF

PLATE 40

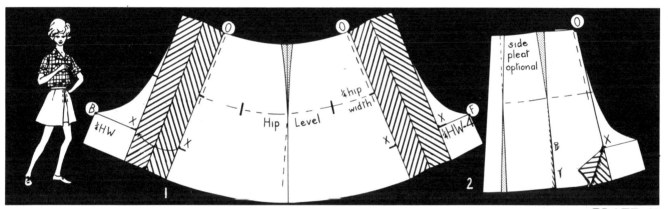

O

O

O

B

¼HW

X

X

Hip Level

¼ hip width

X

X

F

¼HW-4

side pleat optional

B

X

1

2

PLATE 41

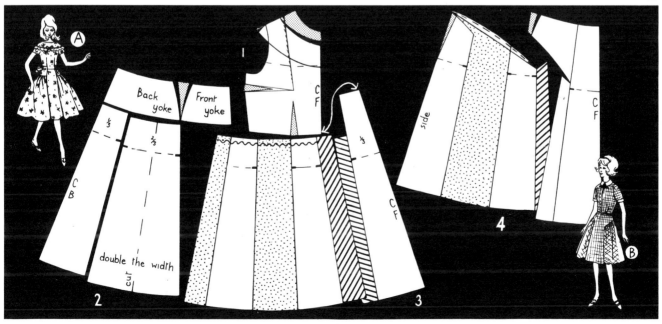

A

Back yoke

Front yoke

⅓

⅔

C B

double the width

cut

2

C F

⅓

C F

3

side

C F

4

B

PLATE 42

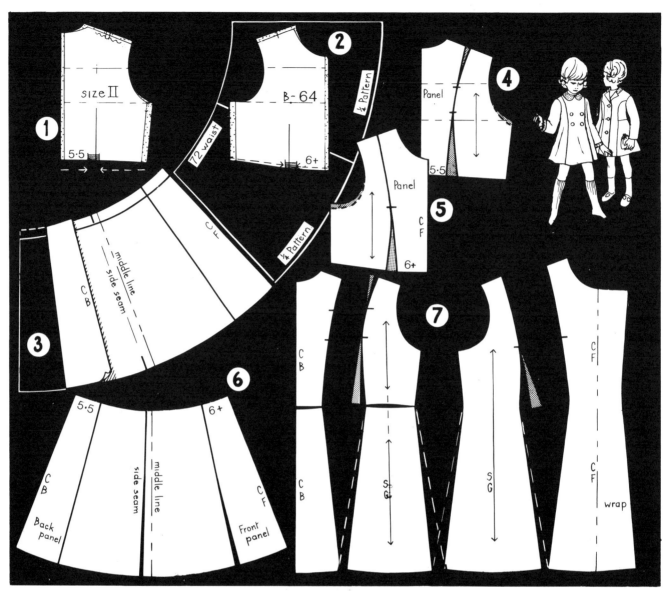

PLATE 43

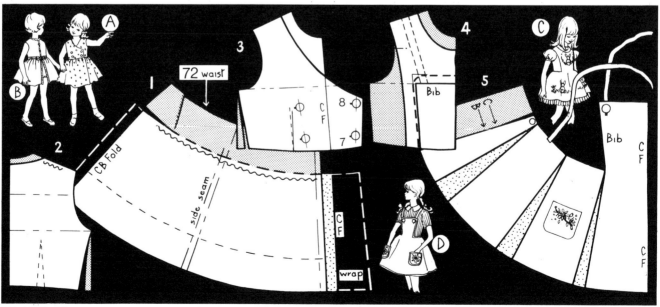

PLATE 44

PLATE 43 – A PRINCESS COAT

Style A is a 7-gore Panel coat, with a DB wrap and a fairly full hem, for which the Quarter-circle skirt is again used. The pattern is cut for Size II – a child of 5 or 6 – and is made to the following measurements:

Breast – 64 + 10 cm (the block) + 8 (10) extra for coat.

Waist – 60 + 10 = 70 cm – the finished coat waist.

Length – 60 cm.

After outlining the Bodice block *add, according to whether the coat will be light or heavy,* 0·5 or 1 cm down CF and CB and 1 cm on the side seam (FIGS. 1 and 2). Raise shoulder 0·5 cm. Move NP back to reduce neckline. Lower armhole 1 cm.

To plan the style first prepare **the skirt part** (Fig. 3). Using only half of the Quarter-circle (the block), which usually has a 72 cm waist, reduce the waist to the required finished size of 70 cm by raising it 2 cm. Fold the pattern lengthwise in half to find the middle line and draw the side seam to the back of it, 1 cm to the back at the waist and 2 cm at the hem. The front waist now measures ¼ finished waist + 1 cm, i.e. 18·5 cm, and the back = 16·5 cm.

For width of panel at the waist allow approximately ⅓ of this, though this may vary with style. This makes the panel 5·5 cm wide in the back and 6+ cm in the front. Carefully *fold over* the back panel waist so that the circular lines at the top *match perfectly*: this will give the right hem width for the back panel. Repeat this for the front. The remaining parts are the Side back and the Side front.

The panel planning can, of course, be done entirely by measurement, but folding over is a useful, quick method, provided the original circle pattern and the folding over are accurate.

On the bodice the waist is planned by simply marking it *from the waist of the skirt*, measuring from CB and from CF, and then from the side seams: the remaining width between the two sections is taken out in the panel darts (FIGS. 4 and 5), to reduce the waist to the required 70 cm. The Panel seams are thus obtained *from the waist planning*, and are not necessarily in the usual position of the Waist darts of the block.

It will be easily understood that the amount which goes into the panel darts is what is added to the block for extra coat width, (or slightly more), since *the original full waist width of the block* is suitable for the coat, which even in this shaped style must be 10 cm looser round the waist.

The Panel seams of the top (FIGS. 4 and 5) are drawn from the middle of the shoulder. Note that there is a small shoulderblade dart but no front Shoulder dart since in this size the latter is still in the waist position. Cut the pattern, cutting away the darts. Cut the skirt part also into the various sections, as shown in FIG. 6.

Place each section of the top above its corresponding skirt part, as shown in FIG. 7, and *outline the whole together* (or paste them together), completely eliminating the waist seam (ignore any gap at the waist, particularly obvious in the back). On the bodice mark SG direction on both Side front and Side back parallel to CF and CB *before* the bodice is cut up for placing above the skirt sections. Of course, on the skirt part the SG is in line with bodice SG.

To complete the coat pattern, add a wrap, in this style, 5 cm (up to 6 cm) at the waist, widening to 7 cm at the top and to 8–9 c m at the hem.

This quick and simple method can be used for various other Princess styles (including dresses) which can be suitably cut from the Quarter-circle (see style B below).

In small sizes the '**flare**' of the skirt part is not always sufficient because of the short length of the skirt, and is often increased by sloping out the side seams more, as shown in the final stage, FIG. 7 (broken lines).

Style B is planned in a similar way, but retains its waist seam in the side sections, which can be slightly more flared, while the panels are continuous and curve into the armholes instead of going up to the shoulder. It has a SB wrap, 4 cm wide all the way down.

PLATE 44 – OVERALL DRESSES AND APRONS

The 'overall' type of dress, open down the front and usually buttoned in the top part only, is worn with panties to match. It is a practical style, easy to launder, as it can be ironed flat. It may be designed in a variety of styles, and can, of course, be made with a simple straight gathered skirt, though the Quarter-circle pattern has the advantage of reducing the bulk of gathers set into the neatly-fitting waist (waist plus 5 cm) while retaining a good width round the hem.

The skirt pattern, i.e. the Quarter-circle, must have a **wider waist** to provide for the gathers, and this is done by cutting 8 cm off the top and then adding 8 cm to the length. This provides most of the fullness, but 2 cm is also added down CB and CF. The side seam is slightly to the back.

Style A – FIGS. 2 and 3 – has a DB front, slightly cut away neckline and a tighter waist. But otherwise it follows the block. For smaller sizes place the waist join 3 cm higher; the skirt must have a good wrap to match the top.

Style B is a still simpler version, open down CF in the skirt part, with only a very small wrap (1–2 cm).

For the panties, a pilch knicker pattern is generally used.

The Aprons are also cut on the Quarter-circle block. They are suitable for play or school wear, e.g. as cookery aprons.

The 72 cm waist of the Quarter-circle is *reduced* by 8–10 cm to make it only just wide enough to meet round the waist and to button with loop (or buttonhole) on CB. Since a Quarter-circle, when very short, does not have much fullness in the hem, the pattern can be widened by slashing from the hem, adding 3–4 cm in each slash. The pattern is now nearer the Half-circle and can be widened further to become one.

The top part of the bib, whether cut in one or separately and attached, can be planned on the Bodice block, as shown in FIG. 4.

Style C has a high front and either a similar back on to which the skirt fastens, or just a 'halter' back yoke.

Style D has a smaller bib in the front, with crossing shoulder straps, fixed to the back waist.

ADAPTATIONS FROM THE KNICKER BLOCK

A very big range of garments worn by children—boys and girls—are adapted from the Knicker block.

PYJAMA TROUSERS—FIG. 12

Outline the knicker block over 1 cm tuck made in the paper to add 2 cm extra width right through. Increase the crutch depth a little for a sleeping garment by adding 1 cm above the waist. Draw new front and back seams, more curved and closer to rectangle (broken lines).

Continue the Middle line ML to the full length of the trousers equal to 2½ times LW or slightly more in the bigger sizes. In this case (Size 2—Hips 68 cm) with a LW = 28 cm, the length is 68–70 cm. On this level rule a line *parallel to the Basic line*. Measure on it the width of the lower edge equally to the right and left from the middle, making a–b = ½ Hips (though it may be less or

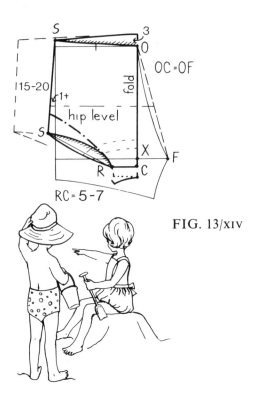

FIG. 13/XIV

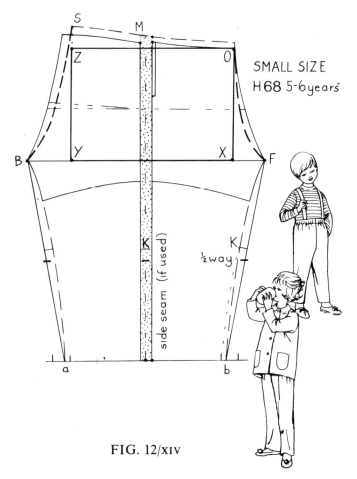

SMALL SIZE
H 68 5-6 years

FIG. 12/XIV

more, e.g. for a gathered ankle finish). Of course these can all be individual measurements taken on the child.

If a seam is to be used down the side, place it slightly (1 cm) to the front of the Middle line. Complete inner leg seams hollowing them out 2 cm on **Knee level** (K) which is marked 2·5 cm above the half-way point in *small* sizes. The waist is wide enough for an elastic finish.

PLAY PANTS—sketch

These simple, pull-on trousers for a small child can be cut from a similar pattern, either with or without the extra width and depth addition, depending largely on whether they will be worn over another garment or not (e.g. pants for outdoor wear). For a more 'tailored' cut see pattern of Shorts and Dungarees below.

PILCH KNICKERS—FIG. 13

These panties are, like all pilch knickers, without a CB and CF seam, but they have side seams. For the adaptation it is sufficient to use the *front part* of the knicker block.

Measure length O–F of the knicker block and apply this length to the CF line, going down below X to point C. From here, at right angles to CF, measure crutch width C–R = 5–6 (7) cm. On the Hip level add

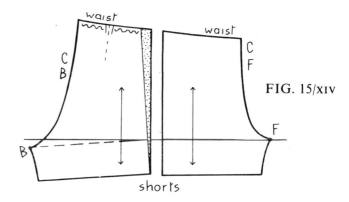

FIG. 14/XIV

FIG. 15/XIV

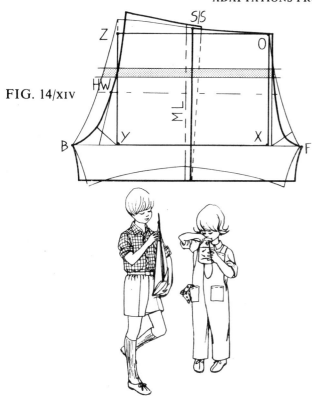

shorts

1 cm beyond the block and through this point draw the side seam, 13–20 cm long. Complete lower edge, as shown, the front part more hollowed out. It must be wide enough to fit round the top of the leg and is often tightened by elastic. Line R–C can go to a fold, or it can be a seam, sometimes slightly curved.

Trace the back of the pattern from the front, adding 3 cm height above CB waist and some extra depth below the lower edge (back of thigh), and sometimes also to the crutch which is then 1 cm longer than the front. The crutch part is usually reinforced, and is often cut separately and faced (i.e. cut double).

Full gathered pantees—sketch and FIG. 13—may also be part of a sun-suit or play suit. The extra width, about half as much again as the pilch knickers, is added at the side. A small addition may be made down CF (to avoid a flat part here and to increase the 'span' between the legs).

BOY'S SHORTS—FIGS. 14 and 15

These are given in a small size—Hips 68 cm (age 5 years).

After outlining the block, make a 3 cm tuck (1·5 cm on the double) right across the pattern to reduce the crutch depth and to fit the shorts closer to the figure.

Move CF line 1 cm forward. Mark the side seam 1 cm to the front of the Middle line ML. Draw a more curved front seam, i.e. closer to the figure. For the back seam first rule a guide line from a point 1 cm inside Z, through HW 1 cm outside the rectangle (Hip width control). Along this line then draw the back seam, as shown in FIG. 14, going up to S for extra height (4–5 cm above the rectangle line).

To complete the lower part, draw the *inner* leg seams 1 cm outside the block and rule the lower edge 5–6 cm below and parallel to the Basic line.

After cutting out the pattern and separating back and front, add to the back a wedge-shaped piece, 2 cm wide at the waist (shaded part in FIG. 15 and overlap in FIG. 14). The straight grain line SG will now be parallel to *new side seam*. If the basic line of the front is continued straight through, it will now pass *above* point B which is thus brought down *below the level of point F* in order to obtain a neater fit in the back.

The finish varies: for small boys the waist can be finished with elastic all round or in the back (and sometimes therefore has to be increased a little by *moving out* point S); or it may be darted or pleated and pulled in by a belt. There is either a front or a side opening.

DUNGAREES—FIG. 16

Dungarees or 'overalls' can be cut from the same pattern as the shorts extending it to full trouser length. If worn over another garment (as overalls) the crutch depth should be reduced less, or not at all (i.e. to add depth above the waist of the shorts pattern).

Continue *the side seam* straight down to the full length (in size 5 years = 65–66 cm), and at the bottom allow, for the back, ¼ Hips + 2 cm and, for the front, ¼ Hips + 1 cm, measuring *outwards from the side seam*. Complete the inner leg seams curving them slightly. If preferred, the width of the lower edge may be reduced a little at the side seam.

The outline of the 'bib' is shown above the front which has no join at the waist.

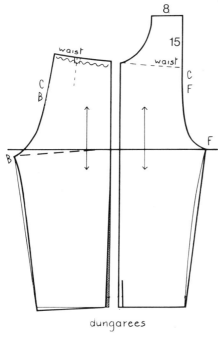

FIG. 16/XIV

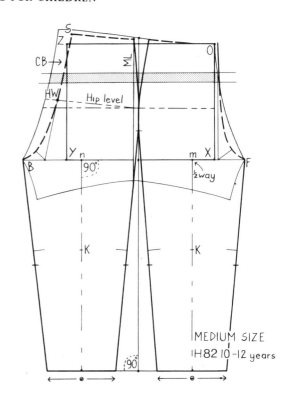

FIG. 17/XIV

SLACKS FOR GIRLS—FIGS. 17, 18

These are given in a medium size (age 9–12) and are **adapted from** the medium size **Knicker block** (H 82).

Reduce the Crutch depth for a closer fit by taking out 3–4 cm right across the pattern, either before or after outlining the block.

Move **the CF (OX) 1 cm forward**. Rule the guide line for **the CB seam** through **two points**: through a point W (or HW) 1 cm *outside* the rectangle, and at the top through point Z (or just outside it for an elastic waist finish). Curve the new seams as shown in FIG. 17, with point S 3 cm above the rectangle. Both seams—front and back—should be *curved closer* to the figure.

Place **the Side seam** 1 + cm to the front of ML and take it down to its full length, in this case just over 2½ times LW. On this level (88–90 cm down), rule the lower edge parallel to the Basic line.

Leg width shaping: On the Basic line, half-way between point F and the Side seam, mark point 'm' and from here drop a perpendicular on to the lower edge: this is the front **Crease line** (or balance line). Repeat this for the back, placing point 'n' *the same distance* from Side seam as the front Crease line. Draw back Crease line. The final width of the leg part is measured equally to the right and left of the balance lines, a quarter of the bottom width, e.g. ¼ of 36 cm (9) each way.

Complete the leg seams, hollowing them out 1–1·5 cm at Knee level, *approximately* 3 cm above the half-way point between the lower edge (Bottom line) and the Basic line.

The waist is usually finished with an elastic.

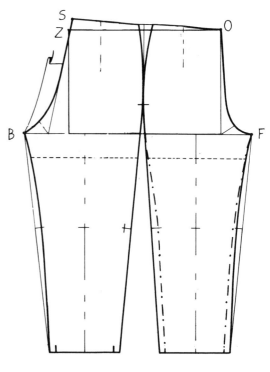

FIG. 18/XIV

TROUSERS FOR BIGGER GIRLS
(pre-teens and teenagers)

Trousers or slacks for bigger girls can be cut by the method given for the basic pattern in Chapter XII. Provided allowance is made for growing by avoiding a tight fit and taking the **Hip measurement loosely** all the proportions can be used and any style in fashion for girls followed.

In all cases **when a Standard skirt block is not available** — whether for children or adults — **a simple draft,** representing the top of a slightly shaped skirt, can be substituted for it. This makes the use of a skirt block unnecessary and the 'Preparatory stage' (pp. 133–134) can be avoided. **N.B.** The circular skirt block given for girls is in any case unsuitable for trousers adaptation.

With the simple draft (FIG. 19) all the instructions given on pp. 134–135 (Method of Adaptation to Trousers) can be followed. They are repeated here only in a very abbreviated form.

Draw a rectangle O–X–Y–Z equal to
½ Hips + 1 (2) cm × Crutch depth (Bodyrise)

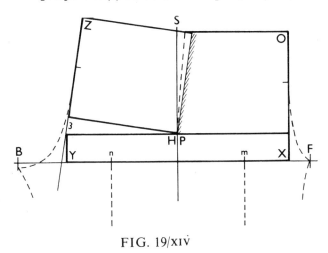

FIG. 19/XIV

For **size Hips 86** make it 44 cm (Y–X) × 26 cm (O–X). Cut it out. Y–X is the basic line, OX–the depth of crutch (Bodyrise). Fold it in half vertically: the crease is the future Side seam S. Draw another line 5 cm above the Basic line and parallel to it — the Hip line. Mark point HP exactly in the middle of it. Cut from the left along the Hip line as far as HP, and then fold out a small dart at the top (i.e. the waist), to the end of the slash (HP). Take out enough to make the gap on the Hip line open 3 cm (the seat angle). Secure the dart by pasting and place the cut out draft, now representing **a skirt top,** on a large sheet of paper, to construct the pattern of trousers round it.

Place it in position to allow 6 cm of paper on the right, about three times as much on the left, and the length of trousers (or a little less) below the rectangle. Trace round to transfer the Basic line (X–Y), the waistline (Z–O), and

the *slanted CB* (i.e. the part *above* the gap), continuing it 12–16 cm down.

Extend the Basic line Y–X right and left. To the right from point X, measure $\frac{1}{10}$ H minus 5 cm for point F, but make it 4 cm (instead of 3·6 cm) as 4 cm should be considered *a minimum* for all sizes. From point F measure *back* along the Basic line ¾ H minus 4 (closer fit 5) cm for point B, (later taken *down* 1·5 cm).

Draw the Side seam along the middle crease of the rectangle, continuing it up to the waist (ignore the 'dart') and down to the Bottom line or lower edge of trousers. This is parallel to the Basic line, after measuring the full length (86–90 cm) from the waist, i.e. from point S.

For **the Crease lines** (balance lines) halve distance F to Side seam on the Basic line and mark point 'm'. Then measure the distance from 'm' to Side seam and repeat it beyond the Side seam for point 'n'. Drop perpendiculars from 'm' and 'n' on to the Bottom line.

Complete **the Fork lines** from F to O and from the *lowered* point B to Z, running them into the rectangle near the Yoke level, i.e. 7–8 cm above the Hip line.

Find the **Knee level** which is 4 (5) cm above the half-point between the Basic and Bottom lines. Measure **Knee width** (e.g. 38–40 cm) allowing a quarter of this (10 cm) to the right and left of each of the Crease lines (this *equal* distribution will not apply, of course, to all styles).

Make the Bottom line width the same, or narrower, or wider (Bell-bottom) — as desired.

Complete **the leg seams,** following style and fashion. For a **wider side effect** — widen at Knee level and below unevenly, giving more width to the Outer and less to the Inner leg seams. For **a tighter effect below the knee** — take additional measurements at Calf and Ankle level (see Chapter XII).

More detailed explanations are given in Chapter XII.

TAILORED SHORTS

These are cut from the pattern of slacks or the trousers, usually down to a length 5–6 cm below the Basic line for the short style (dotted line, FIG. 18) and 12–15 cm below or more for the so-called Bermuda shorts. The actual length is of course entirely a matter of style and fashion. No other change in the pattern is necessary as these shorts, as distinct from the Skirt-shorts given in Plate 40, are merely the top part of slacks (see also Chapter XII — FIG. 7).

In conclusion it must be stated that the patterns given in this chapter represent only a selection of popular garments and styles for children. They can, however, be considered as **basic patterns** from which a big variety of other styles can be produced by simple adaptation. As will be seen, in every case a good line and fit depend considerably on establishing correct and suitable proportions: and this therefore remains the main problem in pattern designing for children.

Hoods appear in a variety of shapes and styles, and they are worn in different ways. They may be large or small, pointed, round, square or flat at the crown, easy fitting, loosely draping round the head or fitting quite close to it, worn separately or attached to the neckline of a coat, jacket or cape; they may also be cut up in various directions by fancy seams. All these details of cut, style and fit must be noted carefully before planning the pattern.

The Basic rectangle (Plate 45, FIG. 1) and the simple Round hood (FIG. 2) are the two useful **basic patterns** from which various other styles can be developed. They represent two ordinary hood styles: a pointed (Pixie) type of hood (style a) and a hood *shaped to the curve of the head* by a middle (overhead) seam (style b).

Measurements:

Heads vary little in size, most measuring between 55 and 59 cm, and therefore a set of **average proportions** can be accepted for general use, being modified a little for the more extreme sizes. Apart from the basic **height and depth measurements,** there are several **check measurements** which may occasionally be required for the correct interpretation and planning of a more fancy hood style.

The first sketch in Plate 45 shows how the **basic height** and the **extended height** are measured. For the first the tape is joined under the chin (average 62 cm), and for the second—at the pit of the neck, with head held high (average 76 cm). The latter measurement is used mainly to control the front fit of a hood which is joined to a garment (the basic height is too tight). Half of each measurement, i.e. 31 and 38 cm, is used in the construction of the basic pattern.

The two other measurements shown in the sketch are sometimes useful, especially for close-fitting hoods. They are the 'depth' of the hood, tight or loose, taken round the back of the head from eye to eye; and the 'overhead' length, from forehead (hairline) to nape (back hairline).

Five styles—a, b, c, d, e—adjacent, illustrate the various methods used in cutting hoods:

Style a is a Pointed hood (the Basic rectangle);
Style b is a Round hood (another basic pattern);
Style c is a Round hood designed for separate wear;
Style d is a close-fitting hood with inset middle section;
Style e is a 'draped' hood with a 'square' crown.

Style a, which is also **the Basic rectangle,** is shown in FIG. 1. A–B and C–D give the loose *basic depth* of the hood = 27 cm; A–D and B–C the *basic height* = 30 cm, dropped 8 cm down to F in the front for the *extended height* A–F = 38 cm (half of 76 cm). C–D is the *basic neckline* and C–F the *final* (dipped) neckline. This is reduced by easing, darting or pleating to the size of the garment neckline into which it fits. The top line is usually a fold. The 'eye level'—a useful reference line (at E) is 15 cm from the top.

For a more pronounced 'pointed' effect point B can be moved to the left and the back seam slanted out towards the top. The square B–P–Q–R (broken line) indicates the part to be cut away for a 'square' crown (by cutting away the point).

Style b or **basic Round hood**—FIG. 2—is the rectangle *shaped to the head* by a seam down the middle. It is not close-fitting in this case, but *may be reduced to fit close* when necessary.

Bisect the right angle by measuring from B 10 cm to points a and b, connecting these and dividing the straight line a–b to obtain point G, through which the bisecting line of the angle is drawn. From B measure down the line 6·5 cm (H) and draw the top curve through the point, as shown in FIG. 2. In some styles the front part is shaped closer to the head (broken line).

The neck width is reduced by a 2–3 cm dart in the back seam and the rest is taken out in a dart, tuck or pleat placed less than half-way towards the back (10 cm from the front).

Style c—FIG. 3—is an adaptation of the Round hood. It has a front turn-back, a flatter curve at the top (often preferable) and a tuck-in 'yoke', so that the hood can be worn separately, tucked inside the coat collar. For the turn-back add an extra 2·5 cm down the front. For the tuck-in add 8–9 cm below the *dipped* neckline, springing out well (7·5 cm) at CB. For the neck reduction (not a tight fit) take out 1·5 cm at the back and use two 3 cm tucks (pleats) 6 cm apart, stitched 4 cm up, releasing width below and above. A split between them helps the yoke to lie flatter. There is a button on the CF.

Style d—FIGS. 4, 5, 6, 7—has a separate middle section joined to side pieces, a very popular cut in hoods, both close-fitting (as shown here) and loose. Reduce the basic Round hood to a closer fit by taking the front line 5 cm in and the basic neckline 4 cm up before planning the style. The overhead measurement from A to C is now 40 cm instead of over 48 cm (as in the loose Round hood). Outline a 7 cm wide middle section (on ½ pattern) following the

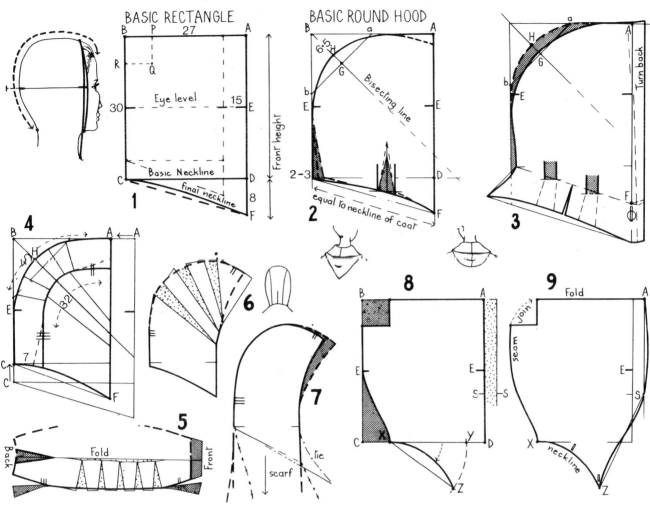

PLATE 45

curve. Measurement will show the lower curve to be 8–9 cm shorter (about 32 cm) than the top one (40 cm). It must be lengthened by that amount to do away with the curve and to make the piece a perfectly *straight band*.

Plan on each side of the bisecting line two sections 4 cm wide on the top and 2·5 cm on the lower curve; cut on the lines (from the inside) and spread as shown in FIG. 5 until the piece is straight. It is not essential that all the gaps (approximately 2 cm each) should be equal. Place pattern *to the fold* (FIG. 5). For closer fit shorten it 2·5 cm in the front and dart at both ends (shaded parts cut away in FIG. 5).

The side piece is also slashed along three lines, the middle one being the bisecting line. Open each slash a full 3 cm to make the top edge match the length of the middle part. Scarf or tie ends can be added, attached or cut in one, straight (in stretchy fabric) or slanted.

Style e — FIGS. 8 and 9 — is a loose style with the front edge long enough to 'drape' on the shoulders (86 instead of 76 cm). It is planned on the Basic rectangle. The crown is 'square' (point cut off), with a short seam across. There is a CB seam, but the top line is a fold. The front edge is turned back 5 cm or more, leaving the front of the head exposed. The neckline of the hood does not meet on the CF (8–10 cm gap).

Use the Basic rectangle *without the neckline dip* (FIG. 8). Add 3 cm down the front, but turn back more later. At CB outline a deep 7 cm dart C–X, going up to E (eye level). At the crown cut out a 6 cm square to remove the point. On the basic neckline, from X, measure 17 cm to Y and then sweep a curve 10 cm down to Z, pivoting from X through Y. Join X–Z and curve the line 2·5 cm up to obtain finally a 18 cm neckline which will not bring the hood round to the CF.

Complete the front edge, taking the line from A down to point S, 5 cm below E, and then down to Z, curving it as shown in FIG. 9. Measure outer edge A–S–Z: it will be about 43 (86) cm and so have extra length for 'draping' on the shoulders.

The final neckline is plain (no fullness) and the hood can either be attached or buttoned to neckline of coat.

Fashion Supplement

by Ann Haggar

Loose Fitting Trouser Adapted from the Basic Trouser

Occasionally fashion demands looser fitting trousers and it is sensible to have a block prepared in readiness to create such styles. The Basic Trouser in Chapter XII serves as a good foundation for such a block.

The main areas requiring adjustment are:

1. **Inside and outside leg seams** which need loosening and re-shaping to create a less thigh hugging appearance.
2. **The side seams from waist points to yoke line** which need to be let out slightly to complete the straighter side seams providing the correct silhouette for a loose fitting block.
3. **CF and CB seams above the hip line** which need letting out.

4. **The front waistline** which needs to be raised slightly. This give more ease over the figure at the front suitable for trousers with front pleats and other similar soft effects.
5. **The crutch area**, especially the front, needs enlarging on this block for a much looser fit. This is a most important adjustment as loose fitting trousers need to be much less close to the body in this area. If this modification is ignored no amount of other adjustment will compensate.

Note: It helps to select the greater bodyrise measurement when beginning to draft the original Basic Trouser, especially with the Loose Fitting Trouser Block in mind.

The Loose Fitting Trouser Block

Method

Outline the back and front Basic Trouser (see Chapter XII) on the same sheet of paper, keeping them on the same level. Leave some space between side seams and a little paper all round.

The adjustments are as follows (refer to Fig. 1):

Outside leg seam

a. Add 0.5 cm at side waist points down to yoke lines. Redraw lines using original block as a guide.
b. Add 2 cm to knee width.
c. Add 2.5 cm to hem width. Connect c–b and then up to Basic Line. This completes the new side seams.

Inside leg seam, back

d. Add 3 cm to knee width.
e. Add 2.5 cm to hem width. Back crutch point B remains unaltered so connect e–d and then up to B in a curved line. The measurement half way may help to achieve a good curve. Note also that this seam is a little shorter than the corresponding front seam. When making up stretch the back between crutch and knee point, possibly under a steam iron, and then sew to front. This promotes a smoother fit on the back trouser.

Inside leg seam, front

d. Add 3 cm to knee width.
e. Add 2.5 cm to hem width.
f. At point F add 2.5 cm outwards along Basic Line. Mark point f.1. This is the new loosened crutch point. Connect e–d with a ruled line and then up to f.1. in a slightly curved line.

CB line

g. Add 0.5 cm to CB waist. Rule down to hip line. This new line should blend well with the unaltered part of the back crutch seam.

CF line

h. Raise CF waist point 0.5 cm off to side waist (a).
i. Add 0.5 cm to CF waist and rule down to hip line, and continue line round into point f.1. creating a new crutch seam. Measurement half way may again help with the curve.

Note: Hem width additions may be made in accordance with the fashion at the time.

Dart positions

Since additions have been made to CF, CB and side seams at waist level to straighten and loosen this area of the trouser, dart volumes may need to be enlarged to guarantee a waistline of the same size. These enlarged darts will be beneficial when designing trousers with waist fullness in the form of pleats, tucks or gathers, which are common when using a block of this kind.

The positioning of the darts can closely follow the instructions given on page 135 except that the darts will have to be larger to cope with additions made to this waist-line. Generally, the area between waist and yoke line can be divided vertically into three portions from centre to side seam. The area nearest the centres may be larger than the other two portions. The dividing lines form the central guide lines of the darts and each dart will need to be approximately 2 cm. As a further guide the darts nearest the CF and CB lines should run on or close to the Straight Grain/Crease Line (SG).

Note: Check the waist measurement before finalizing the dart sizes.

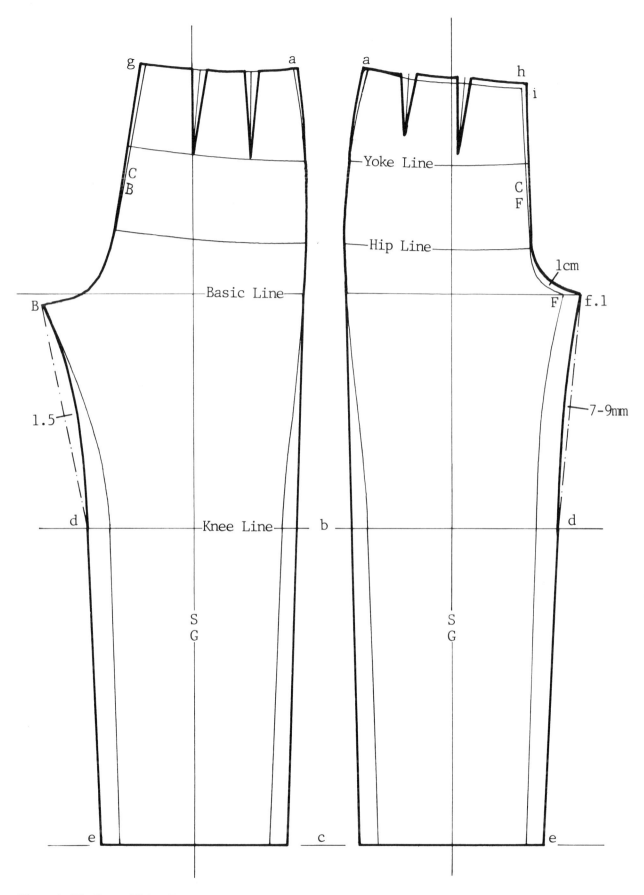

Figure 1. The Loose Fitting Trouser Block. (Scale 1:5)

Style A – Trousers with Pleated Front and Pockets Into Side Seam

Adding pleats

Refer to Fig.3

a. Outline the front block and cut into three sections on lines placed centrally through top of darts, down to but not through hem. These lines should be parallel to the Straight Grain/Crease Line.

b. Add the amount required for pleats remembering that the darts are to be included in this amount, i.e. the dart lines will serve as a basis for the pleat lines.

   Note: The depth of pleats will depend on the weight and thickness of fabric and the design effect required. Some preliminary testing, using the actual fabric if possible, would help to determine the optimum depth of pleats.

c. The hemline should be straightened correcting the break in line caused by the additions.

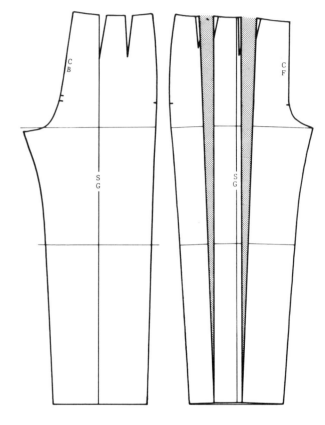

Figure 3.

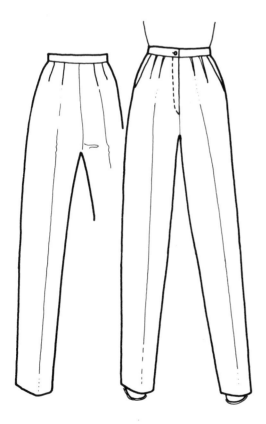

Figure 2. Style A – Trousers with pleated front and pockets into side seam.

Refer to Fig.4

d. The pleat positions are in accordance with the original dart lines and short vertical lines are needed to indicate the folds of the pleats. When the pleats are folded out the waistline may be checked for size and the gaps between pleats cut to the correct angle.

   Note: The back block including the darts remains unchanged. It is quite usual for trousers with pleats in the front to retain the back darts, although the back may also be pleated if required.

   Note: The dart nearest the CB coincides with the Straight Grain/Crease Line and will therefore be almost invisible in wear, if the crease is pressed in.

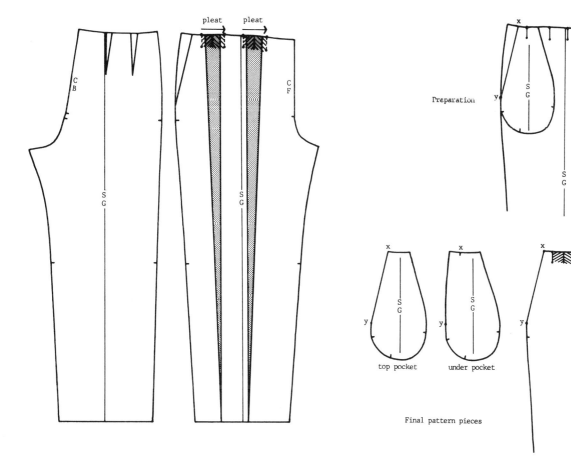

Figure 4.

Figure 5.

Pocket

Refer to Fig.5

e. Plan the pocket position approximately 3 cm in from the side waist point (x) and 20 cm down side seam. Mark point y.

f. To make pocket pattern, sketch in the pocket bag line leaving sufficient length underneath the opening point (y) so that small objects will not fall out when the wearer sits down.

g. Trace off two pocket bag patterns. The **top pocket** faces out the trouser pocket edge (x–y). The **under pocket** lies next to the body and is joined around the curved edge of pocket, matching the balance marks.

Fly front opening

Refer to Fig.6

The fly front has a **grown-on facing on the topside** and a **separate facing on the underside**. A separate pattern has to be made for each front trouser when a fly fastening is required because the underside (or left trouser) needs an extension to allow the zip teeth to be well out of sight.

Topside

h. Draw in fly stitching line approximately 2.5 cm left of CF, curving into CF line at a point 18–20 cm down from waist. Mirror this to the right of CF. Add 1.5–2 cm beyond this, drawing in edge of facing.

Underside

i. First add a 1 cm extension to CF, making it long enough to come below crutch sewing point by the same amount as on the topside.

j. Make a separate facing matching extension in length. The width should be 1 cm less than grown-on facing with corresponding shaping at the bottom.

k. Place a balance mark for correct assembly.

l. The separate facing needs to be cut double, with seam allowances all round.

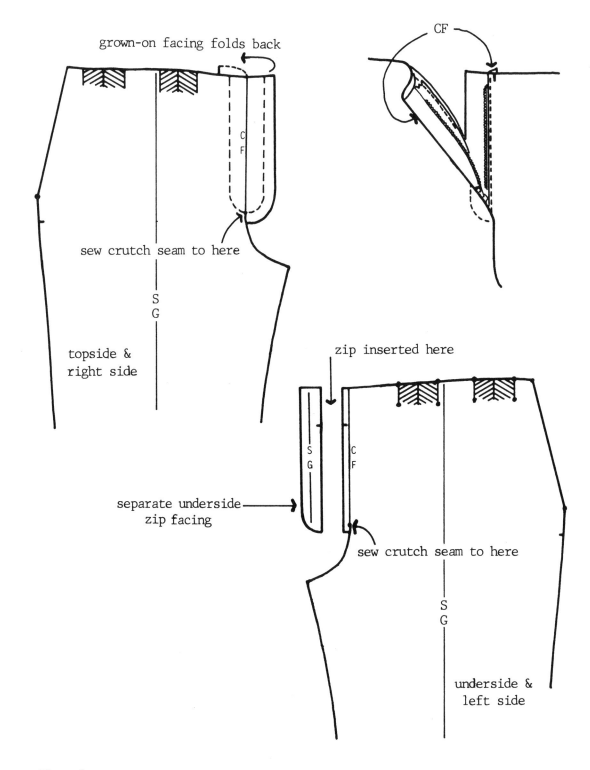

grown-on facing folds back

CF

C
F

sew crutch seam to here

S
G

topside &
right side

zip inserted here

S
G

C
F

separate underside
zip facing

sew crutch seam to here

S
G

underside &
left side

Figure 6.

Style B – Pedal Pushers

Pedal pushers are calf length trousers, so called because they are short enough not to get in the way of bicycle pedals. This style incorporates large patch pockets suitable for such casual trousers and the front waist darts have been converted into soft pleats to complete the look. It would be more appropriate in this case to lose one of the back waist darts, making the area look less fussy. If narrower legs are required the alterations must be made equally on all leg seams.

Refer to Fig.8
a. Outline blocks on same level. Mark in Straight Grain, knee lines and change front darts into pleats.

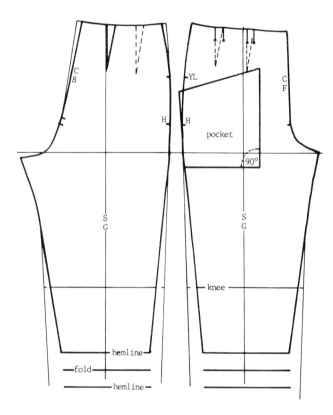

Figure 8.

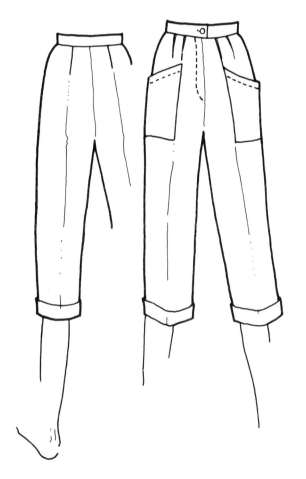

Figure 7. Style B – Pedal pushers.

b. **To remove one of the back darts** measure back dart nearest side seam, and mark *half this amount* at *side waist point* and *half* at *CB waist point*. Using side seam of block re-draw the line down to the yoke line. The new CB point should be ruled down until it hits the original CB in a good line. The unwanted back dart may then be erased.

c. Decide on **trouser length** by measuring down from waist. Mark new hemline (in this case 74 cm from waist). Lines below this are for **turn-up**, in this case 4 cm deep when finished, therefore 8 cm altogether. In addition to this a hem allowance must be made.

d. **To narrow legs** measure in from block lines equally on inside and outside leg seams at hem level, in this case 3 cm i.e. 12 cm on whole leg. Connect these points to Basic Line on outside leg and to points that blend well into the inside leg curve.

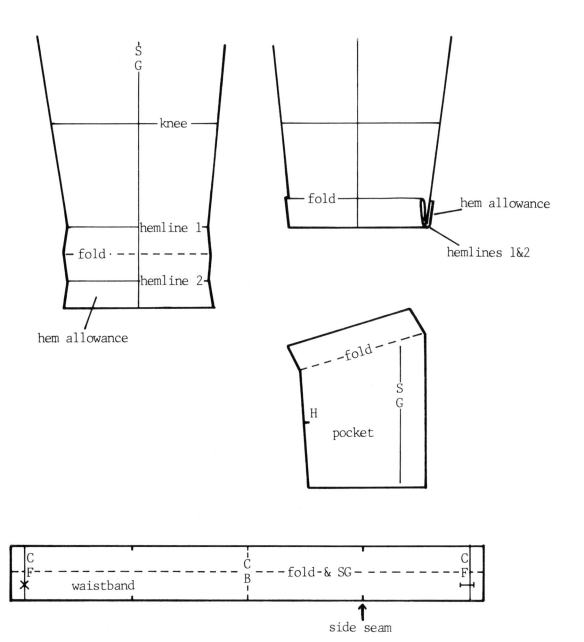

Figure 9.

Refer to Fig.9

e. **To angle the turn-ups** correctly at inside and outside leg seams, fold pattern as shown in Fig.9, and having added seam allowances, cut while still folded.

f. **For pocket** (see Fig. 8), mark outline of pocket on draft (e.g. depth 3–5 cm below Basic Line, width 18 cm from side seam, and heights 23 cm and 18 cm) extending out from side seam by about 1 cm to loosen pocket where hand enters. Trace onto separate sheet, add a facing at the top and seam allowances on other edges.

g. **For waistband**, measure pattern waist excluding pleats and dart. Draft a rectangle using this measurement for the length. Decide on finished depth of waistband, double this measurement and use it to complete the rectangle. Mark both CFs and the CB. Measure back waist only to locate side seam balance marks. Add an amount for button and buttonhole stand beyond each CF.

Style C – Trousers with Waist Fullness (with Drawstring Detail)

When trouser styles with waist fullness are required such as elasticated, drawstring or where gathered into a waistband, it is important to consider not only the width additions at the waist but also the length of the crutch seam. If this seam is too short in relation to the width of the style, a 'drawn in' look can result. The total crutch length measurement should be taken on the body from CB waist, down in-between the legs, allowing the tape to hang as loose as is thought necessary for the style, and on up to the CF waist. This measurement should be checked against the pattern to see if an adjustment is needed. (See comments on Standard Knicker Block – Adjustments of line and fit and Figs. 5, 6 and 7 on page 96.) If this is so the length addition should be made *before* planning the widening of the trouser and in the following manner.

To increase waist to crutch length

See Fig.11

a. Outline the front and back Loose Fitting Trouser Block, placing together at crutch points and with Straight Grain Lines parallel. Draw a right angled line across back and front about two-thirds of the way down from the waist. Cut on this line and add in amount required *equally at back and front*. Secure the adjustment and make good the gaps in CF and CB lines.

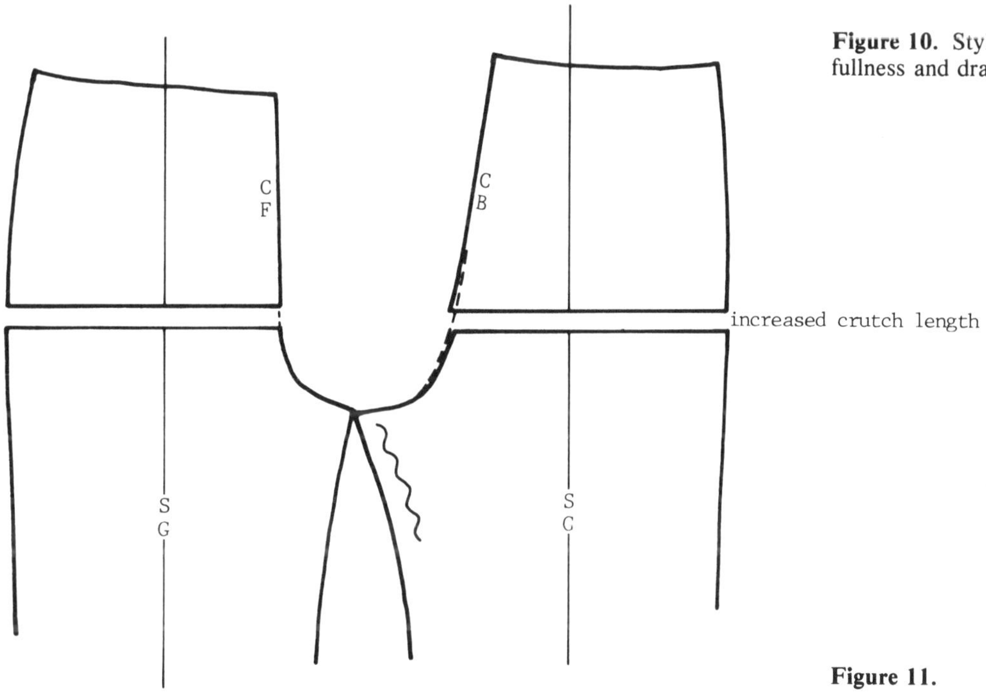

Figure 10. Style C – Trousers with waist fullness and drawstring detail.

Figure

becc
the
com

To wic

Refer

a. Out
   Tro
b. Squ
   legs
c. Squ
   cur
d. Ens
   and
   hem
e. Re-
   the

C F

C B

increased crutch length

S G

S G

Figure 11.

Style E – Playsuit with Elasticated Waist and Side Front Panels into Pockets

Figure 22. Style E – Playsuit with elasticated waist and side front panels into pockets.

Refer to Fig.23

a. Firstly decide on playsuit leg length. Outline the One-Piece Body Block from this new leg length up to the true bust line. Make sure the basic waist level is marked. Disregard the waist darts. These unused darts will contribute to the fullness for the elasticated waist-line.

b. At the true bust line add in some extra underarm to waist length to provide the puffed effect at the waistline. The amount added will depend on the degree of 'puff' (or blouson effect) required and on the chosen fabric. For a light to medium weight woven cotton 5–7 cm would not be excessive.

   Note: Whatever is added on the flat pattern for the puffed effect *always appears halved* when the garment is worn, therefore estimate generously.

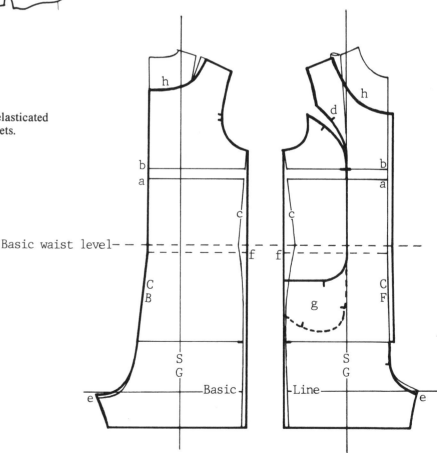

Figure 23.

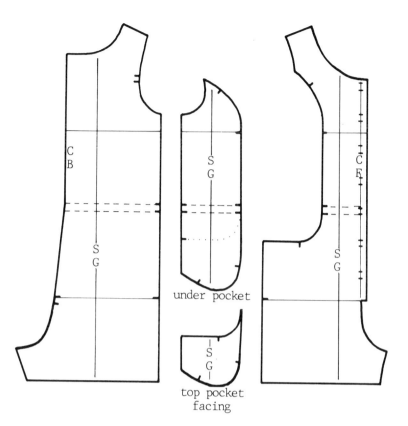

Figure 24.

under pocket

top pocket
facing

c. The side seams may be straightened, thereby adding even more width at the waist for elastication. Using the basic waist level, square up to underarm point and down to hemline widening the hip slightly in the process.

d. Transfer the shoulder/bust dart into the armhole to give the top point of the side body panel.

e. The inside leg seams, originating from the Trouser Block, still maintain the difference in length, providing a smooth fit by stretching the back onto the front leg. *This is unnecessary, indeed detrimental on such a short leg length.* Since the differential is so small it can be dealt with by equalizing the seam lengths, removing from the front inside leg height and adding to the back. *The hemline should remain parallel to the basic line.*

f. Decide on width of elastic to be used and mark in the lower elastic casing line, allowing an extra 0.5 cm so that the elastic may move freely within the finished casing.

g. Draw in pocket line and pocket bag shape (dotted line).

h. Shape neckline as required.

Refer to Fig.24

Trace off back, main front pattern and side panel including under pocket bag. Make pattern for top pocket facing.

Refer to Fig.25

Make facing patterns; join side body panel to front pattern

in area where facing pattern will be planned. Shape inner edge of facing as shown, rounding off to allow ease of neatening. Ensure that inner edge of front facing is kept clear of the bust area (X) in order to avoid an impression of the facing showing through on the finished garment.

Finally, after measuring waist with pattern pieces joined together, make elastic casing pattern in one piece.

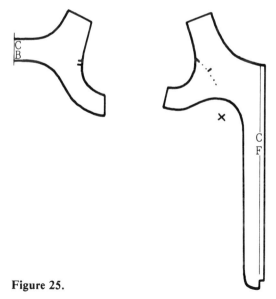

Figure 25.

Grading

Grading is the process by which a range of larger and smaller sizes are produced from the sample pattern using a proportional system of measurement. *It will faithfully reproduce the design without loss of balance, line or fit.*

Many manufacturers use computers and grading machines to handle this aspect of garment production, greatly speeding up the process and offering more consistently accurate results. However, a sound basic knowledge of the subject is essential if full benefit is to be gained from using these machines.

A thorough study of the subject requires knowledge of anthropometry, bodily development and size grouping as applicable to the wholesale garment industry. This section aims only to confer a basic understanding of the subject, not to equip you to become a fully fledged pattern grader. However, even with a basic understanding it is possible to use grading not only for the production of a range of sizes but also for more individual purposes in the design room. For example – a dress pattern has been successfully completed and the designer requires a matching jacket to complete the outfit. If the finalised dress pattern is shortened to jacket length and then graded up one or two sizes (depending on how closely it should fit when worn over the dress) this would effectively speed up the jacket pattern making process by utilising the previously perfected pattern. This particular use of grading is another form of pattern manipulation.

Size ranges are often in 5 cm increments but some manufacturers require an extra size per range, and allowing 4 cm difference between sizes makes this possible. It is wise to establish the required increments between sizes before starting to grade.

To plan the amount of increase per pattern piece remember firstly that *most patterns are cut on the half* (for greater speed and accuracy). Therefore from CB to CF on a 4 cm grade, the half increment will be 2 cm, and this amount would be further divided between the half back and the half front pattern, i.e. 1 cm on each quarter of the garment. Patterns must grow lengthways as well as widthways, so note that *additional length* sometimes means an *increase in girth*, as in the case of an armhole or neckline.

The method of grading illustrated here is to move the pattern pieces from point to point, allowing the size differences in between and marking the outline as you go. *Accuracy is essential or mistakes will magnify as grading proceeds.* The temptation to add the entire increment in one area, e.g. the side seams, must be resisted since this will inevitably result in the loss of line and balance of the garment. Until familiar with the grading movements, keep a careful note of the increases used so that consistent size adjustments are made on all pattern pieces. The cut and spread example of the basic five-piece block (see Fig. 26) illustrates the fragmental division of the grading amounts and the areas in which they are applied.

1. Grading is easier if you arrange the length of the pattern towards you and along the edge of the table. This allows you to see the width increases more readily and is the way in which most grading machines operate.
2. It is helpful to mark the pattern with the grading lines (see Fig.26) showing where the pattern is to be increased or decreased.
3. Make sure there is a vertical line on the pattern. This may be the CF or CB fold or a line parallel to these, e.g. the Straight Grain Line.
4. Square across from this vertical line through the approximate middle of the pattern and preferably at one of the main body levels, e.g. underarm on bodice and sleeve or hip line on skirt and trouser. *All grading movements must take place on or parallel to these two lines (which are known as 'control lines') to ensure correct and accurate grading.*

5. Mark point O at the junction of the horizontal line and the straight vertical pattern edge on CF and CB patterns. This is the *starting point* for the grade.
6. Since size alterations to one pattern piece always affect every other piece to which it will be joined, the possibility of mistakes will be reduced by adopting a uniform method of working.
7. The instructions and illustrations show the basic block patterns graded up one size. **To grade up two sizes** simply double the grading amounts and use the same movements. **To grade down one size** the grading amounts remain the same but *all movements must be in the opposite direction* to the increasing movements.

Note: All grading amounts used in the illustrations are exaggerated for clarity and are therefore not to scale with the blocks.

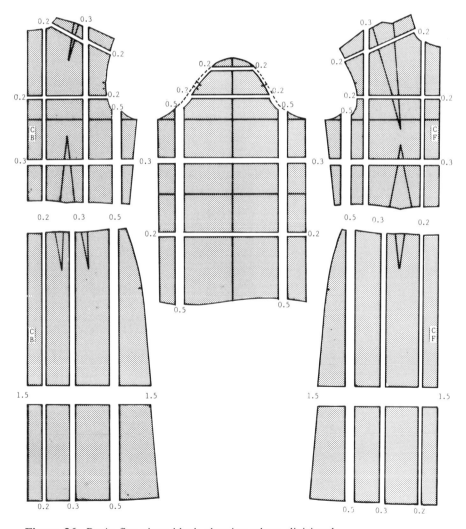

Figure 26. Basic five-piece block showing where divisional grading amounts are applied.

197

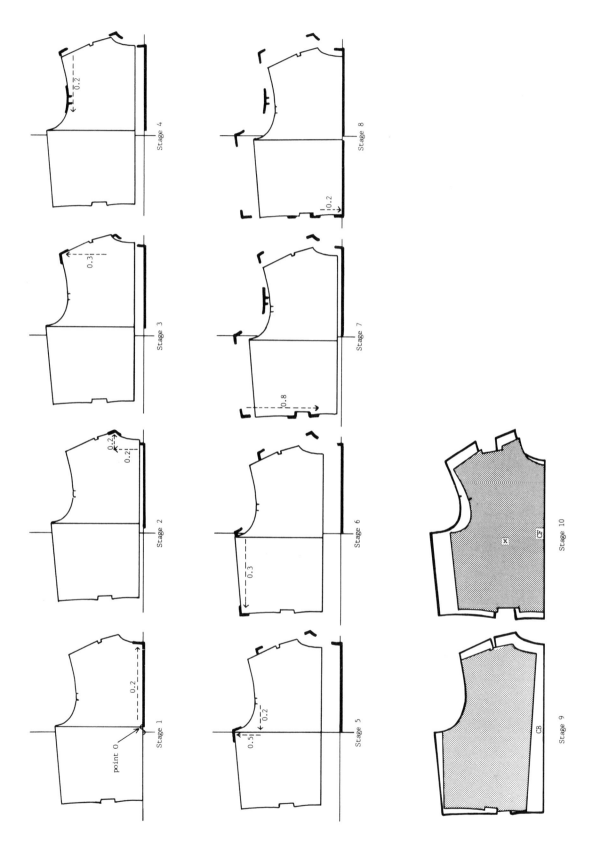

Figure 27. Grading the bodice.

Stage 1 Stage 2 Stage 3 Stage 4
Stage 5 Stage 6 Stage 7 Stage 8
Stage 9 Stage 10

point 0

CB CF

198

Grading the back bodice

Refer to Fig.27

Stages 1–8. Move the pattern stage by stage in the direction of the arrows and by the amounts shown, marking in only the corners of the pattern, especially in curved areas. Note that at stage 2 (neck/shoulder grade) and stage 5 (underarm/side seam grade) there is a double movement, i.e. in both directions (see also Fig.26).

Stage 9. After the final grading movement (stage 8) you will have an unfinished outline. Complete this by using the original pattern to fill the gaps, placing it centrally between the newly marked corners. See stage 9 of Fig.27 showing the completion of the armhole. (Do not be tempted to re-draw the armhole balance marks at this stage. They should have been applied during stage 4 and should need no further adjustment.)

Positioning the darts correctly.

Stage 10. The **waist dart** may be marked in at stage 7. This is in keeping with the positioning of size increases as seen in Fig.26.

The **back shoulder dart** should be marked in whilst completing the shoulder seam outline at stage 9. Simply place original pattern centrally between corners of graded outline and mark in dart points. Remove pattern and join up dart lines.

Grading the front bodice

This is graded in exactly the same way as the back bodice. The **front shoulder/bust dart point** (X) should be marked in at stage 2 with a drop of 0.5 cm towards waistline.

The **top of the bust dart** (where it enters shoulder seam) should be marked in at stage 9, by placing original pattern centrally between neck and armhole corners.

The front waist dart is marked at stage 7, exactly the same way as the back.

Grading the skirt

Refer to Fig.28

The front and back skirt are graded in the same way as the bodice. In this illustration the back skirt has been used. The CB line will serve as the vertical guide line and the hip line (straightened to a right angle against CB) provides the horizontal control.

Stage 1. Start at point O. Mark in CB line between hip and waistlines. Move 0.2 cm and mark **first dart position**.

Stage 2. Move a further 0.3 cm and mark **second dart position**.

Stage 3. Move 0.5 cm and mark in **side waist point**. Then, noting line on original pattern which indicates the point from which length alteration takes place, draw down **side seam** to this point.

Stage 4. Drop pattern by 1.5 cm and (ensuring that original CB is parallel to graded CB) mark in **hemline**. Align both CBs, complete hemline and draw CB up to point O.

Figure 28. Grading the skirt.

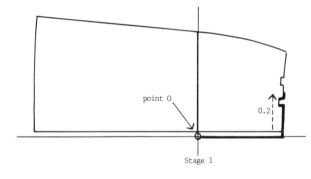

Stage 1

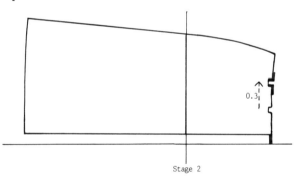

Stage 2

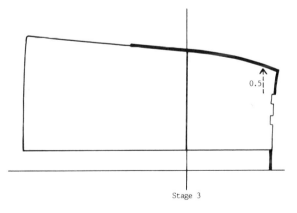

Stage 3

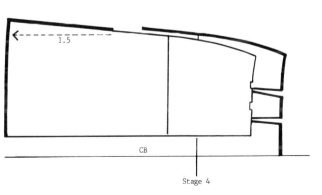

Stage 4

Grading the sleeve

Refer to Fig.29

The sleeve is moved somewhat differently from the bodice and skirt. The grading amounts are, however, exactly the same since *the sleeve must fit back into the armhole after grading*. It is easier to keep a check on the grading and to ensure that the same amounts are added to front and back sleeve head by starting to grade from the junction of the Straight Grain Line and Depth of Crown Line. Mark this point O and continue as follows:

Stage 1. Mark SG Line and DC Line on paper, lengthening lines past pattern outline. Starting from point O, move pattern up 0.2 cm and mark in **balance marks on each side of the head**.

Stage 2. Move up again by 0.2 cm and mark in top of head including **shoulder balance mark**. Move back to point O.

Stage 3. Move pattern outwards in both directions by 0.5 cm – *to match amount added to armhole in same area.* Mark in underarm points. These are the only obvious width increases added at this stage. (The head is widened automatically during stage 6.) Move back to point O.

Stage 4. Now deal with the **underarm length**. Move down 0.3 cm and mark in elbow line. Move down 0.2 cm and mark in wrist level *at centre only*.

Stage 5. **For wrist area**, move pattern over 0.5 cm and mark underarm/wrist point. Move pattern back on itself and mark in opposite wrist point.

Stage 6. **To complete sleeve head**, place original sleeve head halfway between points 2 and 3 and draw in curve *but not balance marks*.

Stage 7. Balance marks are continued through from their position at stage 1 using a set square.

Stage 8. This shows completed sleeve outline with original sleeve laid on top showing the size difference.

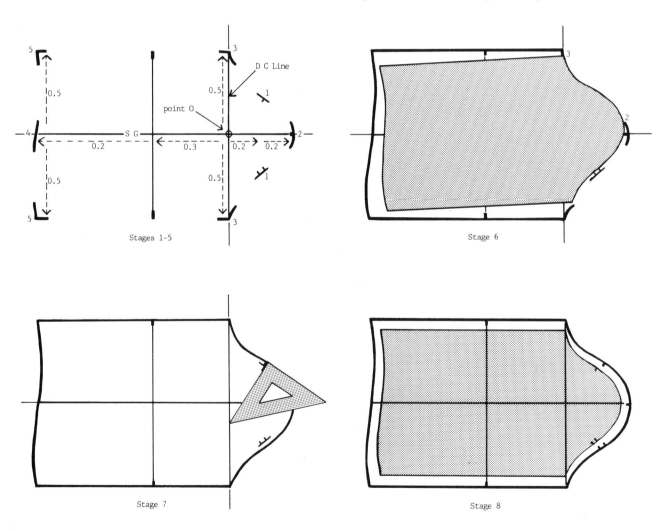

Figure 29. Grading the sleeve.

Grading the trouser

Refer to Figs.30 and 31

The skirt grade may be used as a guide to grading the trouser. Indeed for that area of the trouser pattern exactly resembling the skirt, i.e. the whole area *from waist to hip line, the grades are identical.* Therefore use the skirt grading instructions up to stage 3, *outlining the side seam down to hip line only.* Then continue as follows:

Stage 4. From hip line (H) add in **waist to crutch length increase** of 1 cm and mark upper thigh area from a to b. Move pattern again, adding in **upper leg length increase** of 1.5 cm and mark in knee level (K) and point c. Move pattern a third time adding in **final leg length increase** of 1 cm and mark in corner of hemline, point d.

Stage 5. Move pattern back towards inside leg seam by amount introduced widthways through pattern (1 cm). Mark point e. Then add in a further 0.2 cm and mark point f.

Stage 6. From point f (keeping Straight Grain Lines on original pattern and grading paper parallel) move pattern up towards waist, marking inside leg seam. Include the same grading amounts as allowed on outside leg. If the pattern is moved correctly, gaps will appear opposite those which occurred in stage 4. This is made easier if you have marked the original pattern with the grading positions as already suggested in 'Preparation for Grading'. **Mark knee level** (K). Move pattern towards waist again by 1.5 cm and mark in **crutch point** (g). As a final check after this last move – there should be a 1 cm gap between hip line on original pattern and hip line marked on grading paper.

Stage 7. Use the original pattern to join up the grading gaps as shown.

Stage 8. This shows the completed graded pattern with the original size laid on top – showing the size difference.

Note: The back trouser is graded in exactly the same way.

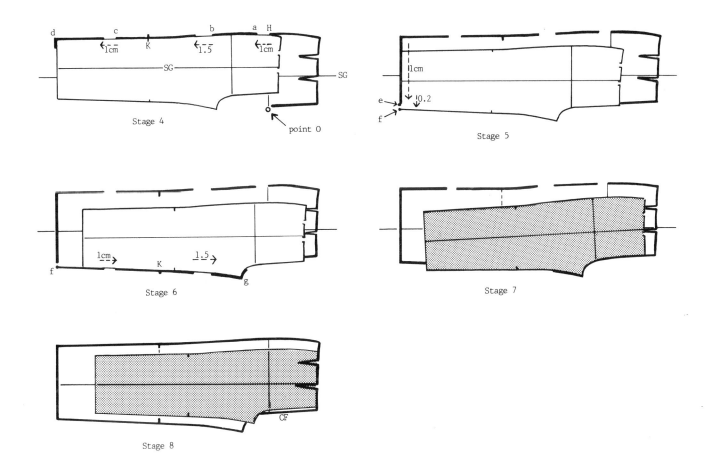

Figure 30. Grading the trouser.

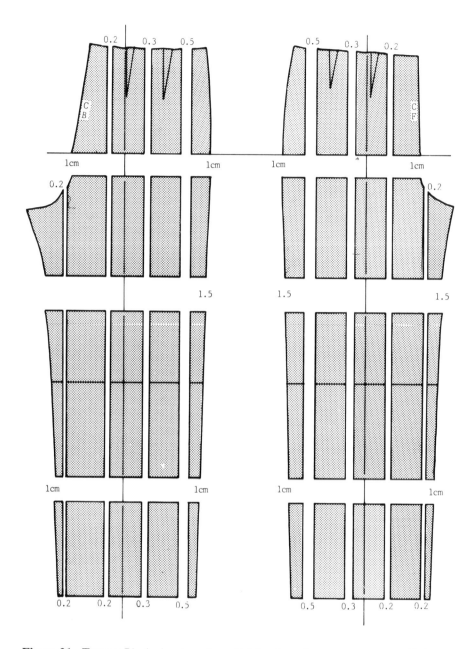

Figure 31. Trouser Block showing where divisional grading amounts are applied.

INDEX

203